My Day

by ELEANOR ROOSEVELT

The BEST of ELEANOR ROOSEVELT'S
ACCLAIMED NEWSPAPER COLUMNS
1936–1962

Edited by David Emblidge
Introduction by Blanche Wiesen Cook

MJF
BOOKS
NEW YORK

Published by MJF Books
Fine Communications
322 Eighth Avenue
New York, NY 10001

My Day
LC Control Number 2004109643
ISBN-13: 978-1-56731-703-9
ISBN-10: 1-56731-703-0

This special edition published by MJF Books in arrangement with Da Capo Press, a member of The Perseus Books Group.

Eleanor Roosevelt's "My Day"—Her Acclaimed Columns was originally a three-volume hardcover series initiated by editor Rochelle Chadakoff and published by Pharos Books. Rochelle Chadakoff edited volume one (1936–1945); David Emblidge edited volumes two (1945–1952) and three (1953–1962). David Emblidge has re-edited all the material to create this one-volume compilation.

Printed in the United States of America.

MJF Books and the MJF colophon are trademarks of Fine Creative Media, Inc.

QM   10   9   8   7   6   5   4   3   2

Contents

1953–1962
First Lady of the World

Preface

*W*ith the passing years, Eleanor Roosevelt rises higher in the public's estimation as the country's preeminent First Lady. Historian James MacGregor Burns, in his magisterial *The American Experiment* (1989), singles out Mrs. Roosevelt as his one hero of social change, praising her for political wisdom, concern for the downtrodden, internationalism, and crusading for women's rights.

Other First Ladies have made substantial contributions to the nation's cultural and political life. But it is difficult to find another who comes close to matching Eleanor Roosevelt's sheer energy and diversity of interests. She was a dynamo.

Mrs. Roosevelt produced at least five hundred words for every "My Day" column and often more, six days per week, with virtually no interruptions, for nearly twenty-six years (1936–1962). Never a great prose stylist, she required the help of her loyal secretaries to clean up, type, and transmit the "My Day" columns by wire or phone to United Feature Syndicate in New York. Eleanor Roosevelt had the good fortune to be blessed with a high energy and chronic insomnia: She often wrote "My Day" in bed at the end of a packed sixteen-hour day.

"My Day" was not Eleanor Roosevelt's only regular column; she wrote for magazines as well. Nor was she simply a journalist. She wrote or co-authored numerous books, countless speeches, and hundreds of letters. One of her children, remarking on the frustration their mother must have felt when palsy eventually made it impossible for her to hold a pen, said she had been "the writingest woman alive."

No activity, work, or subject was too humble to gain Eleanor Roosevelt's attention. No glittering gala event with royalty or famous entertainers was too sophisticated for her tastes. From one day to the next, readers watched Mrs. Roosevelt shift, for example, from gardening at her beloved

Hyde Park, New York, cottage to negotiating as chairman of the United Nations Committee on Human Rights. She found as much fascination in child rearing as in visiting a foreign capital.

"My Day" columns from 1936 through April 1945 show us Mrs. Roosevelt as First Lady during her husband Franklin's four terms as President. FDR, hampered by polio, sent his wife into the country and the world many times to be his eyes and ears. She reported back with an astute sense of the nation's social and political needs. During the Depression Eleanor Roosevelt went to the coal mines, the Dust Bowl farming communities, and the ghettos as well as to universities, factories, and high-society events. She was First Lady to all the people. A pacifist at heart with a clear-headed realism concerning international affairs, she had been tempered by the disaster of World War I and its failed diplomatic aftermath. The onset of a second global conflict in the late 1930s dismayed her. Her own sons enlisted for the war effort after the Japanese attacked Pearl Harbor in 1941, and Mrs. Roosevelt suffered anxiety and relief about their travels and homecomings as did countless other American mothers.

In "My Day" we see Mrs. Roosevelt recovering from the shock of the President's death (April 1945) and, with surprising quickness, finding her own way as a widowed working woman. President Harry Truman asked her to serve as a delegate to the United Nations; eventually she chaired the Committee on Human Rights. By 1952, when Truman left the White House, Eleanor Roosevelt's official standing at the UN was over, although in subsequent years her work as an interested citizen in support of the UN occupied a large share of her time. When Adlai Stevenson's campaign for the presidency failed, despite Mrs. Roosevelt's support, 1952 marked the end of the long Democratic control of the Executive Branch. That year also saw the beginning of the painfully slow truce negotiations in the Korean conflict. Throughout this period, Mrs. Roosevelt inveighed against the scourge of Red-baiting and McCarthyism.

As the President's wife, Eleanor Roosevelt had been generally circumspect in expressing her opinions, letting loyalty to the President's programs override her natural tendencies as gadfly. With the President gone, she took off the padded gloves, becoming an indefatigable, outspoken fighter for a whole rainbow of causes, many of them far from popular.

Eleanor Roosevelt, it was said, "typified . . . the realization of the dreams of the female Crusaders of the 19th century who threw off the restrictions of the Victorian age." So began one obituary for Mrs. Roosevelt in November 1962. She lived to be seventy-eight but had time to acknowledge her advanced age only in her last few weeks. Otherwise she lived with an intensity that left many younger relatives, co-workers, and friends breathless.

A longtime advocate of civil rights, Mrs. Roosevelt had some dramatic gestures to her credit. She resigned from the Daughters of the American Revolution because the group refused to let the black contralto Marian Anderson sing in Washington's Constitution Hall. She resigned from New York's fashionable Colony Club because it refused to consider a Jewish friend for membership. She used "My Day" to promote desegregation as it gained important momentum in the 1950s through Supreme Court decisions, the work of Dr. Martin Luther King, Jr., and congressional equal rights legislation.

America's role in the world during the cold war was a frequent "My Day" topic. Like most Americans Eleanor Roosevelt took seriously the threat of Communist attack from abroad. But rather than arming America to the teeth, Mrs. Roosevelt tried to build bridges of friendship with the Soviets, visiting the Kremlin, interviewing Khrushchev, and even having him to tea in her New York apartment—where, it was reported by a secretary, "she gave him a piece of her mind." There were occasional attacks on her character and ideas by right-wing groups who claimed she was a Communist "pinko" herself, and there was even a threat on her life. She shrugged it all off.

Mrs. Roosevelt was the quintessential grandmother, though some biographers say she was less than an ideal mother. Late in her life it was hard for her to keep track of all the grandchildren, great-grandchildren, cousins and their children, nieces and nephews—but she did an admirable job. The good fortunes and failures of her own offspring were largely kept out of "My Day," but there is a sweet dose of reminiscing about jolly days with her children when the family had time to vacation and play together.

Late in her life Mrs. Roosevelt developed a loving friendship with Dr. David Gurewitsch, who was fifteen years younger and knew her first as his patient. Dr. Gurewitsch appears in numerous "My Day" columns.

Mrs. Roosevelt rarely stayed in any house, apartment, city, or town for more than ten days in a row. In her final decades she crisscrossed the U.S. many times and made several long foreign trips as well as one 'round-the-world junket.

For someone who never held elective office, Eleanor Roosevelt wielded a great deal of political power. In 1956, as in 1952, she actively supported Adlai Stevenson for President. Behind the scenes, she helped rebuild a tattered New York State Democratic Party. She gave Stevenson another push in 1960, hoping the White House could finally be his, and then, after soul-searching and after being charmed during a visit to Hyde Park by John F. Kennedy, she gave her support to the Kennedy campaign and presidency.

Mrs. Roosevelt remained productive and busy with new projects right up until the end. She was always fiercely independent. Treated like royalty wherever she went abroad, Eleanor Roosevelt neither asked for nor expected any consideration at home for having been the wife of a President. When Congress pondered granting presidential widows a pension, Mrs. Roosevelt said she would decline. She would rather proceed on her own resources. Of those resources it was estimated she gave away more than a million dollars to a wide range of charities and needy individuals. Just as she had resisted her children's pleas that she sit for a portrait (though in due time she gave in), Eleanor refused to allow a statue of herself to be placed in a hall dedicated to famous living people. "I can't see why history should be one bit interested in me," she explained. As her United Feature editors wrote, "History apparently thought otherwise."

Editorial note: This book collects many of the best of Eleanor Roosevelt's "My Day" columns. Mrs. Roosevelt often touched on more than one topic in a single day's column. Some "My Day" columns as presented here are excerpts, focusing our attention on a particular subject. Most of the columns in this book are, however, intact, just as Mrs. Rossevelt wrote them.

Acknowledgments

or their help in preparing the cloth edition of *My Day*, on which this paperback selection is based, I thank my editor at Pharos Books, Eileen Schlesinger; the archivists in the FDR Presidential Library, Hyde Park, New York; the reference librarians at the Berkshire Athenaeum, Pittsfield, Massachusetts; and Sheila Buff, who introduced me to this editing project and provided hospitality on my visits to Hyde Park. For both insight and polishing on this paperback edition, I am grateful to my editors at Da Capo Press, John Radziewicz and Fred Francis. I am especially grateful to Assistant Editor Marcy Ross for her attention to detail and her efforts to clarify Mrs. Roosevelt's reaction to the disturbing news of the Nazi holocaust. Our thanks also to Karen Anson of the Franklin D. Roosevelt Library for help in locating photographs for this book.

Finally, I thank the many people young and old—Roosevelt admirers and skeptics—whose unsolicited stories about this great lady confirmed for me the fact that Eleanor Roosevelt had indeed experienced a marvelous transformation from a plain young girl with a shrill voice and no particular self-confidence to a stature unattributed to any other woman in the twentieth century: "First Lady of the World."

David Emblidge
Great Barrington, Massachusetts
September 2000

Introduction

*E*leanor Roosevelt was the great communicator long before she entered the White House. Political activist, public citizen, devoted partisan, dedicated to movements for peace and justice, she was an educator, columnist, editor, broadcaster. She wrote for popular magazines and scholarly journals; she gave endless interviews and was a popularly featured news-source. As Theodore Roosevelt's niece and Franklin Delano Roosevelt's wife, she found politics was her birthright, public affairs her passion.

Eleanor Roosevelt was convinced that governments exist for only one purpose: to make life better for all people. But, she always said, you cannot depend on politicians to do anything about that: You must organize door to door, block by block, community by community. Change required popular movements of activism and persuasion. And she was proud to be part of many movements: the women's movement, the peace movement, the movement of 1930s race radicals that protested lynching, segregation, discrimination, and bigotry. As an organizer, Eleanor Roosevelt spoke everywhere and wrote about every significant and controversial issue.

As the candid wife of a lifelong politician, she wrote with vigor, determined to make a difference. In 1925, she founded an influential monthly with her Val-Kill partners Caroline O'Day, Nancy Cook, and Marion Dickerman. They co-owned, and Eleanor Roosevelt edited, the *Women's Democratic News*, a journal of information and activism. In 1935 it was folded into the monthly *Democratic News*. During the 1920s Eleanor Roosevelt also wrote regular columns for various magazines, notably *Redbook* and *Collier's*. She also edited a monthly magazine of advice for mothers, which she hoped would provide the kind of knowledge she had lacked. Filled with misinformation by today's standards, *Babies Just Babies* also featured marvelous photographs and international perspectives. It did not survive her resignation in 1934.

A loyal supporter of her husband's presidency, Eleanor Roosevelt was eager to promote the best of his programs, and to enlarge the scope of the New Deal. Initially, women were discounted, unprotected, or marginal to New Deal efforts. Eleanor Roosevelt was the first First Lady to leap for her pen to criticize her husband's efforts. FDR always encouraged his wife, and respected her efforts. He told her if she and her allies could "warm up" an issue, he would run with it. To do that, she went on monthly lecture tours, which took her to every state. She broadcast weekly on major radio stations, mostly for the NBC network. She wrote hundreds of letters a month; held regular (usually weekly) press conferences for women reporters only; wrote countless articles a year for various journals and newspapers. Then in 1935 her great friend Lorena Hickok ("Hick"), who had been the highest paid woman political journalist for the Associated Press, said to Eleanor Roosevelt: You know, you send me these long 10-, 12-, 15-page letters, filled with your daily doings. The entire nation would like to know what you are doing every day, and what you think about it all.

Eleanor Roosevelt had sent her friend such detail because she expected Hick to write her biography, and the First Lady intended to compile a record for history. But they both agreed that a public daily letter to the readers of America would be informative and important. It might even galvanize the kind of public spiritedness Eleanor Roosevelt considered essential to a democracy faced with such crises as the Great Depression and the rise of fascism. Launched in 1936, "My Day" became one of America's most popular syndicated columns. Eleanor Roosevelt was a pro who never missed a deadline. She dictated her column six days a week to her hardworking assistant Malvina (Tommy) Thompson, whenever she had a moment in a car, in a plane, in the tub, from a sickbed, or walking through the park. Refreshing and blunt, often surprising and personal, Eleanor Roosevelt's scope was vast, her voice generally intimate.

Readers felt directly addressed, included in the affairs of state, and connected to Eleanor Roosevelt, who shared her moods and her meanderings. She wanted people to write to her and share their thoughts, as she did. Almost every column included public concerns, as well as her own agonies and joys. Some columns included recipes and gossip. Others detailed her own life's chores as mother and grandmother—friend, ally, and hardworking woman in peace and war. Severely attacked by conservative critics who disagreed with her liberal views, she was often dismissed as an amateur who wrote simply to millions of Americans. Others considered her a genius, able to communicate to people in every hamlet and neighborhood. Some thought her heroic and fearless, able to reveal the rumi-nations of her heart; others considered her flamboyant and unwise, ex-posing herself from within the confines of a public fishbowl.

Scorned and reviled, celebrated and loved, Eleanor Roosevelt by the 1940s was the First Lady of the Radio, as well as America's most depend-able political columnist. To most readers of "My Day," she was an unsur-passed and cherished communicator of America's best values. If she made hundreds of dollars per broadcast and thousands per lecture, and many more thousands for her daily column, only Republicans chafed—espe-cially when they learned that she gave virtually every dollar she made away to causes she believed in, through the American Friends Service Committee.

Here, for the first time, collected in one volume are samplings of Eleanor Roosevelt's important, enduring, and unprecedented "My Day" columns.

Blanche Wiesen Cook
East Hampton, New York
September 2000

1936–1941
Up from the
Depression

1936

ven Alice Roosevelt Longworth, often critical of her cousin, admitted that Eleanor Roosevelt was a most impressive First Lady. Early in 1936, *Ladies' Home Journal* asked the daughter of President Theodore Roosevelt to describe "The Qualifications for a President's Wife." Mrs. Longworth observed that the current Lady of the House was "The first wife of a president to have a public life and career. . . . She broadcasts on commercial and other programs. She writes for a number of magazines and newspapers. She holds press conferences. She travels thousands of miles investigating conditions in all parts of the country, doing on a tremendous scale what the lady of the manor did in the days when she looked after the tenantry. She makes as many speeches as the President, if not more. She is here, there and everywhere, gracious, friendly, interested always with something to say."

The author managed to get her barb in: "If the 'old style' qualifications for a President's wife included a not too obvious interference in politics and government . . . possibly now she ought to screen well and have a good radio voice."

Eleanor Roosevelt must have flinched after reading that last line, for she was sensitive about how she looked in photographs and her sometimes shrill voice. But she was a practical woman who carefully considered criticism, worked on weak points, and moved on.

Mrs. Roosevelt was eager for new challenges. In 1936, she quickly accepted the offer to begin "My Day," a diary allowing the First Lady to describe White House life and her varied activities and to comment on events affecting America.

There were rumblings in 1936 of trouble to come. In Europe the Chancellor of Germany, Adolf Hitler, ignored the Versailles Peace Treaty and marched his troops into the demilitarized Rhineland. The Italian dictator, Benito Mussolini, had invaded Ethiopia in 1935. In July, civil war broke out in Spain. The left-wing Spanish Loyalists received munitions from Russia and support from celebrated writers such as Ernest Hemingway and W. H. Auden. Germany and Italy assisted General Francisco Franco's Nationalist troops. China, too, struggled with civil war. Generalissimo Chiang Kai-shek battled the Communists, as Japan tried to take over northern China. Meanwhile, England's King Edward VIII, ruled by his heart, gave up the throne for the woman he loved.

Americans concurred that neutrality was the best foreign policy. The country was on the rebound from the Depression, but an ongoing recession slowed recovery. While the American Federation of Labor (AFL) and the Congress of Industrial Organizations (CIO) struggled for control of the labor movement, more than a million workers had recently joined unions and often organized work stoppages.

Since 1936 was an election year, the First Lady joined the President on his whistle-stop tours through the country. Some people considered Mrs. Roosevelt a potential candidate for Vice President, but she would never consider holding public office. She thought she could accomplish more as a concerned citizen.

More than any of her other endeavors, "My Day" gave Eleanor Roosevelt an opportunity to be something larger than the wife of a politician. As her husband won a landslide victory, Mrs. Roosevelt built up her own following. Originally, twenty newspapers published "My Day"; before the end of the year the column appeared in nearly sixty papers, some owned by publishers who were anti-Roosevelt.

Mrs. Roosevelt wasn't the only person with a White House background to start a newspaper column in 1936: cousin Alice Roosevelt Longworth wrote for a rival news syndicate. The competition between the cousins went beyond Eleanor's involvement with the Democrats and Alice's loyalty to the Republicans. Growing up together, Alice took a wicked delight in making fun of Eleanor's unswerving goodness. Each of their columns reflected their distinct personalities: Eleanor Roosevelt often went out of her way to write something flattering, while cousin Alice exercised her caustic wit. At the Women's National Press Club, members presented a skit showing the columnists at their desks, where instead of inkwells, Mrs. Roosevelt had a bottle of maple syrup and Mrs. Longworth had a bottle of vinegar. The writers' rivalry did not last long; Mrs. Longworth soon ended her career as a columnist.

Eleanor Roosevelt appreciated how "My Day" brought her closer to the American people. She turned fifty-two on October 11, 1936. Still in good health and in good spirits, Mrs. Roosevelt was aware that growing older had its benefits: "One can no longer be interested in one's self, but one is thereby freed for greater interest in others, and the lives of others become as engrossing as a fairy story of our childhood days."

Soon after Franklin and Eleanor Roosevelt moved into the White House, Americans learned to expect the unexpected from the First Lady. Mrs. Roosevelt was the first President's wife to drive her own car, to travel by plane, to take many trips by herself. She crossed a dam in a cable car and accompanied coal miners into a mine shaft. She earned her own money, hosting radio shows, giving lectures, and writing articles. She also encouraged other women to work and held press conferences covered exclusively by women reporters. Now Mrs. Roosevelt added another first—a syndicated column.

Editors may have wished that Eleanor Roosevelt revealed more than the contents of her briefcase in this initial column: It would have been interesting to learn details from that education report on the Civilian Conservation Corps; and a more experienced journalist would have explained that "punging" was another term for sleighing. But the column attracted many readers. One editor reported that 'My Day' has made many lacking education and social contacts regard Mrs. Roosevelt as a neighbor."

WASHINGTON, DECEMBER 30, 1935—I wonder if anyone else glories in cold and snow without and an open fire within and the luxury of a tray of food all by one's self in one's room. I realize that it sounds extremely selfish and a little odd to look upon such an occasion as festive. Nevertheless, Saturday night was a festive occasion, for I spent it that way.

The house was full of young people, my husband had a cold and was in bed with milk toast for his supper, so I said a polite good night to everyone at 7:30, closed my door, lit my fire and settled down to a nice long evening by myself. I read things which I had had in my briefcase for weeks—a report on educational work in the CCC camps, a copy of "Progressive Education" dealing with the problems of youth, the first copy of a magazine edited by a group of young people, a chapter in manuscript and I went to sleep at 10:30. Because I haven't been to bed for weeks before 1 A.M. and often later, this was so unusual that I work this morning with a feeling that I must have slept for several years.

Yesterday was a grand contrast, with sixteen for lunch. My guest on my right was Mr. Regan of Groton School, who long watched over our boys and the boys of many other people and who is, I think, one of the best beloved masters in the school. He certainly is a very wise man and has a delicious sense of humor. One youngster who is staying with us here remarked: "Every meal is different in this house. Yesterday we talked about philosophies of government. Today we talked about movies and punging." I smiled to myself for it would be very hard to be dull with only two people over 30 at the table, all the others bursting with youth and energy.

~

Mrs. Roosevelt didn't relish being in the public eye, but found a philosophical way of coping with the problem. Here, she muses on how to maintain a private life while the world is watching.

WASHINGTON, JANUARY 7—Someone sent me a most amusing present. When I came into my room this afternoon, I thought I was being visited by a zoo, for it was surrounded by four polar bears. On closer inspection, however, I found that the polar bears were guarding a goldfish bowl, with three lovely lilies growing out of the center and a red rose floating to the surface and the goldfish swimming around.

The donor had a sense of humor, for to me a goldfish bowl is certainly suggestive. I doubt if anyone living in the White House needs such a constant reminder, for whether they write themselves, or just trust those who write about them, no goldfish could have less privacy from the point of view of the daily happenings of their existence.

There is, however, one consolation to anyone who lives in the public eye, namely, that while it may be most difficult to keep the world from knowing where you dine and what you eat and what you wear, so much interest is focused on these somewhat unimportant things that you are really left completely free to live your own inner life as you wish.

Thank God, few people are so poor that they do not have an inner life which feeds the real springs of thought and action. So, if I may offer a thought in consolation to others who for a time have to live in a "goldfish bowl," it is: "Don't worry because people know all that you do, for the really important things about anyone are what they are and what they think and feel, and the more you live in a 'goldfish bowl' the less people really know about you!"

~

On January 7, 1936, the New York Times *carried this headline:* SUPREME COURT FINDS AAA UNCONSTITUTIONAL; 6 TO 3 VERDICT DOOMS OTHER NEW DEAL LAWS; ROOSEVELT STUDIES UPSET; MORE TAXES NEEDED.

As the Times *reported, "The Supreme Court by a two-thirds majority vote today demolished the Agricultural Adjustment Act (AAA) as completely as last year it destroyed the NRA [National Recovery Act]. These two were the major legislative devices of the New Deal for orderly recovery in industry and agriculture and for economic parity between them."*

The Supreme Court decided that the AAA was an invasion of a state's right to regulate local business. Although $979 billion had been collected for the AAA, the Supreme Court also banned the use of processing taxes to regulate crop production. A sidebar was headlined: ROOSEVELT RECEIVES DE-CISION WITH A SMILE; STARTS CONFERENCE ON STEPS TO BE TAKEN.

WASHINGTON, JANUARY 8—Needless to say, the big thing in the past twenty-four hours has been the Supreme Court decision. I thought it was going to be the budget, but that was completely overshadowed.

It seemed to me that after a long afternoon of reading and rereading and trying to thoroughly digest legal opinions, we would have a rather quiet and subdued swim at 6 o'clock.

One of our sons who was still home, a young friend of his and one of the men who had been working with my husband appeared with me at the pool. My husband was already in the water and when I reached the door, I dropped my wrapper, plunged into the water and, swimming about very quietly, I inquired hesitatingly how they all were feeling.

To my complete surprise, instead of either discouragement or even annoyance, I was told that everyone was feeling fine, and on that note we finished our swim. Then we went up to dress for dinner and the family met again at the dinner table.

I prepared for some candid opinions on current events. Instead I found that we were discussing history.

My memory for dates is extremely bad, but between us we settled the dates of the Dark Ages, the Middle Ages, the Renaissance and how long the Holy Roman Empire remained a reality, and when it continued in name but was merely a figment of the imagination.

Then we took up what happened in different countries during the Renaissance and reluctantly we got up from the table at 9:15. We still violently discussed the history of the past at a time when I imagine most supper or dinner tables which gave any thought at all to questions of government discussed those of the present day.

My husband plunged into work on a speech and I went off to work on an article. Midnight came and bed for all, and all that was said was "Good night, sleep well, pleasant dreams."

With the new day comes new strength and new thoughts.

∼

*Marian Anderson was that rare thing among singers: a genuine deep con-
tralto with a repertoire ranging from baroque to spirituals. Anderson started
her career at age six with the choir of a Baptist church in Philadelphia. At age
twenty-three she soloed with the New York Philharmonic and later spent ten
years in Europe studying and singing. Marian Anderson's appearance at the
White House carried special significance—she was one of the first blacks to be
invited to entertain a President of the United States. Mrs. Roosevelt would
later champion her right to sing in other public venues.*

WASHINGTON, FEBRUARY 21—My husband and I had a rare treat Wednesday night in listening to Marian Anderson, a colored contralto, who has
made a great success in Europe and this country. She has sung before
nearly all the crowned heads and deserves her great success, for I have
rarely heard a more beautiful and moving voice or a more finished artist.
She sang three Schubert songs and finished with two Negro spirituals, one
of which I had never heard of before.

~

*Helen Keller always viewed March as an important month. On March 3,
1887, Anne Mansfield Sullivan had come to Tuscambia, Alabama, to teach
a little girl who was blind, deaf, and mute. With Sullivan's support, the once
unruly child became a woman of great social vision.*

*Before Keller graduated cum laude from Radcliffe in 1904, she had writ-
ten numerous magazine articles and two books. In 1913, Keller formed the
American Foundation for the Blind. It was a tribute to her hard work that
by 1937 thirty states had established commissions for the blind.*

WASHINGTON, MARCH 26—Last night's meeting of the National Library
for the Blind was quite an inspiring occasion. Miss Helen Keller's efforts
for those who are similarly affected and her willingness to give of herself
was a very touching sight.

She spoke of the few books that were available in Braille when she was
in college and what it would mean for the blind to have the constantly expanding field of a library of such books.

The National Library for the Blind is a nationwide organization and I
hope it will enlist the interests of the people throughout the country. As I
sat on the platform and looked at the people who in spite of their handicap were doing so much, I could not help but think of what an obligation
their example puts on the rest of us.

~

State Senator Franklin Roosevelt (1911–1913), the aristocratic Harvard graduate with matinee-idol looks, had the frequent company of a rumpled little newspaperman. Short on polish, Louis Howe was long on political savvy. He was the central figure of the Old Guard that supported Roosevelt when he was James Cox's running mate in the 1920 presidential race.

The 1920 campaign created a permanent bond between Roosevelt and Howe. Sara Delano Roosevelt, FDR's mother, and the Roosevelt children resented the attention FDR willingly gave Howe.

Eleanor Roosevelt was a reluctant convert: "I was as determined that I would not like him as he was that I should," she admitted some years later. "I could not see what Franklin saw in him, nor why everyone thought him such a political genius. But he kept on coming to my desk until I became interested in spite of myself."

After FDR was crippled by infantile paralysis in 1921, Howe suggested that Mrs. Roosevelt bolster her husband by keeping alive his political interest. As FDR's "eyes and ears," Eleanor Roosevelt involved herself in the New York State Democratic Party. Howe also advised her on politics and speechmaking (Stop giggling. Think out what you want to say and just write down your first sentence and your last sentence).

Occasionally serving as a mediator between Mr. and Mrs. Roosevelt, Howe lived in the White House the last year of his life.

WASHINGTON, APRIL 20—We can, of course, think of little else today but the loss of our old and dear friend, Colonel Howe. For over a year he had been ill. It has been quite evident that his one great desire was to get back to the work which he has done for so many years, but his heart was not up to the spirit that would have driven him back into harness. Last night he simply slept away after having a very cheerful talk with the doctor.

There were few people for whom he really cared, but those who had the privilege of calling him their friend know that he could always be counted upon. There never was a more gentle, kindly spirit. He hated sham and cowardice, but he had a great pity for the weak and helpless in this world, and responded to any appeal with warmth and sympathy. His courage, loyalty and devotion to his family and friends will be an inspiration to all of them as long as they live.

$\sim$

Mrs. Roosevelt had been coached by her husband on how to inspect an institution. As governor of New York he relied on his wife to tour state facilities, a task often too cumbersome for him. Here she reports on an institution that failed inspection.

This was the type of "My Day" column that conservative Democrats dreaded—the First Lady firmly supporting social reform. She followed up by inviting the girls from the reform school to a garden party at the White House. The occasion was controversial because most of the girls were black. The First Lady did comply with common segregation practice by supplying separate refreshment tents for white and black guests. Nevertheless, Mrs. Roosevelt continued to scandalize many Americans with her liberal ways.

WASHINGTON, MAY 8—I have often said that I thought the District of Columbia should not only stand out for the beauty of public buildings but that its public institutions should be models for the rest of the country. I would, however, be ashamed to have anyone visit the District of Columbia Training School for Delinquent Girls.

Never have I seen an institution called a school which had so little claim to that name. Buildings are unfit for habitation—badly heated, rat-infested with inadequate sanitary facilities. Children are walled in like prisoners, in spite of ample grounds and beautiful views.

The girls are without an educational program or a teacher. There is no psychiatrist to examine and advise on the treatment of these unfortunate children, who at such an early age have found the social conditions of the world too much to cope with. There is practically nothing but incarceration for the juvenile delinquent.

I am more ashamed than I can say that this is my first visit and I am grateful to the new superintendent, Dr. Smith, for drawing the attention of Congress and the commissioners to the conditions existing in this institution. Congress has already granted an appropriation to remedy some of the worst features. It will, however, take more than appropriations to set this institution straight.

~

Mrs. Roosevelt usually went to sleep well after midnight, but no matter what her bedtime she rose at 8:30 a.m. To her staff and the reporters who had to keep up with the First Lady, she seemed tireless. Although an indomitable nature led Mrs. Roosevelt to ignore minor illnesses, the flu did keep her off her feet.

"The Land of Counterpane" is a poem Robert Louis Stevenson wrote for A Child's Garden of Verses, *the last stanza of which reads:*

> I was the giant great and still
> That sits upon the pillow-hill,
> And sees before him, dale and plain,
> The pleasant land of counterpane.

Washington, September 18—For the first time in many years I had to give up doing something which I had agreed to do, and I find myself not exactly a willing prisoner in what Stevenson called "The Land of Counterpane." It is just one of those ridiculous things you have to laugh about even if they do annoy you.

Everyone who is sent in to make a test, or find out what is the matter with me, goes away saying that as far as his particular branch of medicine is concerned I am a perfect specimen. Yet they won't let me get up, nor do I feel that I want to do so, for whoever the little bug may be, he is doing a pretty good job in temperature.

If I believe in the old Irish fairy tales, I think that in the intervals of sleep last night some little Irish gnome came and played "Chopsticks" on my ribs and up the back of my head. It is so unusual for me to be in bed that each new person arriving looks at me with a more concerned expression than the last. Even my brother, who is very much the way I am and who thinks things are better downed afoot than abed, comes in to give me a worried once-over twice a day.

I am quite sure that if I kept going as I did until Tuesday I could not feel worse than I do now. I feel I deserve little crowns of glory for doing exactly as I am told, though down in my heart I know that I could not very well do anything else.

It is strange how long the nights are, even though one sleeps most of the time. It seems they never come to an end. I am happy that I usually sleep very well. Ordinarily I do not even mind lying awake, but at such a time as this, there isn't any particular way one can lie in bed and be comfortable.

I can readily understand people who become so worried about not being able to sleep and who get themselves into such a fearful state of mind that life hardly is worth living. When you are ill you begin to notice many things in a room which you do not think much about the rest of the time—the scratches on the furniture, faded spots in the hangings, the peculiar angle at which some pictures hang. I have many photographs in my bedroom of people of whom I am really fond, and I am very apt to think about them and go back over pleasant times together and make plans for the future.

~

While Mrs. Roosevelt supported most New Deal projects, she became devoted to Arthurdale, a resurrected Appalachian community. In the early 1930s, her friend Lorena Hickok wrote to Eleanor Roosevelt about this pathetically impoverished area where a Quaker group was struggling to bring help and hope.

These were truly the forgotten families of the Depression: Some of the men had not worked for eight years after the closing of Morgantown's Crown

Mine. Mrs. Roosevelt visited the community in West Virginia and was shocked by the physical and spiritual hunger. She would later recount how one little boy ran away with his pet rabbit when his older sister calmly told the First Lady that, pet or not, the family would soon be forced to eat the rabbit.

Back in Washington, Mrs. Roosevelt paid for one little girl to have her "bad eyes" treated and filed a report with the President. The community became an opportunity for FDR to put a cherished plan into action. The Arthurdale project inaugurated the Subsistence Homestead Act. The government bought a nearby farm and selected 200 families as homesteaders. They would live in prefabricated homes (outfitted, at Mrs. Roosevelt's insistence, with refrigerators and indoor plumbing) and work in the fields or in the community's furniture factory.

ARTHURDALE, W. VA., DECEMBER 2—It is more than six months since I was here last, and then summer was on its way. Now the trees have lost their leaves and winter will soon be with us to stay. We were greeted by rain, and the roads were covered with snow which had become rather icy slush.

I was very much interested to go through the school, meet the new principal and many of the teachers and finally to sit at luncheon opposite two of the high school boys who are running the Arthurdale newspaper. They were laboriously trying to take down the names of everyone at the luncheon table.

The president of the Arthurdale Association sat next to me and I was impressed by his cooperative spirit and his interest in all questions affecting the welfare of the community.

The chicken farm, run by a co-operative, is doing very well. The entire output of eggs is being sold to the state sanitarium at Hopemont, not very far away. The Homesteaders have done well with their pigs and the dairy co-operative is about to start. They are planning to specialize in Jersey cows producing cream which will be saleable in Washington.

The vacuum-cleaner assembly plant is working out nicely and the manager told me his workers are proving as skillful as any he had come across in other parts of the country. I visited the craft shop and bought some Christmas presents and had tea at the tea room, which is a new development.

The last forty houses, which I have just been through, are delightfully planned and so livable that I would like to have one. Such houses as I had an opportunity to stop in today looked comfortable and homelike. On the whole, I think Arthurdale is becoming a community able to work out its own problems and find a satisfactory solution for them, which may be helpful in other parts of the country.

1937

The sign, THIS SHOP CLOSED. SIT-DOWN STRIKE was not unusual in 1937. But no one expected to see a strike at the White House or pickets carrying placards with such slogans as UNION HOURS FOR FIRST LADIES, NO MORE THAN 300 HANDSHAKES A DAY, NO MORE INAUGURAL TEAS.

The First Lady on strike? It could only happen during a skit at the Women's National Press Club both to rib and to honor its member Eleanor Roosevelt. The journalists paid tribute to Mrs. Roosevelt's packed schedule while acknowledging her ambivalence about her very public White House role.

Eleanor Roosevelt could not hide the fact that she was a reluctant First Lady—indeed, she still seemed to agree with a verse penned by FDR before his first term:

> Did my Eleanor relate
> all the sad and awful fate
> of the miserable lives
> lived by Washington wives . . .

At any rate, 1937 was a very busy year for her. She traveled 43,000 miles, made 100 speeches, shook countless hands, and was hostess to 22,353 people for tea and 319 overnight guests. She stayed true to her promise always to be herself, even when she caused controversy. The First Lady triggered debate by advocating birth control and divorce. Her opinion that housewives should be paid wages made front-page news.

Sometimes she traveled on special assignment for FDR. *Vanity Fair* called her "reporter-at-large" for the White House.

"No one who ever saw Eleanor Roosevelt sit down facing her husband, holding his eyes firmly and saying to him, 'Franklin, I think you should . . . Franklin, surely you will not . . .' will ever forget the experience. . . . It would be impossible to say how often and to what extent American government processes have been turned in a new direction because of her determination," observed economist Rexford Tugwell, a member of FDR's Brain Trust. Although the First Lady wasn't included in the Brain Trust, many considered her the New Deal's conscience. Mrs. Roosevelt adhered to her motto—"Go out and see for yourself"—often accomplishing her objective: "to make others see what you've seen."

Despite heavy rain and missing grandchildren, Franklin Delano Roosevelt's second inauguration was less dramatic than when he became President on March 4, 1933. Two days after that first inauguration, FDR declared a bank holiday and placed an embargo on gold. It was a bold move to help the Forgotten Man.

In 1936 the Forgotten Man hadn't forgotten FDR: voter turnout increased by 8 million votes. Roosevelt would now be the first President to be inaugurated in January. Standing bareheaded in the rain, President Roosevelt told the cheering crowds that when the New Deal began: "We were writing a new chapter in our book of self-government. We have always known that heedless self-interest was bad morals. We now know that it is bad economy." Roosevelt pledged to keep administering his alphabet soup, because, as he said, "I see one-third of the nation ill-housed, ill-clad and ill-nourished."

WASHINGTON, JANUARY 21—If anyone asked me my impression of the day so far, I would say umbrellas and more umbrellas! The President's usual luck in weather doesn't always hold, and today bad weather reigns, the rain simply coming down in torrents.

At 10 o'clock we went over to St. John's Church, and here began some of the mishaps which are bound to happen on a day like this. Two of my grandchildren had gone over ahead of me and, for some reason, the policemen refused to let their car stop and they went round and round the block. The service was half through before they were brought in!

I brought them home with me in the car and from that time on I kept my family together. Up at the Capitol I could not find some of my friends whom I wanted to get under shelter, so, with my youngest son I wandered around through the section where their seats were, trying to find them. I was greeted by all kinds of people who did not happen to be the particular ones I was looking for!

Finally the ceremonies began and, wet and cold as we all were, and hardened as I am to official occasions, I could not hear the oath of office being taken by the Vice President and the President and not realize what it meant for them to assume this responsibility without a catch in my throat. I had read the President's speech before, but even in the rain I felt these were words of sincerity which well expressed the feeling at the opening of the second stage in a long period of change.

As we went to the inaugural, they drove my husband's car with the top up, but he insisted on having it down for the drive back, so when we reached the White House his head and feet were soaking and I was pretty well soaked through. In about a minute and a half I slipped a wet dress off and a dry one on and received my luncheon guests and now we must go out to view the parade.

~

Photographers were discouraged from taking pictures of the President in his wheelchair. The public was rarely reminded that FDR could not dance and even had difficulty walking. It took extreme effort for FDR to greet guests for an hour. Eleanor Roosevelt, often alone on the reception line, had her own strategy: "After every 500 guests, take a sip of water."

WASHINGTON, JANUARY 30—Last evening we held the Congressional reception. This is one of the largest receptions and perhaps one of the most difficult to handle with fairness to all concerned.

There was a time when several thousand people were asked to these receptions. I can remember, many years ago, spending well over an hour progressing up the stairs to the East Room, and even longer, gradually approaching the President and his wife. In those days the entire Cabinet was lined up also to shake hands with the guests.

Now we attempt, for the sake of our guests as well as ourselves, to limit the numbers so that the entire line can pass the President in little more than an hour.

More than a certain number, however, would mean that no one would have a pleasant evening. As it is, after the President goes upstairs, I always go back into the dining room and down the corridor to the East Room to have a look at those who are dancing and I really think it is possible for people to enjoy themselves.

This morning I am on the trail of a new "Scamper." Our small grandson, Bill Roosevelt, who is staying here at the moment, has read and enjoyed both of my daughter's books about "Scamper," and every morning since his arrival he has demanded to know where Scamper can be found.

We used to have bunnies in an enclosure at the back of the White House, but the number of dogs in the White House made it rather difficult to keep them safely apart. Now all the dogs are gone, so I am satisfying Bill by starting in on bunnies again. They will doubtless be very entertaining playmates for any visiting children, unless Bill becomes so fond of one we have now that he will insist taking it home with him.

I started to be a growling lion on the floor this morning, only to discover I was being too realistic and my grandson had run away. Then I had to change into a bucking bronco and put him on my back while my brother held him on. That was entirely successful and ended in roars of laughter as we both collapsed on the floor.

The President had suggested a constitutional amendment allowing him to name up to 6 more Supreme Court members, one for each justice age 70 or older who would not resign. Having inherited the bench from Herbert Hoover, a frustrated FDR couldn't see the point of fighting Congress to win support for New Deal programs only to have bills declared unconstitutional by a conservative court. Casualties already included the National Recovery Act and Child Labor and Wage bill.

~

Ex-President Hoover accused FDR of trying to pack the Court. John Nance Garner, FDR's vice president, lobbied against the proposal. Journalists parodied FDR's idea to the tune of Cole Porter's "It's De-Lovely," saying of the plan "it's delousy." The ultimately defeated scheme was FDR's biggest disappointment.

Mrs. Roosevelt was one of few who supported changing the format of the Supreme Court. Here she quotes a letter written by an unidentified supporter (some suspected it was FDR's handiwork).

WASHINGTON, FEBRUARY 13—From reading the papers of the last few days I have almost begun to feel that fear motivates much of our thought. So I was glad to come across a letter from which I quote:

"People's fears are an odd thing anyhow. Here are these people all so scared for the Supreme Court, because it 'protects our liberties.' *Whose* liberties has it protected?

"Here they are terrified lest the Constitution be interpreted as it was meant to be interpreted in each age according to that period's own ideas, instead of those of the past generation. It seems to me it would be more intelligent to be afraid of strangling democracy by letting a fossilizing process harden the Constitution into a cocoon which must be violently broken because it *could* not grow up with the life within. Life implies growth, and the Constitution was never meant to be used as the Bible was by our most puritanical Puritans.

"'The letter killeth.' Do these people really want to be ruled by a frozen document? If so, they are the ones who are going back upon the American spirit, not we.

"I do hope that there are enough men and women of vision in Congress who are not ridden by these fears, which seem most inappropriate ones in the mouths of self-governing people. It seems to me, it would be better to have less in the Constitution than more, because it has all got to stand interpretation and reinterpretation through the ages.

"Suppose we fill it up with stuff about employers and labor, and two hundred years from now, we are all employing one another in cooperative fashion. All that instead of being fundamental law is really changeable human provision for certain conditions. There is very little actual fundamental law. Really only 'love one another.' The rest is all interpretation— even the Ten Commandments.

"You know, I really hate to see even the Child Labor Amendment added, but I am working for it because it is no less inappropriate than others in the Constitution and there seems to be no hope of accomplishing the end otherwise."

Curiously enough, I never thought very much myself about what could be considered fundamental law. If it is really "love one another," how woefully short we fall of New Testament standards!

∼

When Eleanor Roosevelt insisted that she wanted to take drives without a Secret Service escort, Louis Howe gave her a gun, and Earl Miller, the bodyguard she befriended, taught her how to shoot.

ALVA, OKLA., MARCH 13—While I was speaking this morning, my eldest son called me all the way from Washington. The story, which has seemed to be of the greatest interest to everyone out here, had reached Washington and they were worried. It is too bad that it is not absolutely accurate, for, according to newspaper reports, it caused one youngster great disappointment.

He was the son of my hostess at one of my stops and he had read that I carried a gun with me. Someone had evidently forgotten to mention what I actually said—namely, that when I motored and was driving my own car by myself, the Secret Service had asked me to carry a pistol. I did it and learned how to use it. I do not mean by this that I am an expert shot; I only wish I were. If inheritance has anything to do with it I ought to be, for my father could hold his own even in the West in those early days when my Uncle Theodore Roosevelt had a ranch in the Dakotas. These things do not, however, go by inheritance. My opportunities for shooting have been few and far between, but if the necessity arose, I do know how to use a pistol.

~

Though many would disagree today, Mrs. Roosevelt held a firm belief that women and math don't mix well.

WASHINGTON, APRIL 21—Last night we had a rather prolonged dinner because I actually had the temerity to discuss a time-taking question of mathematics with the gentlemen, my husband and my brother.

I know women should never discuss mathematics, our minds don't function that way. But, on the whole, it didn't work out so badly because everything was so carefully explained to me and I was so persistent that I think they finally got my point of view—which was in this particular case that mathematics made little difference, though it does seem to loom very large in the masculine mind.

As soon as we went upstairs I said good night and went to work at my desk. There is one thing quite certain, and that is that visitors who come for anything but formal entertainments should be prepared to entertain themselves from dinnertime on, unless the President happens to be having a movie. Otherwise both of us retire to our respective studies and a guest who expects to be entertained will have a disappointing time.

~

Despite her mother-in-law's disapproval, Eleanor Roosevelt rejoiced in her role as a working wife. Her endeavors included co-owning a furniture business based at Eleanor's Hyde Park, New York, home, "Val-Kill"; hosting a radio show; journalism and book writing; and teaching at a private school.

Eventually White House obligations prevented Mrs. Roosevelt from actively continuing some projects, so she turned her energy to lecture tours and broadcasts. Her earnings, most of which were given to charity, usually topped the President's salary.

HYDE PARK, JULY 24—I am particularly happy today that the Senate has followed in the steps of the House and sent the bill repealing the so-called married persons clause of the Economy Act to the President for his signature. This bill has worked a great deal of hardship among government employees. It was probably necessary as an emergency economy measure, but it is very satisfactory to feel Congress considers the emergency to be at an end.

The other day I received an appeal from an organization which has as its purpose the removal of any married woman, whose husband earns enough to support her, from all employment. Who is to say when a man earns enough to support his family? Who is to know, except the individuals themselves, what they need for daily living or what responsibilities are hidden from the public eye? There are few families indeed who do not have some members outside of their own immediate family who need assistance.

Added to this, who is to say whether a woman needs to work outside her home for the good of her own soul? Many women can find all the work they need, all the joy they need and all the interest they need in life in their own homes and in the volunteer community activities of their environment. Because of this I have received many critical letters from women complaining that other women who did not need paid jobs were taking them. That they were working for luxuries and not for necessities, that men who had families to support were being kept out of jobs by these selfish and luxury-loving creatures.

I have investigated a good many cases and find that, on the whole, the love of work is not so great. Those who are gainfully employed are usually working because of some real need. There are a few, however, who work because something in them craves the particular kind of work which they are doing, or an inner urge drives them to work at a job. They are not entirely satisfied with work in the home.

This does not mean they are not good mothers and housekeepers, but they need some other stimulus in life. Frequently they provide work for other people. If they suddenly ceased their activities many other people might lose their jobs. As a rule, these women are the creative type.

It seems to me that the tradition of respect for work is so ingrained in this country that it is not surprising fathers have handed it down to their daughters as well as to their sons. In the coming years, I wonder if we are not going to have more respect for women who work and give work to others than for women who sit at home with many idle hours on their hands or fill their time with occupations which may indirectly provide work for others but which give them none of the satisfaction of real personal achievement.

~

Eleanor Roosevelt was a news junkie, devouring several newspapers daily. "My Day" often parsed recent headlines. The New York Times *headlines reported a Soviet flier and five passengers attempting a flight from Moscow over the North Pole to New York. In Spain, Franco's troops seized the once autonomous Catalan territory. Japan shook the world by taking over*

China's most important seaport, Shanghai. The House ignored FDR's pleas for a balanced budget, adding $20,367,500 and passing the third deficiency appropriation bill for nearly $100 million. Mrs. Roosevelt's critique of congressional budgeting rested on her grasp of ordinary domestic affairs.

HYDE PARK, AUGUST 17—I hate the newspapers these days and yet I can't wait to see them. We are hunting for the Russian fliers and I only hope they will be found safe and sound. Then, there is war news from China and Spain and difficulties here between employers and their employees.

The only really pleasant piece of news on the front page of the first paper I looked at this morning was a column on the possibility of balancing our own budget. That will be pleasant news to some people, for many have wondered if an attempt was ever going to be made to do this. I have heard wails and groans over the fact that they could see no signs in this Administration of an interest in economy.

Like almost every other woman I know of moderate means, I am always terribly nervous until all my bills are paid and I know I still have a balance in the bank. Anything borrowed hangs over my head like a cloud. I do hope, however, that in this budget balancing business we make our economies without making people suffer who are in need of help. There are wise and unwise economies, as every housewife knows and, figuratively speaking, the women of the country should be watching their husbands to see that the national budget is balanced wisely.

～

Mrs. Roosevelt was in Boston to help her son John through the ordeal of having four wisdom teeth removed. While there she wrote a column inveighing against discrimination toward "mature workers."

BOSTON, OCTOBER 27—There is no doubt about it, the hours spent sitting around in a hospital are conducive to doing a great deal of knitting—if that happens to be the only kind of work you have at hand. I started a sweater not very long ago in the hope, which I confess was faint, that it would be finished as a Christmas present. These two days up here make me very hopeful it will be ready before that date arrives.

I have also read a great many communications and articles sent on from my Washington mail. One of the articles was of special interest. It appeared in one of our larger magazines. It deals with the topic of the curtailment of employment for people beyond 35 or 40 years of age. It is interestingly written and gives some actual stories of what has happened in the past few years to people who found themselves obliged to look for new occupations between the age of 35 and 65. An old-age pension steps in to care for people at 65 or 70.

The writer makes an excellent point, it seems to me, when he says that the policy many employers have of hiring only very young people will mean we will only have some 15 years in which to earn the necessary money to care for our children until they are of working age. That working age seems now to be in the 20s. We must also provide for our own old age which is to begin, apparently, after 15 years of work.

Of course, looked at in cold-blooded fashion, this is preposterous—for in our own experience we know that the most vigorous and able people of our acquaintance, doing the most important work in the world, are people between 40 and 60.

We always seem to go to extremes in this land of ours. We neglect to help youth get its first job and [we] give youth [a] feeling there is no place in the world in which it fits. Then we bring complete discouragement to the mature worker of 35 or 40 by telling them time after time, "We prefer to employ people between 25 and 35."

How contradictory we are—and how lacking in real understanding. These mature years should be used productively to increase the buying power of the nation.

It would be legitimate to ask employers to contribute to constructive thinking which leads to more employment, that they help to find places for young people entering industrial life. But to have no place for them is like writing a death warrant to the expansion of our industries.

1938

*P*resident Roosevelt began 1938 by asking Congress for appropriations to build up the armed forces, especially the navy. In February, British Foreign Minister Anthony Eden resigned in disagreement with Prime Minister Neville Chamberlain's belief that appeasing Hitler would maintain peace. By March, Nazi troops invaded Austria.

FDR signed the landmark Fair Labor Standards Act in June, starting the minimum wage at 25 cents an hour and fixing the maximum work week at 44 hours. Detroit's "Brown Bomber," Joe Louis, defended his heavyweight title by knocking out Germany's Max Schmeling.

In September, with backing from Hitler, German-speaking people in Czechoslovakia demanded self-determination, triggering the Munich crisis. Germany, England, Italy, and France then conferred on a "peaceful" solution to the struggle in Europe. By autumn, Czechoslovakia was dismembered, with parts claimed by Germany, Hungary, and Poland.

The night before Halloween, another type of invasion stirred up America. Orson Welles's realistic radio drama *Invasion from Mars* (adapted from H. G. Wells's *War of the Worlds*) frightened unprepared listeners and caused a substantial panic.

In November, a Jewish refugee killed a German diplomat in Paris. In revenge, SS troops smashed, burned, and looted Jewish homes, synagogues, and shops throughout Germany in a night of terror known as "Kristallnacht." The Nazis also shattered the lives of more than 20,000 Jews who were sent to concentration camps. President Roosevelt called a press conference to condemn Hitler, and Britain considered plans to evacuate the 700,000 Jews living in Germany.

During 1938 many Americans found refuge from the ever-changing world in the First Lady's newspaper column. Writing in *The Nation*, Mary

Marshall observed, "To the prisoners of newspapers where wars are always raging, 'My Day' is like a sunny square where children and aunts and grandmothers go about their trivial but absorbing pursuits and security reigns. In the sense of security it generates lies the deepest appeal of 'My Day.'"

After balls celebrating FDR's birthday raised substantial funds to fight infantile paralysis, the National Foundation for Infantile Paralysis formed in 1937. Right before the 1938 fundraising drive, vaudevillian Eddie Cantor coined the name "March of Dimes" and asked Americans to send contributions to the White House. The result: $1.8 million in donations during that year.

FDR also observed a private birthday tradition, celebrating with supporters of his 1920 bid for vice president. This Old Guard included Missy LeHand, James Farley, and Frances Perkins. New Dealers like Secretary of the Treasury Henry Morgenthau, Jr.; Secretary of State Cordell Hull; and Secretary of the Interior Harold Ickes made up the New Guard.

WASHINGTON, JANUARY 30—I reached Washington yesterday just in time to welcome my very large family, which had arrived for the President's birthday. All four boys are here, three daughters-in-law and one fiancée, and we all miss Anna and John and feel they should be here too!

After greeting my children, we went down in a body to welcome all the movie talent which had come to help out in the President's Birthday Balls. We had a very jolly pleasant luncheon in the State Dining Room. As usual, my family seemed to make more noise than any of the guests. After our guests had met the President, the children took them on a tour of the offices and the White House. When they finally returned to my room, we discovered that some of the related history was not exactly accurate! Then we had pictures taken and they started off to prepare for the evening's work.

The Old Guard, which dates back to the 1920 campaign, and the New Guard, which comprises more recent additions, all dined with us last night. I think the birthday dinner was as jolly a dinner as we have ever had. An added feature this year was a double celebration, for Franklin Jr.'s wife Ethel was also born on January 30.

A little after 10 o'clock, I started off with three gentleman escorts to visit each of the hotels where a ball was going on. The crowds seemed larger and happier, as though they all rejoiced in being able to take part in this fight against infantile paralysis. By 12:45 we were back at the White House and I confess that it was with difficulty that I did a short half-hour's work at my desk.

Miss Dickerman and I had a grand ride this morning. Sad to say, my horse Dot is lame, and I don't enjoy any other horse's gait quite as much. Everybody at Fort Meyer was interested in the horse's condition for I am to ride Dot in the horse show Tuesday night. As we rode along the bridle path, several people asked Captain Reybold, rather apprehensively I thought, "How is Dot today?" I felt that she was more important than I have ever realized.

~

Mrs. Roosevelt, a popular speaker, was self-conscious about the high pitch and register of her voice, which many in her audience found irritating. Here she talks candidly about her decision to begin voice lessons.

NEW YORK, FEBRUARY 22—I came to New York on the midnight train last night, and I have today taken my first lesson to improve my speaking voice. It seems stupid not to have done this before, but I am always so busy and I never realized until lately that as one grows older it is important not to strain one's voice. One must take advantage of anything which can make life easier for oneself and pleasanter for other people.

~

Franklin Roosevelt—gentleman farmer, good Samaritan stricken by infantile paralysis the day he helped put out a forest fire—knew the value of land. During the President's first hundred days in office he nurtured into existence the Civilian Conservation Corps, to improve the country's natural resources and put unemployed young men to work.

The U.S. Army set up camps where men between eighteen and twenty-five lived and worked for a minimum of six months. The pay started at thirty dollars a month. FDR made sure some camps were open to blacks and Indians. In peak years, the CCC employed 500,000. U.S. involvement in World War II ended the CCC, but by 1941 more than 200 million trees had been planted on 17 million acres around the country.

NEW YORK, APRIL 16—A dinner was given last night to celebrate the fifth birthday of the CCC camps and I went to read a message from the President. I was very happy to be able to spend a few minutes with these people who have made this nationwide program possible. I feel the work of the CCC camps has enriched many communities.

Aside from the fact that it has taken boys who might have drifted into evil ways and kept them busy, it has given them better health and skill with which to face the world. Someday we will have fewer floods because of the trees which the CCC has planted, better soil because of the soil erosion program which they have helped to carry on, and innumerable improvements which can be seen everywhere throughout the country.

I returned to find our son Franklin Jr. had just arrived. He was talking to his father and had not decided whether he would stay the night and rise early to drive to Charlottesville, or whether he would proceed at once. In my most organizing spirit, I started to make his plans for him. He looked at me with the funniest expression and said "I don't like being organized. I'm going to flip a coin!"

The coin decided that he would go, but he finally stayed.

~

Joe Louis, the "Brown Bomber," was world champion heavyweight boxer for twelve years, winning the title after a historic fight. Louis seemed indestructible until 1936, when Germany's Max Schmeling became the first fighter to knock out Louis. Hitler hailed Schmeling's victory as proof that Germans were the master race.

Nevertheless, Louis was soon proclaimed world champ. Hitler wanted Schmeling to challenge the champ and win the title. The fight became more than a sporting event; it became an issue of national pride. The exciting match was over in two minutes and four seconds, with Louis the victor.

HYDE PARK, JUNE 23—Of course, all I've heard for the last few days is "The fight" so, though I was working on a manuscript last night, when 10 o'clock came I turned on the radio, lo and behold much noise and excitement and then, puff, it was all over in two minutes.

Much money came into New York City, and it was probably good for business in general. People traveled from many parts of the country. Restaurants, hotels, taxicabs—the ramifications of the way money is spent when an event of this kind occurs are infinite. So it is helpful, but I think a good many people must have felt that their entertainment was rather short.

Joe Louis is a great fighter: There seems to be no one left for him to fight. We congratulate him and hope that he has some wise member of his family who takes his money away and puts it away so that when he no longer has any opponents, he will be able to do something else to make life interesting and pleasant.

I'm always sorry for the man who is beaten or the team which loses. Much effort has gone into training and preparation and it must be such a terrible letdown. I've never seen a fight and probably never shall, but every time I see a crew race or a football game, I grieve over the boys who are beaten and slump in their boat, or the team that has to go off the field cheering the victors when their hearts are filled with despair.

~

In 1938, ten-year-old Shirley Temple was at the peak of her career. Already, she had been in the entertainment business for six years—singing and tapping her way through ten films—and was considered the biggest box-office draw of the 1930s.

It is possible that FDR was the "gentleman present who became the star's willing slave for the day."

POUGHKEEPSIE, JULY 10—My grandchildren [Sistie and Buzz] came home on Friday evening and yesterday was a red-letter day for us all. Mr. and Mrs. Temple brought Shirley for a picnic. In addition to Shirley, Sistie and Buzz, we had two children who live here, and Mr. and Mrs. George Bye's little niece, Lois Rosenbauer. When I met Shirley in Hollywood last spring, I was impressed by her natural simplicity and charm and marveled at what her mother had succeeded in doing. She had kept her a child in spite of having to make her mature in so many ways.

Newspapers, photographers and newsreels were all anxious to follow the party but it was everybody's wish that since Shirley was on a holiday, it should be made as pleasant a picnic as possible. Only the Fox Films, with whom she is under contract, were allowed to take a few shots. I was amused when we walked out together for the first picture to have her tell me just what to do. "We should walk," she said, "from far back and wave at the camera as we come out." When I did not realize the camera was following us, she said, "They are still taking us," and we turned for a final wave together. After that was over, there was no more preoccupation with pictures.

The children ate their picnic food with the zest which all children should have for outdoor meals. They watched their chops broil and worried over the chance of their burning, for I have never yet mastered the art of removing enough fat to prevent my charcoal fire from flaming up again as the fat burns. Secretary and Mrs. Morgenthau, who are fond of Shirley, had sent up some of their delicious raspberries and that with ice cream seemed to be a very satisfactory dessert. Shirley demanded to know why I did not have on the badge she had given me in Hollywood. I reminded her that while she did give me two, they were meant for Sistie and Buzz; then they had to explain that the badges were at home in Seattle.

As a sign of her special favor, she handed one of her badges to a gentleman present who was her willing slave for the afternoon. She informed him if he did not wear it he would have to pay a fine, and if he lost it, an even greater one, and the money all went to the Babies' Milk Fund in Los Angeles. After the picnic was over, I took everyone over to see my mother-in-law at the big house and told Shirley about the Gilbert Stuart portrait of Isaac Roosevelt which hangs over the mantlepiece in the big library.

I doubt if this bit of history meant as much to her as a chance to go out with her father and the other gentleman, who had dedicated his day to her, and to see the horses. I only hope the entire family was as sorry to leave as we were to see them go. All of us here are wishing for chances in the future to meet again. A well brought-up charming child is a joy to all who meet her.

∼

Mrs. Roosevelt's column appeared in 75 papers and had 4 million readers when excerpts were collected into a book, My Days. *Reviewing it,* Time *magazine observed: "More remarkable than the fact that one of the most active gadders in the U.S. can find time to turn out a daily column is the fact that in so doing, she has consistently avoided boners. . . . But most gratifying to millions of women readers, who write her thousands of letters, is Mrs. Roosevelt's ability to make the nation's most exalted household seem like anybody else's."*

HYDE PARK, AUGUST 12—I don't know if other authors feel as I do when a copy of a new book first appears from the publisher, but I always have a little sense of wonder that I actually wrote so many words and that anyone thought it worthwhile to publish. This morning there came into my hands a new book. It will not be out until the 22nd, so I cannot really tell you about it, but I can't help imparting a little of my own thrill.

Not long ago someone sent me an article by a very well-known journalist who indicated that, as a family, we all like publicity, for otherwise we would not write so much and talk so much and do so many things that put us in print, or in the public eye in one way or another. The gentleman forgets it is not entirely our own doings which put us in the public eye. But I must plead guilty to the writing and the talking for I did both before my husband became the President and I hope I shall continue to do so after he ceases to be president. I have no illusions about being a great speaker or a great writer, but I think in some of us there is an urge to do certain things, and if we did not do them, we would feel that we were not fulfilling the job which we had been given opportunities and talents to do.

Frequently, too, there is an objective approach to oneself in viewing one's activities. In much of my own life, for instance, I stand back and look at myself and think that isn't you as an individual, that is you as the personage you may happen to have to be for this period of time. I imagine that comes from having been a shy child with very little personality and having become accustomed to do things because they were expected of me and not because I wanted to do them.

~

James Roosevelt joined his father's staff in 1937, although his mother predicted it would cause trouble. James did not handle the tension of being dissected by the press, politicians, and the public with his mother's equanimity; he developed a serious case of ulcers. With his mother in tow, he went to the Mayo Clinic for treatment. Writing from Minnesota, Mrs. Roosevelt praised Neville Chamberlain's efforts to avoid another European war.

ROCHESTER, MINN., SEPTEMBER 16—The bellboys, the taxi drivers, the people who pass me in the street, all ask how James is feeling. I am glad to be leaving with such a light heart and a feeling that all is going to progress smoothly and well from now on. Jimmy could not be in a more friendly atmosphere.

I open the newspaper every day with a feeling of dread, and I turn on the radio to listen to the last news broadcast at night, half afraid to hear that the catastrophe of war has again fallen on Europe. It seems to me that the Prime Minister of England did a fine thing when he went to visit the German Chancellor in a last effort to prevent bloodshed. It seems insanity to me to try to settle the difficult problems of the day by the unsatisfactory method of going to war. If you kill half the youth of a continent, the problems will be no nearer to solution but the human race will be that much poorer.

~

On September 21, without much warning, a vortex of rain and wind hit the beach towns of Long Island and slashed its way up the coast. In Westhampton, only 6 of 150 buildings remained standing. During the flash floods, people drowned in the streets. Gathering speed as it worked its way through New England, the hurricane smashed into Massachusetts with gusts of 186 mph. The savage storm wrecked homes, uprooted trees, and killed at least 700 people.

NEW YORK, OCTOBER 2—We experienced so many painful impressions yesterday that it is hard to tell you which seemed the most terrible. Many people lost members of their families and friends. There are still many people missing.

A rocking chair with a little child's chair not far away in the middle of a field seemed the epitome of desolation. All around was wreckage of one kind and another. Along the shore we could see a few houses still standing, leaning crazily in different directions. In some places the land, as well as the house, has disappeared, and prized possessions with which families had old associations are gone forever.

Of the big cities, Providence, R.I., seems to have had the hardest time. There we saw the best example of the curious, freakish things which a storm can do. Two huge coal barges were evidently picked up by the waves, washed over the top of a little brick harbormaster's house and neatly set down side by side, about a foot apart, between his brick house and a gas station which was not even scratched. These barges now stand by the main highway, and I imagine they will be there for many a long day, for it hardly seems possible to get them back into the water.

The great loss of trees, particularly the tall giants which have been the pride of many of these New England towns, gives one a curious feeling of desolation, perhaps even greater than the damage to the houses along the village streets. Nature does repair her ravages fairly quickly but it will be a long time before these giants will reappear in the streets, parks and village greens of New England.

Everyone who went through the storm on the coast felt that it was a terrifying experience. All of them praise the WPA [Works Progress Administration] men and the CCC boys and NYA [National Youth Administration] boys, in just the way I heard them praised in Springfield, Mass.

~

Eleanor Roosevelt often remarked how hard it was for her children to grow up in the White House. When FDR became President, the Roosevelts' oldest child, Anna, was twenty-six and the youngest son, John, was sixteen. As adults, the children would often chide their mother for being either too disciplined or too aloof.

HYDE PARK, NOVEMBER 11—My journeys are over, and I hardly realized that I have covered so much territory and seen so many of my children and grandchildren.

A newspaperwoman on one of my stops tried to catechize me on the proper relationship between parents and their children. It grew out of [a] remark I made that I was horribly neat, and she wanted to know if one could be too neat. Because I had nothing better to say, I answered, "Yes, if one nags one's family too much on the subject, and makes life miserable for everyone." Thereupon she asked if I had succeeded in making my children as neat as I was myself. She had brought her son down to meet me, so I gathered she found it very difficult to make him live up to her own standards.

The answer, of course, is that having children is, perhaps, the beginning of an education for them, but it is certainly the beginning of an education for their parents. All their young lives their parents are learning self-control, patience, a sense of values, how to respect other people's personalities and yet not neglect teaching some things which, if they are not learned young, must be learned in later life with far greater hardship.

When these early years are over, this type of education comes to an end. The parents think they have done all they can do in the way of home discipline and education, and a new phase of mutual education begins. Parents then find that having developed individuals, they must permit those individuals to live their own lives, to have their own experiences, to make their own decisions, sometimes to make their own mistakes.

I don't know how other parents are, but I know that for myself, I can stand back and look at my children and what they do and think, once they are grown up, with a certain amount of objectivity. On the other hand, I know quite well that there is a bond between us and that, right or wrong, that bond could never be broken. I am proud of them when I think they have acquitted themselves well, regardless of what the rest of the world may think. Even when I disagree and feel impelled to tell them so, I know that I understand them better than anyone else, perhaps. They are always my children, with the right to call upon me in case of need.

The greatest contribution the older generation can give, I think, to the younger generation, is the feeling that there is someone to fall back upon, more especially when the hard times of life come upon them. That is so even when we know that we have brought those hard times upon ourselves.

Funny that a newspaperwoman, in a casual interview at an airport, should force me to think of one of the most binding relationships in life. I have been immersed in personal things for several days, and it is rather a strange transition back to a life which is completely taken up with public affairs.

1939

*E*arly in 1939 activist Joseph Lash met Eleanor Roosevelt. Writing to a friend, Lash, just 29 and a "self-styled revolutionary," dismissed the First Lady as "a good woman utterly lacking in knowledge of social forces . . . who thought that she could reform capitalists by inviting them to the White House for dinner and a good talking to." Lash, himself, dined at the White House and received a talking to from both the President and the First Lady, but he also got a chance to see Eleanor Roosevelt put her beliefs into action. By year's end, Lash's derision turned into devotion. He wasn't alone in his high esteem for Mrs. Roosevelt. A 1939 Gallup poll showed the First Lady outranking the President, winning 67 percent approval compared to FDR's 58 percent.

In an April 17 cover story, *Time* rendered this tribute: "Mrs. Roosevelt is an oracle to millions of housewives. She would bring them face to face with right and wrong. . . . Her audience has grown and so have her skill and temerity so she can venture past platitudes. Now people accept her for what she is. . . . Sophisticates who would scoff now listen."

This was the year when the Supreme Court ruled sit-down strikes illegal, and July Fourth celebrations were dimmed when the New York Yankees' Lou Gehrig retired—a form of spinal paralysis slowly immobilizing the great first baseman.

Also in 1939, Eleanor Roosevelt dared to serve hot dogs to the visiting King and Queen of England and visited both the San Francisco and New York World's Fairs. As the year wore on, she came to the painful realization that the U.S. must abandon isolationism and neutrality to aid the beleaguered Allies. World War II was under way. A mother of four sons, the First Lady reluctantly decided that America must strengthen its armed forces.

Some accused Mrs. Roosevelt of being influenced by the President or by the Communists, but most would have agreed with this observation in a *New York Times* article: "After her hundreds and thousands of miles of industrious travel and sightseeing and myriads of questions and explanations, the probability exists that she is, except for the President, the best informed individual on the American scene."

When Howard University planned to present the acclaimed contralto Marian Anderson in concert, she was banned from Washington's Constitution Hall. The Daughters of the American Revolution, who espoused a "No Negroes" policy, controlled the hall.

Having welcomed Marian Anderson to the White House in 1936, Eleanor Roosevelt could no longer support the DAR's policy and resigned from the organization. In a Gallup survey, 67 percent of Americans agreed with the First Lady, and her resignation triggered much debate about segregation.

FDR's Secretary of the Interior Harold L. Ickes and NAACP leader Walter White helped Anderson find a new concert space: the foot of the Lincoln Memorial. At the free concert, more than 75,000 people listened to Marian Anderson's renditions of "Nobody Knows the Trouble I've Seen" and "America."

WASHINGTON, FEBRUARY 27—I am having a peaceful day. I drove my car a short distance out of the city this morning to pilot some friends of mine who are starting off for a vacation in Florida. I think this will be my only excursion out of the White House today, for I have plenty of work to do on an accumulation of mail, and I hope to get through in time to enjoy an evening of uninterrupted reading. I have been debating in my mind for some time, a question which I have had to debate with myself once or twice before in my life. Usually I have decided differently from the way in which I am deciding now. The question is, if you belong to an organization and disapprove of an action which is typical of a policy, should you resign or is it better to work for a changed point of view within the organization? In the past, when I was able to work actively in any organization to which I belonged, I have usually stayed until I had at least made a fight and had been defeated.

Even then, I have, as a rule, accepted my defeat and decided I was wrong or, perhaps, a little too far ahead of the thinking for the majority at that time. I have often found that the thing in which I was interested was done some years later. But in this case, I belong to an organization in which I can do no active work. They have taken an action which has been widely talked of in the press. To remain as a member implies approval of that action, and therefore I am resigning.

~

In 1932, Mrs. Roosevelt, with daughter Anna as assistant, became the editor of Babies—Just Babies. *Her first editorial began: "Babies, just babies, can you think of anything more wonderful?" Mrs. Roosevelt withdrew from the magazine before FDR's 1933 inauguration, but firmly held to her sentiments. A doting grandmother, she flew to Seattle to be with Anna while she had her third baby.*

Anna married John Boettiger six months after divorcing Curtis Dall. Boettiger was one of Mrs. Roosevelt's favorite reporters, although he had worked for the anti-Roosevelt Chicago Tribune. *The First Lady enjoyed playing Cupid in her daughter's romance and frequently visited the couple on the West Coast.*

SEATTLE, APRIL 1—What a different point of view one can have on life in 24 hours. The night before last, John and Anna and I were still waiting for a baby's arrival, and no one can tell me that is ever an entirely carefree time. No matter how many times we have seen babies come safely into the world, we always think before the event of all the dreadful possibilities that surround all human ventures. When, yesterday afternoon, Anna was safely back in her own room at the hospital and the baby was brought in for John and Anna to inspect together, the sun shone outside. But it would have made no difference, for the sun was certainly shining in our world as far as all the people who love Anna were concerned.

I feel sure that the baby is going to grow up able to take care of himself in life, for he began at once to make himself heard and to move his arms and legs like a little prizefighter. His shoulders are broad too, like his father's, so he ought to carry burdens.

Sometimes I think one's subconscious mind shows the trend of one's thoughts: Anna kept murmuring yesterday, "So many social problems and I can't solve them," as though she were searching for the answers and could not get her mind quite focused on them. The baby was saddled at once with responsibility, for the first thing Anna said about him was "He is so tiny now, but some day he may do something really big."

Sistie and Buzz came down to see the baby in the afternoon and were a little awed by anything which looked so small, even though we told them what a big baby he is. However, at supper the baby's future status was settled. In discussing the difficulty of adding to the Johns already in the family, Buzz suddenly remembered that Robin Hood had a Little John as his constant companion, so he announced that he would be Robin Hood and the baby would be Little John.

This is one occasion when an event actually occurred in the family and was telephoned to the President before the press was aware of the news. This so rarely happens that I could hardly believe it was possible. Judging from my husband's tone of voice, it gave him great joy to hear it in Warm Springs, Georgia, half an hour after the baby's arrival. And then to be able to announce it to the press.

When you love people very much, isn't it grand to be able to join in their happiness? Like everything else in the world, however, there is a price to pay for love, for the more happiness we derive from the existence and companionship of other human beings, the more vulnerable we are when there is any cause for apprehension. It takes courage to love, but pain through love is the purifying fire which those who love generously know. We all know people who are so much afraid of pain that they shut themselves up like clams in a shell and, giving out nothing, receive nothing and therefore shrink until life is a mere living death.

~

As a new bride living at the Roosevelt estate in Hyde Park, Eleanor Roosevelt felt that much of her life was controlled by her mother-in-law. While Sara Roosevelt usually exercised firm rule over Hyde Park, FDR had final say during King George VI and Queen Elizabeth's visit. Lowly hot dogs and beer were served at the Hyde Park picnic. The royal couple also sampled other American favorites: smoked turkey, cured ham, baked beans, and strawberry shortcake. Evidently, foreign relations did not suffer.

ARTHURDALE, W. VA., MAY 26—Oh dear, oh dear, so many people are worried that "the dignity of our country will be imperiled" by inviting royalty to a picnic, particularly a hot dog picnic. My mother-in-law has sent me a letter she received, which begs that she control me in some way and in order to spare my feelings she has written a little message on the back: "Only one of many such." But she did not know, poor darling, that I have received "many such" right here in Washington. Let me assure you, dear readers, that if it is hot there will be no hot dogs, and even if it is cool, there will be plenty of other food, and the elder members of the family and the more important guests will be served with due formality. It might be possible to meet the desire of these interested correspondents if there were not quite so many who berate me for too much formality and too much courtesy. I am afraid it is a case of not being able to please everybody and so we will try just to please our guests.

~

The First Lady was making a round of WPA projects when she wrote this column on the road in Tennessee. Grading it "excellent," Harper's magazine observed that Mrs. Roosevelt "is adept at rolling up the curtain on her life and inviting her readers to look in the window as if it were a play."

JOHNSON CITY, TENN., MAY 31—I looked out of the window of the train this morning while I was waiting for my breakfast, and it suddenly occurred to me that scenes from a train window might give a rather good picture of the variety in the conditions and occupations of our people in different parts of the country. I saw a little girl, slim and bent over, carrying two heavy pails of water across a field to an unpainted house. How far that water had to be carried, I do not know, but it is one thing to carry water on a camping trip for fun during a summer's holiday, and it is another thing to carry it day in and day out as a part of the routine of living. On the outskirts of the town, I saw a wash line. On it hung two brown work shirts, a pair of rather frayed and faded blue dungarees, two child's sun suits and a woman's calico dress. Not much sign of wasteful living here.

Through its open door, I had a glimpse of the inside of a cabin in the hollow below us. It was divided into two rooms, one of them the bedroom with two beds in it. These beds took up about all the available space in the room and it must have been necessary to leave the door open for air. There was a pad which looked rather like the cotton mattresses that have been made on WPA, and a quilt spread neatly over each bed. I didn't notice any sheets or pillows.

There has been rain down here and the fields look in good condition. We passed a man plowing in a field with two women not far away hoeing. Beyond, in a grove of trees, there stood a stately house and under the trees was a baby carriage. I caught sight of someone in a flowered dress sitting on the porch. Then I again saw a yard of an unpainted house in the outskirts of a small town and a happy looking woman rocking a baby on the porch while a group of youngsters played in the yard. Happiness may exist under all conditions, given the right kind of people and sufficient economic security for adequate food and shelter.

~

It was a sad day for the First Family when the Roosevelts' daughter-in-law Anne (wife of their youngest son John) suffered a miscarriage. Mrs. Roosevelt later noted that during this time she relived the sorrow of losing their second son (the first Franklin Jr.), who died in infancy.

BOSTON, JUNE 3—I find myself unexpectedly in Boston. The night before last, our youngest son called me in Washington and said that the doctors were a little worried about his wife during the day. Even when I reached New York late yesterday afternoon, there was no further news.

Today I took a friend to the World's Fair and returned to my apartment rather late. As I entered the door, the telephone was ringing. It proved to be my son, who told me that things were not going very well with his wife. It always seems particularly hard when young people meet the first disciplines of life. We know these have to come to all of us but it never makes it any easier. I wondered what to do, feeling that it was probably too late to make the night train, when my husband called me on the telephone. I voiced my doubt of being able to make the midnight train and he said firmly: "What are you thinking about? It is only 1 o'clock." And so it was by Standard Time, which I had entirely forgotten. Then he added: "You can get the train that goes through the Pennsylvania Station at 12:45," which I did.

I was fortunate enough to obtain a section and realized how spoiled I had been lately, for traveling so much with Miss Thompson has made it possible to have a compartment. I had almost forgotten how to dress and undress in a berth. Fortunately, the technique is soon reacquired. I can't say, however, that the night was a very restful one and I was glad to arrive here this morning. If I did nothing else, I was able to answer the questions of the various reporters and take that much off my son.

To have hoped for a baby and then not to have it is always a very bitter disappointment, but these two young people realize that they have much to be thankful for in that Anne herself is well and strong. They are young and the future lies before them and they have the courage which makes us proud of youth. Like all other disappointments and sorrows, it will probably make them more conscious that, in the real things in life, everyone stands on the same level and God sends us disciplines in order that we may better understand the sufferings of other people.

~

Under Hallie Flanagan's direction, the Federal Theatre staged more than 50,000 performances in forty states. During the program's four-year run, millions of Americans viewed its productions, most of which were free. The controversial New Deal WPA project received $25 million in government funds and created employment for thousands of actors and stagehands.

The Federal Theatre, however, got bad reviews from William Randolph Hearst and Martin Dies's House Committee on Un-American Activities, who viewed some plays as Communist-inspired. Some critics complained that the program didn't develop any hits or memorable stars. Others, how-

ever, noted that it introduced T. S. Eliot's Murder in the Cathedral *and allowed Orson Welles to direct a memorable all-black* Macbeth.

Unfortunately, Mrs. Roosevelt couldn't be the Federal Theatre's much-needed angel, and Congress cut the program's funds in July.

HYDE PARK, JUNE 20—After my ride, I sat in the sun and read the newspapers, completely forgetting I had an appointment with Mrs. Hallie Flanagan at noon. She appeared on time, however, and I confess that I am just as concerned as she is about the proposed ending of the Federal Theatre Projects. There seems to be nothing I can do to help. Apparently the House of Representatives has decided that it doesn't matter what happens to people who have definite talents of a particular kind. Only 5 percent of people on the Federal Theatre Project are non-relief, so apparently the 95 percent can starve, go on local relief, or dig ditches, if they can find ditches to dig.

I know that this project is considered dangerous because it may harbor some Communists, but I wonder if Communists occupied in producing plays are not safer than Communists starving to death. I have always felt that whatever your beliefs might be, if you could earn enough to keep body and soul together and had to be pretty busy doing that, you would not be very apt to have time to plot the overthrow of any existing government.

However, the wisdom of Congress must never be questioned and I can only hope that in the Senate some changes may be deemed wise. If this is an era, as some people think, of civilization, then this project may serve as an instrument to that end.

～

The Grapes of Wrath *sold 300,000 copies its first year and brought John Steinbeck a Pulitzer Prize. Steinbeck described the disappointment that shatters the American Dream: people deprived of what they yearn for most—the security of home and work. In the novel, Oklahoma farmers (Okies) displaced by a prolonged extreme drought (the Dust Bowl) seek a simple life and new work in California, confronting complex obstacles that come their way. The book's characters and plot are grounded in Depression era realities.*

HYDE PARK, JUNE 28—Now I must tell you that I have just finished a book which is an unforgettable experience in reading. "The Grapes of Wrath," by John Steinbeck, both repels and attracts you. The horrors of the picture, so well drawn, make you dread sometimes to begin the next chapter, and yet you cannot lay the book down or even skip a page. Somewhere I saw the criticism that this book was anti-religious, but somehow I cannot imagine thinking of "Ma" without, at the same time, thinking of the love "that passeth all understanding."

The book is coarse in spots, but life is coarse in spots, and the story is very beautiful in spots just as life is. We do not dwell upon man's lower nature any more than we have to in life, but we know it exists and we pass over it charitably and are surprised how much there is of fineness that comes out of the baser clay. Even from life's sorrows some good must come. What could be a better illustration than the closing chapter of this book?

~

As a child, Eleanor Roosevelt saw how drinking dissipated her father and later she witnessed its same impact on her brother Hall. A confirmed teeto-taler herself, Mrs. Roosevelt nonetheless permitted liquor in the White House. Her husband won the presidency in 1932, running as the "Wet" can-didate, opposed to Prohibition, which Congress repealed in 1933.

NEW YORK, JULY 14—A number of letters have come to me complaining bitterly about the fact that I said in an article recently that the repeal of prohibition had been a crusade carried on by women. I know quite well, of course, that the Democratic Party took the stand in its platform that Prohibition should be repealed. I have always felt, however, that the women's organization for repeal, which was a nonpartisan organization, laid the groundwork which finally brought about the vote for repeal.

I was one of those who was very happy when the original prohibition amendment passed. I thought innocently that a law in this country would automatically be complied with, and my own observation led me to feel rather ardently that the less strong liquor anyone consumed the better it was. During prohibition I observed the law meticulously, but I came grad-ually to see that laws are only observed with the consent of the individu-als concerned and a moral change still depends on the individual and not on the passage of any law.

Little by little it dawned upon me that this law was not making people drink any less, but it was making hypocrites and law breakers of a great number of people. It seemed to me best to go back to the old situation in which, if a man or woman drank to excess, they were injuring themselves and their immediate family and friends and the act was a violation against their own sense of morality and no violation against the law of the land.

I could never quite bring myself to work for repeal, but I could not op-pose it, for intellectually I had to agree that it was the honest thing to do.

My contacts are wide and I see a great many different groups of people, and I cannot say that I find that the change in the law has made any great change in conditions among young or old in the country today.

~

The women's auxiliary of the American Legion once gave Eleanor Roosevelt a moniker they considered a dubious distinction: America's No. 1 pacifist. Mrs. Roosevelt calmly accepted this label, troubled by memories of World War I. In 1918 she and FDR, then assistant secretary of the navy, inspected the French battlefields. She never forgot the wounded, mangled young soldiers or the ravaged French towns.

HYDE PARK, AUGUST 1—I read an article last night in the "Atlantic Monthly": Graham Hutton's "The Next War" is a rather interesting analysis of the European situation, drawing attention to the fact that in some ways we are duplicating our behavior of before the 1914 cataclysm. The point which struck me particularly was the fact that we did nothing in 1914 to get at the root of the difficulties between the various nations. Nobody attempted to find any remedies which would allay the causes of friction, and it seems to the author, as it does to me, that this is exactly what is happening today.

What is the sense of spending all this money for more and more armaments? Yes, I know we have to do it so long as the nations are doing it. But, where does it lead? Nowhere but to war, because, while it seems the only possible thing to do as a temporary measure to prevent the outbreak of war immediately, no one goes beyond the immediate necessity and talks about the final elimination of the difficulties which have thrust the various powers into their present situation.

Why can't we get around a table and face the fact that Germany and Italy have started this whole performance because it was the only way in which their people could exist? It hasn't been a very good existence and I don't imagine the German and Italian people look forward to war any more than we do, but desperation is desperation wherever you find it and this course begun by Germany and Italy has driven the other nations into courses which we all are now pursuing.

We invited the nations to sit around a table last spring. But, though I feel very sure that among the people of the world there is a desire for action of this kind, some leaders refused.

It is wearisome to read of the balance of power. I would like to see somebody write about a balance of trade and of food for the world and the possibilities of so organizing our joint economic systems that all of us could go to work and produce at maximum capacity. This would mean much to the next generation in every country. I cannot help feeling that the best minds of every nation should be working out a way to find some solutions, even though temporarily their attitude may have to be: "Gentlemen, if you move to war, we move too with all the power we have."

It may be somewhat impertinent for a mere, unimportant citizen, and a woman at that, to have the presumption to suggest that we are not moving forward toward the fundamental solutions at the present time. But, after all, if war comes, it is the individual citizen—man, woman and child—who carries the war through and pays for it, so we might as well begin to think about it before it is on our backs.

Let's do a little more than think. Let's ask our leaders not to weaken their stand against war, but to tell us what more could be done for permanent peace.

1940

*E*leanor Roosevelt's devotion to the American Youth Congress would become paramount in late 1939 and early 1940. She used "My Day" to defend the organization against the House Committee on Un-American Activities, which attacked AYC for Communist beliefs held by some of its leaders. The First Lady even had a round with Gene Tunney, the ex-prizefighter who led a group challenging the AYC.

In Europe Nazi troops invaded Norway, Denmark, Luxembourg, Belgium, and Holland by the end of May. The Allies were badly shaken though not beaten at Dunkirk, but two weeks later, France fell to Germany.

In September Congress passed the Selective Training and Service Act, and in October, 16,316,908 men aged twenty-one to thirty-six registered at makeshift draft boards. The first call-up of draftees was to be in November, but many men enlisted.

War was not the only controversial issue of 1940; there was great debate over the possibility of an unprecedented third term for President Roosevelt. FDR did not toss his hat into the ring until the Democrats essentially drafted him at their July convention. He called on his wife to complete a mission filled with irony. Although she had long urged the President to find a successor, Mrs. Roosevelt appeared at the convention to show his good faith and to nominate his choice for Vice President. The restless crowds were soothed by her presence.

Even people who had wearied of the New Deal still felt enthusiastic about the First Lady. *Life* reported that since moving into the White House Eleanor Roosevelt had traveled more than 280,000 miles, been to every state but South Dakota, written a million words, given away over a half-million dollars, shaken more than a half-million hands, given hundreds of lectures . . . "and probably not wasted as much time as the average person does in a week." And as the editors declared in their story headline, "Her admirers have their own platform, 'A new President, but the same First Lady!'"

The Tennessee Valley Authority (TVA) remains one of the New Deal's landmark achievements. TVA, the largest public works project up to that time, impacted the river valley's 41,000 square miles in Tennessee, North Carolina, Virginia, Alabama, and Ohio. At Alabama's Muscle Shoals a deep waterfall became a dam and two hydraulic plants. Elsewhere TVA built more dams, sold electricity, produced fertilizer, established flood control, developed river transportation and navigation, maintained reservoirs, and reforested lands. New Deal opponents thought TVA altogether too intrusive and ambitious for the federal government and contested it in the courts. Attorney Wendell Wilkie—the 1940 Republican presidential nominee—represented a southern electric company that contended TVA had usurped its entrepreneurial rights.

WASHINGTON, APRIL 17—Here I am back in Washington! After I had filed my column yesterday in Chattanooga, I started on a busy day. I heard ex-Senator Pope give a most interesting account of what the Tennessee Valley Authority had meant to the industrial development of the region. I was told the story of a woman of 65 who came to town to announce to her friends that the rural electrification project had reached her home and that for the first time she had an opportunity to lighten the homework. She said that she was going to buy every gadget possible and had already invested in an iron and a refrigerator and added that: "If they have something which will milk the cows by electricity, some day I'm going to have that too."

So, on every hand in this area, the TVA has meant a great deal. One finds the program being discussed and, from the figures given, the utility companies seem to have benefited too, for they report a rise in net profits of over $5,000,000 in the last few years.

～

Winston Churchill had just replaced appeasement advocate Neville Chamberlain as Prime Minister of Great Britain. A New York Times *headline read:* NAZIS PIERCE FRENCH LINES ON 62-MILE FRONT, TAKE BRUSSELS. . . ; WASHINGTON SPEEDS ITS BIG DEFENSE PROGRAM.

President Roosevelt told Congress that the crisis in Europe demanded an "impregnable America." Now he asked the legislature to approve a national defense budget of $1.82 million. Although Eleanor Roosevelt wished that *diplomatic negotiations could stop Hitler, she was also a realist with clear memories of World War I. She threw her support behind the president's defense efforts.*

WASHINGTON, MAY 17—No one reading the news today can fail to realize that this is a crucial moment for the world. The President is asking today for a great increase in our national defenses. Of course, as the picture develops before our eyes, it is vital for us to understand the need of the ability to produce mechanized weapons of war in order to protect our manpower. One has but to read the record of what happened to Holland's Army—one-fourth wiped out—to realize why we must have modern weapons of war. This, of course, we must face and must pay for.

We need a united front here as well as the more tangible front of creating war materials. It requires greater cooperation and it will require greater self-sacrifice really to make democracy something for which every citizen will feel he will willingly die, because with its loss, will go economic as well as intellectual freedom.

Much has been said in this country about not wanting to participate in foreign wars and people who have said it, must now face the fact that foreign wars come very close to our own shores. We will always have not only the religious groups, but many groups who feel that war is wrong. I cannot imagine how anyone could feel otherwise with the picture before them today. But when force not only rules in certain countries, but is as menacing to all the world, as it is today, one cannot live in a Utopia which prays for different conditions and ignores those which exist.

I have a great belief in spiritual force, but I think we have to realize that spiritual force alone has to have material force with it so long as we live in a material world. The two together make a strong combination.

～

The Spanish Civil War (1936–1939) pitted Loyalists ("Republicans," leftists loyal to the monarchy, with Soviet support) against Nationalists (rebels with support from Nazi Germany and Fascist Italy). Rebel leaders formed their troops into four columns, attacking Madrid, the Loyalist stronghold. It was said that "fifth column" attackers were secret sympathizers, engaging in espionage and sabotage. In America, "fifth columnist" came to mean a clandestine subversive organization such as Nazi sympathizers. In many communities, anyone who held a political viewpoint at odds with American policy could be branded a "fifth columnist."

Mrs. Roosevelt refers to a "gentleman" who is Gene Tunney, world heavyweight boxing champ in 1926. Tunney read Shakespeare and the Bible, was the director of the Boy Scouts, and founded the Young Voters Exchange. He

NEW YORK, JUNE 23—Something curious is happening to us in this country and I think it is time we stopped and took stock of ourselves. Are we going to be swept away from our traditional attitude toward civil liberties by hysteria about "Fifth Columnists," or are we going to keep our heads and rid ourselves of "Fifth Columnists" through the use of properly constituted government officials?

If we violate the rights of innocent people or even of guilty people, we lose our long established liberties because of our desire to curtail the activities of those who are dangerous as groups or as individuals, by trying to curtail them in unconstitutional and ill considered ways.

On page one of a newspaper this morning articles show the heat and lack of consideration with which many people are acting. One heading reads: "Crowds Force Sect Members to March with Flag in Wyoming." The story tells how six people of a certain religious sect were dragged from their homes and forced to pledge allegiance to the flag.

In public places at this time we might exact this of all people, and the most dangerous Fifth Columnists would be the first to conform. Must we drag people out of their homes to force them to do something which is in opposition to their religion?

Another article states that a leader of great prominence in Catholic Youth, Boy Scouts and Boys Club of America, is going to lead the fight on what he considers subversive elements in a youth-led organization. One of the first things he suggests is that he will demand that this organization advocate the suspension of civil liberties in this country as far as Communists are concerned. He is quoted as saying: "I don't think it is any time to pamper those who are bent on destroying our country. These birds (meaning the Communists) are saboteurs. I fought in one war and I will fight in another to defend my country, but I don't want to do it with a lot of saboteurs at my back."

The gentleman in question is forty-two years old. The people in the youth-led organization are likely to be dead in the front line of battle before he is even called. If they happen to feel that our Constitution should be adhered to, unless it should be changed, they seem to be thinking along the same lines as the Attorney General of the United States.

～

Roosevelt did not relish another four years in the White House. To give delegates a free hand in backing other candidates, the President skipped the Democratic convention. Later, the First Lady recalled, "Listening to the convention proceedings over the radio, we heard my husband nominated by acclaim; but I, at least, felt as though it were somebody else's excitement and that it had very little to do with me."

HYDE PARK, JULY 19—We sat and listened to the radio last night until the early hours of the morning. The world we are going into is certainly an unknown quantity to all of us. For anyone near you, to be nominated today for the presidency of these United States, whether for a first or a third term, is a very serious thing. A heavy responsibility at home for domestic policies, and a heavy responsibility to shape a policy to guide this nation in the peaceful way that our people desire in the troubled world of today.

No one knows what will happen on election day, but during the next few months the two nominees must face the future and tell the people what their experience, their background and their vision makes them see as the mission of this country at home and abroad. Beyond that no one can know. It seems too solemn a thing for me to wish for more at the present time than that the candidates may be given the ability to put their beliefs sincerely before the people. God grant the people will be given the wisdom to choose wisely, not for themselves alone, but with a realization of the weight of their responsibility in the world.

We all went to bed so late that it was rather difficult to get up this morning. So far the day has been anything but a normal day, for, after several urgent messages came through from Chicago last night, my husband agreed that, since he could not go himself to the Democratic Convention, because of his feeling that he should not be so far away from Washington, he would like me to go. I think he hoped I might be able to give the delegates a personal sense of appreciation he feels for their confidence in him, even though the service required is such a heavy responsibility.

~

Anticipating long-term social developments came instinctively to Eleanor Roosevelt. The importance of Spanish as a second language in the U.S. was clear to her as early as 1940. From 1933 onwards under FDR's "Good Neighbor Policy," favoring increased trade and mutual defense among Western Hemisphere nations, improved relations with Spanish-speaking Central and South American countries was a high priority in foreign policy.

HYDE PARK, AUGUST 8—I am entirely convinced that one of the things that must be done, if we are going to develop the Good Neighbor Policy satisfactorily, is to make the Spanish language the second language learned by every school child in this country. We elders had better do what we can too, no matter how haltingly, to learn this language spoken by so many people whom we must understand.

Yesterday, the two South American ladies who came with their husbands to lunch with us were perfectly charming. One of them, in Spanish which I could understand but not answer, told me that in her country she belonged to the Socialist Party which corresponded to the Democratic Party here. She added that the position of women made it impossible for a woman in her country to hold a public office, if she were married and her husband held one. She regretted this because she felt that women had a contribution to make and she had held a position before her marriage. Quite evidently we could have talked at some length and with advantage to both of us had I been able to speak, as well as understand, Spanish. Some day, perhaps, I will have time to learn another language, and I am quite determined that it will be Spanish. In the meantime, I hope that in every school in this country we will teach the children to consider Spanish their second most important language. It should be as easy to talk Spanish as English. This will encourage our Latin-American neighbors to make English their second language. I must say they get on better in English than we do in Spanish.

⁓

Six weeks before Election Day the Roosevelts held a picnic for celebrities and others who campaigned for FDR. One of the President's biggest fans, actress Katharine Hepburn, surprised everyone by making a dramatic entrance from the river by the Roosevelt estate. With characteristic aplomb, the actress rolled up her pants and waded ashore. Rescuing Hepburn himself, gallant country squire FDR told the great Kate, "I'm very flattered that you would go to all this trouble to see me."

HYDE PARK, SEPTEMBER 25—Here it is Tuesday and I must begin by telling you of a picnic which we had at Hyde Park on Sunday. You probably have read in the papers about how many distinguished people came to share our chowder and frankfurters at my cottage. Everyone seemed relaxed and at ease. Even Katharine Hepburn, who landed in a seaplane in the Hudson River at the foot of our place and dashed a mile and a half through the woods to the big house, found the President to bring her over to the picnic.

⁓

Not jaded but sobered by a long personal history in politics—or rather her husband's political career—Mrs. Roosevelt here puts the election process in perspective. The weight of worldly matters, with war already under way in Europe, took nearly all the shine off FDR's imminent third term-victory.

HYDE PARK, NOVEMBER 6—This is Election Day and I have been told with great firmness to get my column in early because the telegraph wires into New York City will soon be busy with election news. Of course, nothing authentic in the way of election returns can come in until the later afternoon, but I suppose newspaper correspondents will be filing stories all during the day about minor happenings here and there.

I am taking my ride but at noon, my husband and I, with his mother, will go up to vote and all the photographers and newspapermen will be on hand to record the process as they have done so often before. I shall feel quite calm, but no one thinks that you should be calm, so, willy-nilly, you find yourself being urged into excitement.

The telephones will ring and people will be rising from the table during meals to answer them. The President will have to talk to many people and in spite of all one can do, election excitement will mount. By the time returns are really coming in, very few of us will be left who are capable of comparing past votes with present figures and making any evaluation of what is really going on.

I remember what it was like the first time my husband ran for the New York State Senate. We had no radio and no news service in the house then, and if I remember rightly it was 32 years since a Democratic State Senator had gone from this district to Albany. The campaign had been an intensive one, and I doubt very much if he has ever worked harder since. I wanted him to win just because he was running, and because I felt he might do something of value for the district. From then on there have been campaigns for various offices. Some were lost and more were won, but I think my feelings have always been much as they were the first time. I think I can say with honesty: "May what is best for the country happen today, and may we all remember that whatever happens, this is just the beginning of some years of useful work."

1941

erhaps President Roosevelt's biggest victory in the campaign for a third term was winning the First Lady's support. As a political pundit, Mrs. Roosevelt upheld the tradition of a two-term presidency. And as the President's wife, she feared another four years in the White House would be a crushing burden for him. The First Lady nevertheless believed that only FDR could successfully manage the challenge of the growing global crisis in 1941.

The war had spread week by week. By the time FDR was sworn in for his third term, German troops had swept through most of Europe and had attacked North Africa, East Africa, the Balkan states, and Greece. The Allied troops valiantly tried to check what appeared to be the Germans' surefire conquest of two continents.

Two developments bolstered the British: President Roosevelt became Prime Minister Churchill's silent partner, and he finally persuaded a stubborn Congress that the Lend-Lease Bill—which supported the Allies with machines and munitions, if not with manpower—was in America's best interests. Then, on June 22, Hitler reneged on his 1939 nonaggression pact with the Soviets, and the Germans launched the devastating Operation Barbarossa against the Russian homeland. Premier Josef Stalin quickly received a promise of support from Churchill and Roosevelt.

Lend-Lease was not the only bill Roosevelt pushed through Congress. On the home front, the Federal Wage and Hour Act prescribed a 48-hour workweek and prohibited mine-owners and manufacturers from hiring workers younger than sixteen.

Lifesaving penicillin, now mass-produced, became widely available. And Washington State proudly opened the Grand Coulee Dam two years ahead of schedule.

To prevent further aggression in the East Indies and Indochina, the U.S. froze Japan's American assets. Japan was also cut off from important oil supplies and had to yield to diplomatic pressure or resort to force. Diplomatic negotiations became more forced in autumn, when General Hideki Tojo and his military junta came to power. On December 6, President Roosevelt sent a message to Japanese Emperor Hirohito, hoping he would consider "ways of dispelling the dark clouds" overshadowing the two countries. At dawn on December 7, the Japanese bombed Pearl Harbor.

Although shocked by the surprise attack, Mrs. Roosevelt had been keenly aware that the U.S. would somehow be drawn into the war. Once a fervent pacifist, she was now a determined antifascist. However, the First Lady urged the President not to make his welfare programs the first casualty of the war. She hoped to protect some of these programs as the assistant director of the Office of Civilian Defense.

Chicago Tribune *publisher Robert McConnick was a founder of America First, a group that advocated isolationism and opposed FDR's "warmongering policies." The group rapidly gained national support because of prominent members such as Charles Lindbergh, Lillian Gish, Henry Ford, Alice Roosevelt Longworth, and Senator Harry Byrd. Eventually, America First claimed nearly 8,900,000 followers and 500 chapters.*

WASHINGTON, MARCH 19—There are strange things happening in this country. I was reading a digest of the news the other day, and was amused to see a grouping of papers that have had similar slants on various questions lately. In the group were "The Chicago Tribune," "The Daily Worker," "Social Justice," "The Table," "The Liberator" and "The Vindicator."

All these publications of late have been harping on the beauties of peace and the necessity of saving our Republic for ourselves. Some of them pin our danger on the international bankers, some of them on the present administration, but all of them harp on the same line. What a queer combination of bedfellows in the journalistic world this makes.

Sometimes I think a few people are becoming a trifle hysterical. To bear this out, I shall quote here a few lines from a letter which I have just received from a lady. There is nothing peculiar about this letter. The writer just assails the President and the present administration and, incidentally, me, for starving the little children of the democracies of Europe. It demands a negotiated peace with Hitler and says it is no more possible to restore the conquered nations in Europe to their freedom than it would be to restore to England her original Thirteen Colonies.

She assures me that she is of British descent, with Huguenot blood running in her veins, that she is a Colonial Dame, and a member of the Order of the Descendants of Colonial Governors. She even dares to identify her-self further as having four Colonial Governors of Carolina on her badge.

All this to prove that she is no Nazi-lover, but for America First and that she does not wish to police the world. She ends with her personal, not very flattering appraisal of the President.

Nothing in this letter, of course, is very odd. Just from my point of view, it is untrue. There is no reason in the world, however, why she should not express her opinions, no reason why she should not write the letter and no one would question her right to do so. But here comes the hysterical line: "I dare not sign my name for fear of a concentration camp." I haven't yet heard of any, have you?

～

Speaking out on behalf of the largest group of unpaid laborers in the Ameri-can economy, Mrs. Roosevelt goes to bat for homemakers. Her underlying as-sumption is that good parenting is the hardest, most important "job" of all.

TUSKEGEE, ALA., MARCH 28—From the way people talk, I get the im-pression occasionally that it is not considered important for girls to be really well-educated if they are going to marry and bring up a family. I would like to register here my thought that marriage and the upbringing of children in the home require as well-trained a mind and as well-disci-plined a character as any other occupation that might be considered a career.

I think we ought to impress on both our girls and boys that successful marriages require just as much work, just as much intelligence and just as much unselfish devotion, as they give to any position they undertake to fill on a paid basis.

The principles of democratic citizenship are taught in the home and the example is given there of the responsibility assured to the individual un-der a democratic form of government. Every man and woman's college should have that objective in view as part of the educational process. Without it no education is complete.

～

Earlier in the spring of 1941 Hitler invaded Yugoslavia and Greece. On May 21, a German U-boat sank the U.S. merchant ship Robin Moore. *Within a week, FDR condemned German aggression, declaring an unlimited na-tional emergency.*

"We will not accept a Hitler-dominated world," FDR told his Allied audi-ence, reaffirming solidarity among the twenty-one American republics and Canada in protecting the independence of the hemisphere.

After the President's speech, it would have been appropriate to hear "God Bless America" from Irving Berlin, the patriotic song's composer and one of the country's most prolific songwriters.

WASHINGTON, MAY 29—The flags of all the Americas decorated one end of the East Room of the White House and were draped over the room's main door. It gave me a curious feeling to sit there and watch the President at his desk, faced by all the microphones. I felt as though all the newspaper photographers in the world were grinding and clicking in front of him. Diplomats are trained to observe the amenities, no matter what they feel, but last night everybody's face showed some emotion as the evening progressed.

I felt strangely detached, as though I were outside, a part of the general public. I represented no nation, I carried no responsibility except the responsibility of being a citizen of the United States of America. Then I looked at the President, facing representatives of all the Central and South American countries, Mexico and Canada. Like an oncoming wave, the thought rolled over me: "What a weight of responsibility this one man at the desk, facing the rest of the people, has to carry. Not just for this hemisphere alone, but for the world as a whole! Great Britain can be gallant beyond belief, China can suffer and defend herself in equally heroic fashion, but in the end, the decisive factor in this whole business may perhaps be the solidarity of the hemisphere and, of necessity, the President of the United States must give that solidarity its leadership!"

Then the President began to speak. For three-quarters of an hour he told us what conditions existed, what obligations lay before us and, finally, what his present step to meet those obligations was to be. More must follow, and day by day each one of us is going to realize that his life is changing, that he has an obligation to perform.

In my capacity of objective citizen, sitting in the gathering last night, I felt that I wanted to accept my responsibility and do my particular job, whatever it might be, to the extent of my ability. I think that will be the answer of every individual citizen of the United States, for when all is said and done, it is our freedom to progress that makes us all want to live and to go on.

After our guests had departed, we went into the Monroe Room to listen to Mr. Irving Berlin sing two new songs, as well as some old songs.

~

Earlier in June, the First Lady was visited in Washington by Navajo Indians from a southwestern reservation. The Native Americans wanted to speak with government officials because of a federal decision to cut back their sheep stock, the tribe's livelihood.

Mrs. Roosevelt was distressed that the Navajos felt forced into deeper poverty and shocked at the woefully inadequate education the children received. Here she makes a detailed report on the Navajos' plight. She ends on a note about blacks getting training but not getting jobs. The ban on Negro enlistment was soon lifted: By 1942 a million blacks served in all branches of the armed forces although still in segregated companies.

WASHINGTON, JUNE 18—I asked Mr. John Collier, of the Office of Indian Affairs, to come in late yesterday afternoon to tell me something about the Navajo situation.

It appears that the land on the reservation, in more than 81 years, has completely changed because of overgrazing. What was once meadow land with plenty of water and beautiful grass is now practically desert. The wooded slopes have disappeared, floods wash away the topsoil and the grass no longer exists. It is quite evident that, in order to bring it back, there must be a drastic curtailment of cattle, wild horses, goats and sheep.

This means that a people, whose average cash income is only about $120 a year must either go on relief, which they want at all costs to avoid, or starve to death. The only other solution seems to be the possibility of carrying through an irrigation project which will allow them to irrigate enough land so they can raise crops to feed their cattle at certain times and also to grow some cash crop if the difficulty of transportation can be overcome.

The decision on the irrigation is, of course, up to Congress. At the present time, I can quite understand the argument against putting money into anything which can be set aside to be done when the defense period is over. Still, if Congress decides that this is necessary, it seems to me that they have a joint responsibility with the Office of Indian Affairs to devise some means by which these naturally independent American citizens can earn their living and not feel dependent upon the government for a chance merely to survive.

Here is another problem which has come to me. You know and I know how bitterly the Negro people are disturbed over their inability to participate in national defense or to obtain employment in defense industries. Here again, there are many difficulties and complications. But there is just one little item into which I think all of us could look in our respective communities.

In New York City there are 2,845 Negro youth workers on NYA, of whom 1,245 are girls. This group comprises 15.6 percent of the program in New

York City. There is no discrimination in training and it is open to all girls. It has been found that the Negro girls are fitted to take training in as many different fields as the white girls, but in New York City and the State, the greatest number of employment opportunities for Negro girls are in domestic service.

The next employment opportunities lie in the operation of power sewing machines, because the International Ladies' Garment Workers Union allows no race discrimination. In all the other fields of training, employment opportunities for Negro girls, as against white girls, are extremely limited.

This living in a democracy is a problem, isn't it?

~

Hamilton Fish, Republican congressman from New York, could boast a political heritage dating back as far as the Roosevelts'. Fish's father was also a congressman and his grandfather was a senator, a governor, and secretary of state. Like Franklin Roosevelt, Hamilton Fish graduated from Harvard. There the similarity ended. Fish was always anti-Roosevelt and especially protested U.S. aid to the Allies. In 1939 he formed the National Committee to Keep America out of Foreign Wars, and he supported America First.

Fish irritated Roosevelt so much that when the President had to tell prominent statesmen that the Japanese had attacked Pearl Harbor, he purposely snubbed Fish.

EASTPORT, ME., JUNE 28—I have just received a slightly delayed communication from my congressman, the Hon. Hamilton Fish. His letter, addressed to the people of the 26th Congressional District in New York State, interests me very much. He suggests in the first paragraph that "an undeclared war is an invention and creation of totalitarian nations, and a negation of democratic processes and our constitutional form of government."

Nowhere in the letter does he seem to suggest that, this being the case and we being a peace-loving people, we may find ourselves the victims of an undeclared war, whether we like it or not, even if we ourselves adhere scrupulously to the "democratic processes."

He encloses in this courteous note, a postal card which reads:

"The United States should:
Enter the war . . .
Stay out of the war . . . "

All I am asked to do is to check one of these statements, sign my name or not, as I like, and return my ballot within three days of receipt.

I understand from a newspaper item which I read that my congressman has received an overwhelming number stating that the United States should stay out of war. That seems to me fairly natural.

If I thought I had a choice in the matter, I should answer wholeheartedly that I did not wish to enter any war anywhere in the world. But it seems to me that my congressman has oversimplified the question which confronts us at the moment.

We would like to stay out of war. The people of Norway, Holland and all the other countries in Europe, even France and Russia, and Germany itself, would probably have liked to stay out of war. But that wasn't ever put before them as a choice. The war was suddenly upon them. In some cases, their government in the form of a dictator decreed it so. In others, because they woke up one morning and found soldiers of an enemy government marching down their streets.

I can think of a number of questions, Mr. Congressman, which you could have asked your constituents that would have been more enlightening to them and to you. Just as a suggestion, why not ask "Shall the U.S. allow any enemy nation to obtain possessions which may menace, under modern conditions of warfare, the safety of the U.S.?" or "Shall we accept restrictions on our trade or the abrogation of our right to travel in neutral waters throughout the world?"

We have always been a proud and independent people, Mr. Congressman. As a woman, I pray for peace not only now, but in the future. But I think we must look a little beyond next week if we expect to ensure an independent U.S.A. to our children. There is such a thing, too, as the moral values of a situation, and I do not think we are a nation that has given up considerations for right and wrong as we see it.

～

According to Eleanor Roosevelt, the First Family worried about her mother-in-law Sara Delano Roosevelt's health all summer. After spending the afternoon with her devoted son Franklin, she developed a blood clot in her lung and had an acute circulatory collapse. A widow for forty-one years, Sara Delano Roosevelt died with her only son at her side.

WASHINGTON, SEPTEMBER 7—An anxious 24 hours culminated a little before noon today in the death of my husband's mother. Had she lived until the 21st of this month she would have celebrated her 87th birthday. One can have none of the resentment which comes when death cuts short a young life, but she was a very vital person with a keen interest in living and I think had she had a few more years vouchsafed her, she would have lived them with avidity and keen enjoyment.

She was born in the year 1854, brought up in a large family and endowed with the Delano beauty. She sailed to China on a clipper ship as well as to Europe on the most modern of today's steamers. Her early experiences were picturesque and interesting. Her life was a rich, full life. She had seen her only son inaugurated as president of the United States three times, and she still felt that her husband was the most wonderful man she had ever known.

I think her family, both in her own generation and in the younger generation, would say that her strongest trait was loyalty to the family. She had no hesitancy about telling her near and dear ones their faults, or criticizing their behavior, but if anyone else in the world were to attack a member of her family she would rise to their defense like a tigress. Whatever the family did, in the end, she accepted and condoned before the world, no matter what her private feelings might be.

She was a very generous person, not only to her family but to many others. She was charitable, but I think she enjoyed even more giving to those whom she knew had once enjoyed a little more financial leeway than might be theirs today, and who would therefore prize some little luxury.

She would give away large sums of money and save small ones. The President's mother always attributed her little economies, like undoing string and folding wrapping paper for future use, to her New England upbringing. She was not just sweetness and light, for there was a streak of jealousy and possessiveness in her where her own were concerned. But when others were bored she would be kind, and had the gift of making all those around her feel that the word "grande dame" was truly applicable to her.

She wanted her son to live up to high standards of character and conduct and never believed that he failed in this. She spoiled her grandchildren perhaps a little, but they had great affection and respect for her. I think even some of the great-grandchildren will remember her when they grow up as a very beautiful, stately old lady who loved them and made them feel that Hyde Park would be their home as long as it was hers.

~

Eleanor Roosevelt never needed to worry about money, and she gave away most of what she earned. Such largess did not, however, numb her to the concerns of middle- and lower-class American households where every penny counted. Here Mrs. Roosevelt worries about a sharp increase in the American housewife's grocery bill.

Washington, November 14—I had some quite appalling news on the cost of living last week. The average housewife must now spend 14 percent more money for the food she will need for the family dinner than she did a year ago. In some cities, the increase in food costs is even greater, running to over 19 percent. If you were preparing a meal of ham and eggs, potatoes, white bread, butter, coffee and milk, the following prices show what you would pay this year in comparison with last year:

	SEPT. 1940	SEPT. 1941	PERCENT INCREASE
Ham (lb.)	25.4¢	34.4¢	35
eggs (doz.)	37.2¢	46.9¢	26
white bread (lb.)	8.1¢	8.5¢	5
butter (lb.)	34.3¢	43.5¢	27
potatoes (15 lb.)	28.8¢	32.8¢	14
coffee (lb.)	20.8¢	25.7¢	24
milk (qt.)	12.3¢	13.9¢	13

In other staple products, the prices have gone up very considerably also.

Sugar (10 lbs.)	51.0¢	60.0¢	18
Flour (10 lbs.)	40.1¢	47.5¢	18
Lard (lb.)	9.3¢	14.6¢	57
Cheese (lb.)	25.7¢	32.7¢	27

The greater part of these increases occurred since last February, and in October of this year prices were still rising. Some of these prices should undoubtedly have increased, particularly if the increase reflects itself in the farmer's pocket.

~

Japan stunned America by bombing Pearl Harbor, the Hawaiian naval base, on the morning of December 7. For months tensions had been rising between the U.S. and the Japanese. Overnight on December 6, President Roosevelt and his closest advisers had puzzled over the possible military implications of an intercepted dispatch to the Japanese ambassadors. Now they had their answer, as did Americans who seesawed on the question of American intervention in the broadening international conflict. Even Charles Lindbergh and Herbert Hoover agreed that the attack ended the debate. The United States was at war.

WASHINGTON, DECEMBER 8—I was going out in the hall to say goodbye to our cousins, Mr. and Mrs. Frederick Adams, and their children, after luncheon, and, as I stepped out of my room, I knew something had happened. All the secretaries were there, two telephones were in use, the senior military aides were on their way with messages. I said nothing because the words I heard over the telephone were quite sufficient to tell me that, finally, the blow had fallen, and we had been attacked.

Attacked in the Philippines, in Hawaii, and on the ocean between San Francisco and Hawaii. Our people had been killed not suspecting there was an enemy, who attacked in the usual ruthless way which Hitler has prepared us to suspect.

Because our nation has lived up to the rules of civilization, it will probably take us a few days to catch up with our enemy, but no one in this country will doubt the ultimate outcome. None of us can help but regret the choice which Japan has made, but having made it, she has taken on a coalition of enemies she must underestimate unless she believes we have sadly deteriorated since our first ships sailed into her harbor.

The clouds of uncertainty and anxiety have been hanging over us for a long time. Now we know where we are. The work for those who are at home seems to be obvious. First, to do our own job, whatever it is, as well as we can possibly do it. Second, to add to it everything we can do in the way of civilian defense. Now, at last, every community must go to work to build up protection from attack.

We must build up the best possible community services, so that all of our people may feel secure because they know we are standing together and that whatever problems have to be met will be met by the community and not one lone individual. There is no weakness and insecurity when once this is understood.

~

British Prime Minister Winston Churchill, along with his advisers Lord Beaverbrook and Field Marshal Sir John Greer Dill, visited FDR to discuss strategy for World War II. (Germany had declared war on the United States after the President's speech on December 8.) At dinner, the very complicated Roosevelt genealogy clearly confused the visitors.

Time magazine described Churchill's introduction to the Senate: "Those who crowded up front saw a pudgy man with cheeks like apple dumplings, blue eyes beneath crooked restless eyebrows and the merest foam flecking of sandy gray hair on his bald pink pate, a long black cigar clenched at a belligerent angle above his bulldog jaw."

WASHINGTON, DECEMBER 27—Last night we had a rather large gathering of various family groups at Christmas dinner. The number of cousins was really quite amusing. I think the complications of family relationships, as regards my husband and myself, became completely baffling to our English guests. I tried to explain to Lord Beaverbrook what relation my husband is to Mrs. Theodore Douglas Robinson, and I think at the end he was as mystified as if I had never attempted an explanation.

When you tell someone that the lovely lady sitting opposite him is your husband's half-niece, that she married your first cousin, and that he was her sixth cousin, whereas you are married to your fifth cousin once removed and are also her sixth cousin and that her children, in order to simplify life, say "Uncle Franklin and Auntie Eleanor" when the relationship is really only that of a half great-uncle, you may well imagine that you have led anyone—no matter how great his interest in genealogy—through a maze from which there is no emerging.

Field Marshall Sir John Dill celebrated his birthday as well as Christmas here last night. I wish I had known sooner, for I would certainly have provided him with a birthday cake.

After dinner, we had newsreels featuring both the Prime Minister and the President, and then sang some Christmas carols together before saying good night and letting the President, the Prime Minister and Lord Beaverbrook go back to work again.

I was a little late at the office this morning on purpose. My office force, however, was all there ahead of me. After clearing up the mail and seeing one or two members of the staff, I listened on the radio to the Prime Minister's speech in the Senate and then came home to a late luncheon. I am planning to devote the afternoon to telling some of the kind people who sent me Christmas gifts how much I am enjoying them.

It will be quite impossible for me, of course, to thank the many people who have sent the President and me Christmas cards and telegrams, but I want to say here how grateful we are for their thought and the confidence and affection which so many of them expressed.

1942–1945

The War Years

1942

*A*lthough not guided by the occult, First Lady Eleanor Roosevelt occasionally visited a palm reader who once explained: "The leadership finger was bolder in your left hand, which shows inherent potentialities, than it is in your right hand, which shows actually what happened. This leads me to believe that many times you've had to cramp your style."

How many times during ten years in the White House did the First Lady feel she must cramp her style? It happened often in 1942. She was subjected to pressure to subordinate her plans to accommodate the President's schedule, and she was the object of continual criticism from his opponents and constant scrutiny by the press. To avoid accusations that the President had succumbed to "petticoat rule," Mrs. Roosevelt used discretion as she introduced new people and ideas to her husband.

The First Lady had fewer opportunities to conduct her back-door diplomacy once the war started. After the Japanese attacked Pearl Harbor, FDR spent long hours in meetings with military advisers. It was difficult to gain access to the President and harder to talk about anything other than the war.

Mrs. Roosevelt played an important part in the war effort. As the nation's No. I volunteer, she organized programs for the Office of Civilian Defense. This first official appointment should have been a victory for the First Lady—a chance to show what she could do. Mrs. Roosevelt devoted all her energy to the program, but she was soon attacked by the press and politicians. The criticism grew so harsh that a frustrated Mrs. Roosevelt felt forced to resign.

Of course, Mrs. Roosevelt wasn't the only one to feel limited during 1942. Although the President started the year by pronouncing that a coalition of United Nations would protect the four essential freedoms, his vision of peace was overshadowed by the fall of Manila and a string of setbacks in the Pacific. The war was paramount. President Roosevelt was equipped by Congress with emergency powers and a record-breaking $42.8 billion military budget.

Each month brought new restrictions and civilians struggled to adjust. The U.S., new to war, ordered blackouts on both coasts. Schoolboys couldn't buy new sneakers or rubber balls or play with spare tires; instead, they searched for scraps of precious rubber, crucial for the war effort. Eighteen-year-old boys joined the front lines. At home, the mail included ration books and long-awaited letters, already scrutinized by censors, from the men overseas. By April, the War Production Board ended the manufacture of products not essential to the war effort.

Most civilian complaints were silenced by "Don't you know that there's a war on?" Thousands of women enlisted in each branch of the armed services, accepting noncombat auxiliary duties. Millions of other women worked in factories or as volunteers.

Civilians were awed by the Allied struggles to control the U-boat infested Atlantic as well as Guadalcanal and Stalingrad. Many Americans wondered how the beleaguered British coped as the war dragged on and their supplies dwindled. President Roosevelt sent the First Lady to visit Great Britain to observe how women were supporting the war effort. During this three-week assignment, the British people came to see Eleanor Roosevelt as America's best goodwill ambassador.

At the Brooklyn Naval Hospital to see Franklin Jr., who had his appendix out, Mrs. Roosevelt also visited the wounded from two navy ships—the Normandie and the Kearny. The Normandie was burned by a mysterious fire while anchored in New York, and 200 of its crew had been injured. A German torpedo hit the Kearny on the way to Iceland, killing eleven sailors and wounding many more.

The wounded were eager for news about the war, but the news wasn't good: Singapore had fallen to the Japanese. Mrs. Roosevelt, however, predicted an ultimate Allied victory and cautioned against vengeance when the Axis nations were defeated.

NEW YORK, FEBRUARY 12—You might be interested to hear a little about the boys in the Brooklyn Naval Hospital. Nearly a whole ward was filled with boys from the "Normandie," who had been overcome by smoke or burned. They all seemed to be recovering, but the experience must have been a very unpleasant one.

I also had an opportunity to talk for a little while with a boy who was very seriously injured on the destroyer "Kearny." He is getting well and will be able to be about again, but his remark was that he wanted to "get back at them."

As I walked through the hospital, I told the doctors that I had a particular interest in the destroyers because my boy is on one. I noticed a smile on the faces of the boys nearest me, so evidently they have a feeling, too, for destroyer duty. I imagine there is greater opportunity for contact between men and officers on a destroyer and, therefore, a greater feeling of belonging to one big family.

Franklin Jr., looked remarkably well, and I expect to find him feeling even better when I go over today. I had a very nice telegram from the head of a group of Navy mothers who visit the hospital and try to make boys who come from a great distance feel at home.

Everyone I met seemed depressed over the news from Singapore. We have been told that we must expect reverses at the start, and yet we want victory at once. The Axis nations prepared their people for many years, physically and mentally, for this struggle. They built up huge reserves of war materials.

They laid their plans well in advance. The people who did not want war tried to plan for a peaceful world. They conditioned their people to peace. Those who foresaw that, whether we wanted it or not, we might be attacked had a hard time getting a hearing. No one wanted to spend money on things which might never be needed, and for that reason our preparation had, of necessity, to be slower.

We should remember now, however, that day by day the opposition in the Pacific and in the Atlantic, in Europe, Africa and Asia is wearing itself out far more rapidly than we are. Some day, when we have reached the full power of our production, the day of victory for those who love peace will come. Then we shall have to remember St. Paul's Epistle to the Romans: "Dearly beloved, avenge not yourselves, but rather give place unto wrath: for it is written, Vengeance is mine; I will repay, saith the Lord."

∼

After five months, Eleanor Roosevelt resigned as assistant director of the Office of Civilian Defense. She had been chosen for the post (with FDR's blessing) by New York City Mayor Fiorello LaGuardia, the OCD director. Both were hounded out of their positions by attacks from the press and politicians.

Just before the First Lady left OCD, the staff screened Woman of the Year, *the first film to pair Katharine Hepburn and Spencer Tracy. Hepburn plays a political columnist and Tracy portrays a sportswriter. Hepburn took a crash course in being a dutiful housewife to prep for the role.*

Mrs. Roosevelt's resignation from OCD became front-page news. Here she explains why it was difficult for a First Lady to hold an official government post.

WASHINGTON, FEBRUARY 23—Friday night, at our Office of Civilian Defense party, I saw for the second time the movie called "Woman of the Year," in which Katharine Hepburn plays a most amusing and delightful role. Every girl who has tried to keep house without training will have sympathy with her struggles in separating the eggs, and those horribly rising waffles!

I was interested yesterday to find that my resignation from the Office of Civilian Defense rated front-page stories in the New York "Herald Tribune" and "The New York Times," and an editorial in both papers. I am beginning to feel puffed up with importance!

Strange to say, this is the first time that I have seen what I know is a valid criticism, not of the Office of Civilian Defense but of my taking part in the organization. They both point out that the wife of any president cannot be looked upon as an individual by other people in the government. She must always carry the reflection of influence or power beyond that of the usual government public servant.

I hoped that this was not true, but I have found out that it was. Therein lies the one really valid criticism against the wife of a President taking an executive job in the government, even when that position is unpaid.

People can gradually be brought to understand that an individual, even is she is a President's wife, may have independent views and must be allowed the expression of an opinion. But actual participation in the work of the government we are not yet able to accept.

Six months after the President created his pledge for a coalition against the Axis powers, he invited representatives of the twenty-six countries who joined the United Nations to the White House. These nations' flags were displayed with the Stars and Stripes at a Flag Day celebration.

That day FDR relied on the words of Pulitzer Prize–winning poet Stephen Vincent Benét.

WASHINGTON, JUNE 16—The Flag Day ceremony in the State Dining Room at the White House yesterday afternoon was very impressive. The flags of the United Nations were placed in a circle and underneath each flag stood the representative of his country. At the table, in the middle of the room, sat the President and the Secretary of State with the Mexican Ambassador and President Quezon of the Philippines, who were joining the United Nations. The President read Mr. Stephen Vincent Benét's beautiful prayer, which I am giving in part in the hope that all will cut it out and keep it with them.

"God of the free, we pledge our lives and hearts today to the cause of all free mankind.

"Grant us victory over the tyrants who would enslave all free men and nations. Grant us faith and understanding to cherish all those who fight for freedom as if they were our brothers. Grant us brotherhood in home and union, not only for the sake of this bitter war, but for the days to come which shall and must unite all the children of the earth.

"Our earth is a but a small star in the great universe. Yet, of it, we can make if we choose, a planet unvexed by war, untroubled by hunger or fear, undivided by senseless distinctions of race, color or theory. Grant us that courage and foreseeing to begin this task today so that our children and our children's children may be proud of the name of man.

"Yet, most of all, grant us brotherhood, not only for this day but for all our years—brotherhood not of words, but of acts and deeds. We are all of us children of earth—grant us that simple knowledge. If our brothers are oppressed, then we are oppressed. If they hunger, we hunger. If their freedom is taken away, our freedom is not secure. Grant us a common faith that man shall know bread and peace—that he shall know justice and righteousness, freedom and security, an equal opportunity and an equal chance to do his best, not only in our own lands, but throughout the world. And in that faith let us march toward the clean world our hands can make. Amen."

~

Three years after Hitler invaded Poland, a radio station asked some of America's leading women to discuss the plight of Polish women. Eleanor Roosevelt was joined by columnist Dorothy Thompson, playwright and politician Clare Boothe Luce, author Pearl Buck, and poet Marianne Moore.

Here Mrs. Roosevelt focuses on the Nazis' brutal treatment of Polish women in the Ravensbrück Detention Camp. Her December 5 column and later ones would address the extermination of Jews in concentration camps.

New York, September 25—Yesterday afternoon I joined in a broadcast to the women of Poland on the third anniversary of the loss of their country's freedom. Miss Dorothy Thompson, Mrs. Clare Boothe Luce, Miss Pearl Buck and Miss Moore were extremely effective in their talks. I hope the broadcast will give some sense of future security to the women of Poland. I was glad to be able to say how deeply the women of this country sympathized with the sufferings of the women in Poland.

Starvation and horror live with them day by day. I wonder more and more at the Nazi psychology when I read descriptions of what happens to people in the occupied countries under Nazi control. How can the Nazis hope to create loyal and friendly citizens in a country which they have conquered by cruel treatment? Certainly, if they want good will, they go about it in a strange fashion.

I have before me a description of the Ravensbrück Women's Preventive Detention Camp. One of the items reads: "People are regarded as ill only when they drop. Prisoners have to go barefoot in streets sprinkled with coarse gravel. In consequence prisoners get sore and festered heels, but they have to go on walking barefoot. No food is provided during the examination period so, if they bring none of their own, they go hungry until they are finally assigned to barracks. One of the punishments consists of transfer to punishment barracks where degenerates are detained. If a Polish woman talks to a Jewess, she is punished with 42 days in a dark cell. There is one month of quarantine on entrance to the camp. Kitchen work starts at 4:00 A.M. and includes the carrying of heavy sacks of food from the lorries."

This is only the description of one camp, and I should not think it would tend to make the conquered people love their conquerors. The Nazi psychology is a strange one, because fear and suffering do not create love and loyalty.

~

Eleanor Roosevelt wanted to participate in the war effort by representing the Red Cross and visiting the wounded in Europe, but that was deemed too dangerous. Noting his wife's restlessness, FDR suggested she accept the Queen's invitation to see the contributions British women were making to the war effort. (FDR wrote to Churchill that Mrs. Roosevelt was not to do anything "official.")

Her secretary, Malvina "Tommy" Thompson, traveled with her, and they stayed briefly with King George VI and Queen Elizabeth. The First Lady received a hearty welcome from the King and Queen, and most British subjects were just as enthusiastic about the visit. Mrs. Roosevelt later admitted worrying about going to Buckingham Palace, "but I finally told myself that one can live through any strange experience for two days."

Because there were many Nazi spies in England, the Secret Service carefully guarded the details of her travel plans.

LONDON, OCTOBER 24—The past few days have been so filled with a variety of experiences that it is difficult to tell you about them. In the first place, I should explain that I find myself this evening in England because, a short time ago, Her Majesty, Queen Elizabeth, felt that it might be valuable for me to see with my own eyes the work of the women in Great Britain, and so she wrote and asked whether I would care to come here.

I was assured that I would be given full freedom to see everything in the way I felt would be most useful to me. I realized at once this would also give me an opportunity to see our armed forces, which have been sent to this country in such great numbers. I hope very much that what I see may mean something to the mothers, wives and sweethearts of our men who are now stationed here. I hope, too, that the opportunity afforded to see the work which the women are doing in Great Britain may also be of use not only to our women at home but also to the children. Since it is family life which changes when women go to work, children have a share of the sacrifice and their interests deserve consideration.

Now you have the background and the reason for this visit. The trip, across what has now become a very small pond indeed, was as comfortable and as delightful as possible.

No one knew I was actually arriving, in spite of newspaper rumors. Since Miss Thompson and I travelled under very unimaginative names and our bags looked like everyone else's, there was no easy method of identifying us. But, as I stepped out of the plane, I heard someone say, "Why, there is Mrs. Roosevelt!"

The countryside looks as green and as calm as ever, but every now and then in the city you come upon a heap of ruins and someone casually says, "A bomb fell there."

Our Ambassador, Mr. John Gilbert Winant, met me at the airport and on the train trip sketched for me the things which had been planned for the next few days. The King and Queen met me at the station, together with a number of officials, both British and American. We were then whisked away from the station very quickly.

At tea I felt as though I had dropped off after a number of years to visit with some friends of my school days in very homelike environment. In a short time I am going to search for my one and only evening dress. Forty-

four pounds of luggage does not give much room for clothes, but I am assured dinner tonight will be very informal.

～

*Eleanor Roosevelt, who lived in London while attending the Allenswood
School, returned to see a city devastated by the Blitz—the German bombing. The King and Queen took her to St. Paul's Cathedral, built in 1683 and
almost destroyed in the 1940 bombings (the bombs bounced off its rounded
metal roof). All over England, families had lost their homes to German
bombs; even Buckingham Palace took a direct hit.*

London, October 27—The King and Queen very kindly gave a luncheon Saturday for the heads of the various women's services, to which
they also invited Mrs. Oveta Hobby, Director of our Women's Army Auxiliary Corps.

After lunch, Their Majesties took me to visit St. Paul's Cathedral. It was
my first view of the destruction which has levelled whole blocks of houses.
It is remarkable that St. Paul's still stands, in spite of considerable damage.
Its firefighters spent night after night sleeping in the crypt, ready to spring
to their posts should they be needed.

I had seen pictures of the fire which had swept the financial district,
known as "the City," after one of the blitzes, but I was in no way prepared
to see such a great area of destruction. When buildings such as the fine old
Guild Hall and many beautiful old churches are destroyed, they are a loss
to the whole world.

But even more poignant is the destruction that we viewed a little bit
later in Stepney. Here the crowded population lived over small shops and
in rows of two-story houses. Today there is only one-third of the population left and each empty building speaks of a personal tragedy. They
showed me one of the big shelters, which at one time housed 1,200 people and where, even now, 300 people come to sleep every night.

It seemed to me as I walked through the brick compartments of that
shelter that I learned something about fear and the resistance to total destruction which exists in all human beings. How could people be herded
together like this night after night without an epidemic being the result?
Yet it was done and the spirits of kindness and cheerfulness prevailed.
Those who had lost so much still managed to smile.

～

*Given Eleanor Roosevelt's dedication to helping oppressed people, some
historians have been bewildered by her uncharacteristic lack of public re-*

sponse to the growing horrors facing European Jews. In Eleanor Roosevelt: 1933–1938, *Blanche Wiesen Cook notes that during the 1930s Mrs. Roosevelt received vivid, disturbing letters from private citizens imploring her to speak out against the Nazi treatment of the Jews. Cook reports, "She volunteered no private or public response to reported atrocities as they intensified between 1933 and 1938." While there were ". . . many and amazing acts of personal generosity toward individual Jews in need or in trouble within the United States. . . ," according to Cook, Mrs. Roosevelt said in private correspondence that she was "obliged to leave all contacts with foreign governments in the hands of my husband and his advisors." Indeed, FDR gave his wife explicit orders to keep hands off all war strategy questions.*

In The Abandonment of the Jews, *David Wyman chronicles the transmission of reports from Europe that confirmed the Nazi extermination of Jews. Wyman indicates that on September 4, 1942, Eleanor Roosevelt received a copy of a telegram written by Isaac Sternbuch, the Agudath Israel World Organization's representative in Switzerland, detailing the killing of about 100,000 Jews from the Warsaw ghetto. Wyman observes that throughout the war Mrs. Roosevelt "cared deeply about the tragedy of Europe's Jews" and took various steps to support refugee assistance efforts but that she and President Roosevelt "saw almost no prospect for rescue [of the Jews] and believed that winning the war as quickly as possible was the only answer."*

The Germans called the mass extermination the Final Solution, but the Jews referred to it as Shoah, *Hebrew for "catastrophe." In the 1960s this annihilation of 6 million Jews came to be known as "the Holocaust"—meaning "burnt whole."*

NEW YORK, DECEMBER 5—There was a small item in the paper this morning which filled me with horror. I noticed yesterday that in many parts of the country work had stopped for a few minutes while people prayed for the Jewish victims of Hitler's cruelty. This morning I saw that, in Poland, it was reported that more than two-thirds of the Jewish population had been massacred.

There seems to be little use in voicing a protest, but somehow one cannot keep still when such horrors are going on. One can only pray that it will dawn upon Hitler that the Lord is not patient forever and that he who puts other people to death by the sword is often meted out the same fate.

～

Writing about the courage of the Polish women's resistance against the Nazis, Mrs. Roosevelt urges American women to participate in the peacemaking process after the war and into the future.

WASHINGTON, DECEMBER 10—I have just received from the Prime Minister of the Republic of Poland, who is visiting in this country, a message transmitted from a secret radio station in Poland: "We send you in the name of the Polish women sincere thanks for the imposing protest which you organized on the 30th of July against the German atrocities on the Polish women. We are enduring awful times here in Poland. We still deplore the loss of our dead in September 1939 and already the shadows of thousands tormented to death in concentration camps in Ravensbrück, Oranienburg and other places hover around us.

"But beyond the pain that stabs us, beyond the despair and longing after the dead, we are dominated by the consciousness that the struggle which we are carrying on will decide the existence of freedom, and no one can remain out of it. We Polish women have, therefore, all joined the ranks of subterranean struggling Poland, and together with our husbands, fathers, brothers and sons we will fight to the end with them. We are prepared either to win or perish. God grant that the sacrifices are the smallest and the sufferings of assaulted nations be reduced to naught."

What courage there is in a message of this kind! Listening to the messages sent from here last July would have cost anyone discovered his life. Sending the reply to London was most dangerous and ten efforts were made before it was finally transmitted. These women, who are keeping alive their faith in freedom in spite of such daily horrors as we can hardly conceive of here, are going to have a right to representation when the machinery for peace is built in the future. I am sure that Russian, Chinese and British women have earned and will demand that same right.

In the last peace conference women had no such voice. In the coming one, women will have a right to a voice and they should be sure to prepare in advance so that their influence will be of the greatest value. Women are idealists and I think they had better study these questions and come to their own conclusions. If they do, I am sure they will find that only cooperation and world understanding and concern for each other is going to keep peace through the years. I hope the women of the United States will awaken to the full sense of the influence which they can wield if they accept the responsibility which all power implies.

1943

*T*he war taught children an unforgettable lesson: The world in 1943 was a very grown-up place. Parents looked grim when they read the papers and listened to radio bulletins, and the khaki uniform turned a big brother into an awesome stranger.

Life on the home front had changed. Sugar was now recruited to make gunpowder and plastics for weapons. Other rationed goods included coffee, meat, butter, and canned goods. Carpools became crucial as civilians tried to conserve their precious gas rations. They also had to safeguard their shoes because leather was limited and people were permitted to buy just three pairs of shoes a year.

One thing America had in plentiful supply was jobs. Factories stayed open around the clock. Two million women joined the workforce and made "Rosie the Riveter" an everyday reality. The government initiated the federal withholding tax on weekly wages—yet Americans still managed to buy $156 billion worth of war stamps and bonds.

While the United States was more preoccupied by fighting in the Pacific and the British were determined to ensure the Germany-first commitment, the Allies steadfastly chipped away at the Axis powers. The Soviet army forced the invading German army to surrender at Stalingrad, a stunning setback for the Reich, which lost 150,000 soldiers and gave up their ambitious plans to occupy Russia. The British pushed into North Africa and the Americans regained control of Guadalcanal.

Once the American troops had strengthened their control in the Pacific, Mrs. Roosevelt embarked on another goodwill trip. Her energetic tour of Australia, New Zealand, and the Pacific islands upstaged the visits of movie stars. Greeted with "How's Eleanor?" Gary Cooper responded, "Well, we saw her tracks in the sand at one of the islands, but we couldn't tell which way they were headed." Mrs. Roosevelt not only stopped at many island outposts, she also "walked miles" through hospital wards. Actress Una Merkel was told that the First Lady had gently kissed a boy with a badly shot-up stomach, an act of kindness that seemed to give him the strength to survive.

On these visits, the First Lady became more than a representative of the President; she was the emissary of every mother with a boy in uniform. Mrs. Roosevelt told a reporter, "No one thing has meant more to me, for I have been able to find out firsthand not only what war looks like close-up, but also all the many things that have been done for our men. I have been able to tell large numbers of women how their boys were treated, and how they looked and felt and thought. And that was a precious opportunity which I should not like to have missed."

During World War II, the Selective Service required eighteen-year-old men to register with their draft boards, triggering an important question: If eighteen-year-olds were responsible enough to defend the country, why weren't they responsible enough to vote? The debate would not be settled for another twenty-nine years.

NEW YORK, JANUARY 21—I have noticed lately a number of articles in the papers and even some cartoons on the subject as to whether we should lower the voting age, since we have lowered the draft age. This question has been academically discussed for some time, but now it becomes more than an academic question.

If young men of eighteen and nineteen are old enough to be trained to fight their country's battles and to proceed from training to the battlefields, I think we must accept the fact that they are also old enough to know why we fight this war. If that is so, then they are old enough to take part in the political life of their country and to be full citizens with voting powers.

~

The wife of China's leader, Madame Chiang Kai-shek, came to the U.S. to lobby for support of her country's forces in their war against Japan. In an extemporaneous but artful speech to the Senate, she charmed the most cynical politicians. Describing Madame Chiang's appearances in the House and Senate, Mrs. Roosevelt echoed the sentiments of Congress in her praise of this diminutive but powerful woman.

WASHINGTON, FEBRUARY 19—The speech by Madame Chiang was not only an interesting occasion, but quite unique. It marked the recognition of a woman who, through her own personality and her own service, has achieved a place in the world, not merely as the wife of Generalissimo Chiang Kai-shek but as a representative of her people.

We left the White House to go to the Capitol, and people along the way waved and smiled their recognition of Madame Chiang Kai-shek. I went at once to the gallery overlooking the Senate Chamber, where she was to appear and deliver an extemporaneous, short speech.

When I saw her little, slim figure in her straight Chinese gown coming down the aisle, she seemed overshadowed by the men around her. I could not help a great feeling of pride in her achievements as a woman, but when she spoke it was no longer as a woman that one thought of her. She was a person, a great person, receiving the recognition due her as an individual valiantly fighting in the forefront of the world's battle.

I hurried from the Senate to the House Gallery to hear her deliver a speech. Then we went to the Senate Foreign Relations Committee, where Senator Tom Connally and Representative Sol Bloom greeted us. Here, Madame Chiang tried to gain a few minutes to correct her extemporaneous speech. For she knows, as we all do, that one may say things in rather careless fashion which in print look very different from the way they sound when spoken.

I shall remember for a long time the applause which both sides of the House gave her when she made a plea that we look upon Japan as our major enemy. It was evident that the plea struck a responsive chord in the hearts of the men and women before her. This balance between our two fronts certainly brings up difficult questions for decision, but I imagine we shall have to trust our military authorities to plan the wisest strategy in both oceans.

～

The First Lady chastises U.S. housewives for not saving cooking fat more diligently. Mrs. Roosevelt expected every American to support the war effort.

FORT WORTH, TEX., APRIL 24—A call has gone out from the government to every housewife in this nation. If she does not actually run her own kitchen, then she should see that whoever holds sway there understands the importance of her particular war job—the salvaging of fat for the use of the Government. Fats contain glycerine, glycerine makes gunpowder, explosives and medicine.

The Japanese occupation of the Far East has cut off much of our imports of oils and fats. However, our need and the needs of our allies have increased, and the place where we must meet them is in our own kitchens.

We should get a minimum of 200,000,000 pounds annually. The continental U.S. Army camps are salvaging about 60,000,000 pounds of waste fat a year. The Navy reports another 11,400,000, but so far our household fat salvage collections are only running at the rate of 90,000,000 pounds a year.

A recent consumer study made by the Office of War Information reveals the astounding fact that nine out of ten women know that the country has a fat salvage program, but only six out of ten are saving their kitchen fat. Only three out of ten have turned over any of these fats to be made into glycerine.

One pound of used cooking fat will produce enough glycerine to make a pound and a half of smokeless powder. It is estimated that American women throw away a billion pounds of waste kitchen fat every year. That means that we are throwing away a billion and a half pounds of smokeless powder. We cannot afford to do that. Our boys fighting in every corner of the globe need that powder and this is one of the ways in which every woman can contribute to fighting the war.

I have heard many a woman ask how she could do her bit when her days were filled to overflowing with housework and the care of the family. Here is one very important way, and don't let's forget it.

~

In 1933 Nazi Propaganda Minister Joseph Goebbels staged a book burning of titles—including many literary classics—the Third Reich considered decadent and subversive. Here Eleanor Roosevelt decries that event, while noting with satisfaction that the books burned became more popular in other countries as a result.

WASHINGTON, MAY 11—Today is the tenth anniversary of the very notorious day when Hitler, in Nazi Germany, ordered the burning of all books by such authors as Pearl Buck, Albert Einstein, Sigmund Freud, Ernest Hemingway, Selma Laegerlof, Sinclair Lewis, Thomas Mann, Stephen Vincent Benét and Sigrid Undset.

In doing this, Hitler thought he would destroy the ideas that inspired these authors and that came to the world through their words. He succeeded in Germany, but in the world he stimulated interest. Instead of making people pay less attention to what these authors had to say, it made many more people read them. Their contributions are probably far greater than they would have been without Hitler's effort at suppression.

In the democracies of the world, the passion for freedom of speech and of thought is always accentuated when there is an effort anywhere to keep ideas away from people and to prevent them from making their own decisions. One of the best ways of enslaving a people is to keep them from education and thus make it impossible for them to understand what is going on in the world as a whole.

In the case of Germany, however, the people have always had the tools of learning. They have been a highly educated nation. Hitler had to use other methods, and he chose to go back to the practices of medieval days and burn the books whose philosophies were opposed to his. He knew that if these thoughts reached the people, they might stir up unrest and opposition to his own regime.

The second way of enslaving a people is to suppress the sources of information, not only by burning books but by controlling all the other ways in which ideas are transmitted. In the end, and that end seems to be drawing closer every day, the people whom Hitler has enslaved will have to come in contact again with the world of free expression and thought; then Hitler will have to face the judgment of his own people.

To me this is one of the hopeful elements in an otherwise difficult situation. If the German people had accepted Hitler as a free people, with access to the thought and expression of the rest of the world and freedom of expression at home, we would face a nation of Hitlers. Now we may hope that we shall face an enslaved nation, where access to freedom of thought and expression may make great changes in the people.

~

When America went to war, the President made it clear that strikes would be considered unpatriotic. Union members were willing to work forty-eight hours and six days a week but resisted the request to take a no-strike pledge. The mining industry was particularly plagued by work actions all year. By June 2, mines in three states were shut down due to union stoppages, and FDR ordered the miners back to work. Here Eleanor Roosevelt takes to task both John L. Lewis, the mine workers' controversial leader, and mine operators for hurting the war effort.

WASHINGTON, JUNE 3—Most of us have heavy hearts about the coal strike these days. Perhaps many of us have a share in the blame. Basically, however, one undeniable fact is plain. In wartime a promise was given not to strike and, at that time, the War Labor Board was set up as the final court after conciliation had failed.

One thing keeps coming up before me. Sons of the men who work in mines are flying planes, or shooting guns or driving tanks, in far-off places. Coal is vital to the production of war weapons.

When everything else is said and done, this is the question that the parents of these boys will ask themselves as they sit idly day by day—"Are we making it harder for our boys?" They trust you, Mr. John L. Lewis, are you letting them down? Mr. Operators, how will your sons feel?

～

In the summer of 1943, race riots erupted around the U.S. over shortages in housing, food, and transportation. Hardest hit were Detroit, Los Angeles, and New York. Thousands of people were injured or arrested, and some deaths resulted as well. Mrs. Roosevelt lamented the violence and hoped that Americans eventually would see racial issues as "new frontiers" to conquer.

FRANKTOWN, NEV., JULY 14—Some days ago, as the newspapers have recorded, I came to spend a few days in this beautiful valley. There are farms around us settled long ago by some hardy Swiss pioneers. Gurgling streams run down even now from the mountains. Wildflowers bloom in the meadows, the pine trees and cottonwoods give you shade.

I have walked in the early mornings with the sun coming up, and again in the evening under the moon and watched the stars come out, and renewed my understanding of our pioneers who gave us this vast land of ours. They had no fear of new adventure, there was no pattern to follow in their lives, they accepted men as they proved themselves in the daily business of meeting emergencies.

Have we lost this spirit, do we fear to face the fact that we have new frontiers to conquer? I was sick at heart when I came here, over race riots which put us on a par with Nazism which we fight and make one tremble for what human beings may do when they no longer think but let themselves be dominated by their worst emotions. We are a mixed nation of many peoples and many religions, but most of us would accept the life of Christ as a pattern for our democratic way of life, and Christ taught love and never hate.

We cannot settle strikes by refusing to understand their causes; we cannot prepare for a peaceful world unless we give proof of self-restraint, of open mindedness, of courage to do right at home, even if it means changing our traditional thinking and, for some of us, a sacrifice of our material interests.

～

In late July, Franklin Jr.'s destroyer, the Mayrant, *was patrolling the Mediterranean off Sicily when it was nicked by a bomb. Mrs. Roosevelt describes*

*that moment dreaded by mothers of soldiers—the official phone call—and
the horrific responsibility of telling other loved ones the news, good or bad.*

HYDE PARK, AUGUST 2—Friday's "Herald Tribune" carried a little item
that the destroyer on which our son, Franklin Jr., is executive officer, had
been bombed off the coast of Sicily. They were not directly hit and they
fought off the bombers, but I know the way it feels when someone calls
you up and says in what you know is an intentionally casual tone,
"Franklin Jr., is all right."

That happened to me Thursday evening, and then followed what details
were known so far and my heartaches for those whose boys are not "all
right." Finally, I asked whether Franklin Jr.'s wife had been told and, learning that she still knew nothing, I promised to telephone her.

I had just started to speak to her when I realized I was talking without
any response. In a minute she came back on the wire and said: "Please
start all over again, I did not hear what you said—the first words gave me
heart failure." I realized then that I hadn't been much better as a news-
giver than my husband was.

Such things are bound to happen. You know it. In fact, most of us tell
ourselves over and over again that we are prepared for whatever may happen. If peace comes without having to face some real tragedy, there are a
good many of us, I imagine, who will not only be relieved but hardly able
to believe it. Nevertheless, any news, even when it turns out to be good
news, makes one catch one's breath just for a minute.

The news from Italy makes one feel that the people want peace. There
has always been an underground movement in Italy and many of its representatives are here in this country. I am sure that they hope from day to
day that the people, themselves, will dictate whatever action their government takes. These people, working in the underground movements all
over Europe, have had extraordinary courage.

Death stares them in the face every minute of the day and night and yet
they go about their daily business unconcerned, knowing that the slightest slip might mean detection, sometimes leaving the country and then
voluntarily going back to danger. The United Nations will have to lean
heavily on them in the postwar period, for they are the ones who are
known by their neighbors as having suffered with them and therefore will
be completely trusted.

~

*In August 1943, reports indicated that the Nazis had already massacred 2
million Jews just in the Treblinka, Poland, death camp. Allied statistics esti-*

mated 16 million European refugees. *Although FDR had sent a pledge to the Emergency Conference to Save the Jewish People in Europe that American efforts "to save those that could be saved will not cease until Nazi power is forever crushed," historians continue to debate whether effective action was taken.*

Here Mrs. Roosevelt further reflects on the Nazi atrocities and acknowledges that all nationalities have good and bad people among them.

HYDE PARK, AUGUST 13—I talked a little while yesterday morning with a representative from the group which is trying to formulate plans to save the Jewish people in Europe. Some people think of the Jewish people as a race. Others think of them purely as a religious group. But in Europe the hardships and persecution which they have had to endure for the past few years, have tended to bring them together in a group which identifies itself with every similar group, regardless whether it is religious or racial. The Jews are like all the other people of the world. There are able people among them, there are courageous people among them, there are people of extraordinary intellectual ability along many lines. There are people of extraordinary integrity and people of great beauty and great charm.

On the other hand, largely because of environment and economic conditions, there are people among them who cringe, who are dishonest, who try to take advantage of their neighbors, who are aggressive and unattractive. In other words, they are a cross-section of the human race, just as is every other nationality and every other religious group.

But good or bad, they have suffered in Europe as has no other group. The percentage killed among them in the past few years far exceeds the losses among any of the United Nations in the battles which have been fought throughout the war.

Many of them for generations considered Germany, Poland, Rumania and France their country and permanent home. It seems to me that it is in the part of common sense for the world as a whole to protest in its own interest against wholesale persecution, because none of us by ourselves would be strong enough to stand against a big enough group which decided to treat us in the same way. We may have our individual likes and dislikes, but this is a question which far transcends prejudices or inclinations.

It means the right of survival of human beings and their right to grow and improve. You and I may be hated by our neighbors, but if we know about it we try to change the things within us which brought it about. That is the way civilized people develop; murder and annihilation are never a satisfactory answer for the few who escape, grow up more bitter against their persecutors, and a day of reckoning always comes, which is what the story of Moses in the bulrushes teaches us.

I do not know what we can do to save the Jews in Europe and to find them homes, but I know that we will be the sufferers if we let great wrongs occur without exerting ourselves to correct them.

~

Eleanor Roosevelt wanted to accept Madame Chiang Kai-shek's invitation to visit China, but the President decided it would be more beneficial for the First Lady to visit American soldiers in the Pacific Islands.

The visit was kept secret, and Mrs. Roosevelt traveled alone. Her over–10,000-mile journey to Australia took more than fifty hours of flying time. The Australians expected to treat the First Lady like visiting royalty, but her informality and curiosity enchanted them. She talked to as many servicemen as possible and even greeted a Maori in the traditional way by rubbing foreheads.

CANBERRA, AUSTRALIA, SEPTEMBER 6 (DELAYED)—There is a curious sense of excitement about seeing a continent for the first time. It seemed so improbable to me that I would ever take this trip that I still feel a little as though I were in a dream world.

My first glimpse of Australia was its wooded and indented shore with fine sand beaches, and here and there rocks and high cliffs. Our glimpse of Sydney was from the air, except for a brief stop at the airport for weather reports. Then we went on to Canberra. The Governor General Gowrie and Lady Gowrie, the Prime Minister John Curtin and many Commonwealth Ministers and their wives met us at the airport. A larger group of cameramen faced us than I had ever seen, even at home.

It would seem that the United States and Australia had many reasons to be similar. Certainly parts of our country resemble this country. Mr. Curtin told me that he had recently been on what we would call a ranch which extended over 30,000 square miles. I don't know whether even Texas could do better than that, and I know that my son Elliott, who owns a ranch there, is going to be jealous.

News has come through that the Eighth Army has landed in Italy and we are all anxiously waiting for further details. The Russians also seem to be steadily advancing. How times have changed in the space of one year, and yet we must not relax in any of our war efforts since all of us desire to shorten the war and the only way to do so is to increase our shipping capacity and our production of planes and munitions and fighting men.

When you are at home this whole theater of war seems very far away. It is not until you get here that you realize what a colossal job our men have done and what difficulties of transportation have had to be overcome, without taking into account the hard, desperate fighting which had to go on at the same time. Talk to any servicemen who did the first magnificent job out here and they will say how different things are now.

It must have been bad for everyone when they had to try to do too much with too little. I hope I shall see some of the Australian men as well as our own while I am here, for I have always had such admiration for the fighting record they established in the last war and to which they have added so much in this war.

1944

*M*rs. Roosevelt was preoccupied by war in 1944. Like most mothers, she waited for word on her sons' safety; she comforted her four daughters-in-law and thirteen grandchildren. She read the newspapers carefully for reports on the Allies' invasion of Normandy and on their power plays in the Pacific. And she prayed for peace.

The *New York Times* observed that the war had a powerful impact on the First Lady: "The impression is inescapable that war is always in the front of her consciousness. It breaks frequently into her conversation. She is less buoyant of spirit—as mothers of sons in the service are apt to be—and more given to thoughtful interludes, listening while others talk, content to comment only now and then in her usual animated fashion."

The antidote to the ravages of war came when representatives of the Four Powers—the United States, Great Britain, the U.S.S.R., and China—met at the Dumbarton Oaks mansion in Washington at the end of the summer. They agreed that the coalition would safeguard world peace and sketched out a plan for the United Nations Security Council and General Assembly.

Like most Democrats, Mrs. Roosevelt accepted the fact that her husband would run for a fourth term. He faced reelection under favorable domestic circumstances. Average weekly wages had climbed from $23.64 in 1939 to $45.70 in 1944. The gross national product had grown from $88.6 billion to $198.7 billion, although the U.S. now spent $183 billion on munitions.

While the war consolidated FDR's political position, it drove a wider wedge between the Roosevelts personally. She disapproved of his transformation from Dr. New Deal to Dr. Win-the-War. He cringed when she kept emphasizing the importance of social welfare programs.

Perhaps what most frustrated Mrs. Roosevelt was the increasing difficulty of communicating with her husband. They had conflicting concerns, different circles of friends, and disparate schedules. She would later explain, "Love is usually selfish; but when sufficiently disciplined a family may be glad that a man has the opportunity to fulfill his heart's desire and will work with him in every way they can to help him achieve his objectives but something of the personal relationship must be lost. It is the price paid for a life spent almost entirely in public service."

Anxious to combat racism in the U.S, Eleanor Roosevelt worked with social reformers like Mary McLeod Bethune, the National Youth Administration's director of the Division of Negro Affairs, and Walter White, the national secretary of the NAACP. However, Mrs. Roosevelt's efforts on behalf of the nation's nearly 13 million blacks always created a backlash in the conservative white community.

Frequently, Mrs. Roosevelt used "My Day" to promote a better understanding of minorities. Here she urges that something be done to improve the squalid living conditions for blacks.

WASHINGTON, JANUARY 5—I have a number of letters asking me why I am so interested in Negro housing in Washington when white people find it so difficult to get decent housing, not only in Washington but in many other places in the United States. The answer is that there are more people to speak for white tenants than there are for colored tenants.

Aside from that, if we allow restrictions of areas in any city which has an increasingly large colored population, we shall have, as in Washington, colored areas where health is bad. Overcrowding will affect the moral conditions for young people as well as old and make the city less safe for all its inhabitants. More people will be needed and the institutions such as prisons, hospitals, etc., will be overcrowded. A heavier tax burden will pile up on the citizens of the community.

There is a shortage of habitable homes for Negroes all over this country. Private builders in Washington are being urged to construct 2,767 homes for them.

The response of the builders is excellent because they recognize that there is a postwar market for medium- and low-cost houses. Builders, however, are meeting with some unfortunate obstacles. In areas which have been long established as Negro there has been an infiltration of a few white families. Now, citizens' associations and property owners want to take over parts of these Negro communities for white tenancy alone.

In Bradbury Heights there is opposition to the erection of apartments on an undeveloped site which is in the center of a Negro residential district. Most recent obstacles are petitions for rezoning of special sections of these areas.

This rezoning will affect the building of 744 garden-type apartments by requiring that in one case single-family homes be built and in the other case row houses in groups of three or less be put up. This would raise the cost of each unit and would put them beyond the means of colored war workers.

Devious ways can be used to achieve the object in view—namely, pushing the colored residents into a segregated little city of their own. This area will be as far out as possible, where transportation and utilities will be less available.

This proposal to herd our citizens according to race and religion has many serious disadvantages and should be fought, I believe, by all people interested in the future peace and unity of our nation.

~

Uncle (and former President) Theodore Roosevelt set a breathtaking example for his young fifth cousins Eleanor and Franklin. Favorite niece Eleanor Roosevelt emulated his energy and compassion. Franklin Roosevelt may have chosen to be a Democrat rather than a progressive Republican, but when he first ran for political office, he made sure to get his uncle's advice. Clearly Eleanor Roosevelt also saw Theodore Roosevelt as an inspiration to all young Americans.

NEW YORK, JANUARY 6—January 6 marks the 25th anniversary of Ex-President Theodore Roosevelt's death. I want to recall the great contribution which I feel that he made to the young people. I think it has a special bearing on the problems which we face in the present day. Theodore Roosevelt never failed to convey to young people that he believed they should take an active part in the public affairs of their community and of their nation. He thought every man and woman faced first their family responsibilities, but he was quick to point out that these could not be faced fully without recognizing the tie that the family had to the community. Theodore Roosevelt made you feel that every act in your daily life was a part of your citizenship. I am sure that today he would preach to young people their obligation to participate in the government of their community, the nation and the world, and the necessity for bringing their influence to bear as individuals and as members of any groups.

He believed that every man had an obligation, if he were physically able, to carry arms in times of war. He had very little patience with those who kept aloof from public life because they disliked criticism or might have to deal with disagreeable situations. He had very little patience with those who wished to advance their own personal fortunes, regardless of the fortunes of the American citizens as a whole.

Many of us have forgotten that his interest in the American people generally brought him the accusation of being a traitor to his class—an accusation which other people have suffered under during the course of our history.

As I look back I think perhaps the inspiration which Theodore Roosevelt gave to young people was one of his enduring contributions, not only to the youth of his generation but to the youth of all generations.

~

The Roosevelts considered divorce after Eleanor discovered Franklin's love letters from Lucy Mercer, her social secretary, but stayed together for the sake of their children. However, they didn't interfere when their married children wanted to divorce their spouses. Here Mrs. Roosevelt muses on the charm of romance and the rarity of a truly happy marriage.

NEW YORK, FEBRUARY 8—Saturday night we went to see Katharine Cornell and Raymond Massey in a play called "Lovers and Friends" by Dodie Smith.

The reviews have been none too good on this play and so I wonder whether the fact that I liked it so much was because the people seemed to me real people and behaved somewhat the way they would have behaved when I was a young woman!

I confess I thought the husband lacked a little subtlety in announcing his love affair, but the rest of the play was full of subtle meaning to me. While perhaps one should not expect evenings of entertainment to teach one any lessons, there is one in this play which men and women would do well to learn.

It is obviously true that the first flush of being "in love" may change into something deeper and calmer—or more superficial. I have known only a few very happy marriages. By that I do not mean just people who get along together and live contentedly through life, but people who are really excitingly happy. These people have somehow preserved the ability to rejuvenate their love so that neither the man nor the woman need wander off to find the romance they long for somewhere else.

The play shows that it is not the people who happen to attract each other temporarily who really matter. It is the lure of romance—finding someone new to tell about yourself, someone who will give you a feeling that what you say is important and that they have never heard it before, someone who will give you the feeling that you are more important and alluring than a previous engagement, or a book, or even a career. This may be a lesson worth learning—or perhaps you think I'm wrong.

～

Mrs. Roosevelt discusses how the demands placed on the average housewife often outweigh the obligations she faces as First Lady. It was her way of honoring wives and mothers.

WASHINGTON, FEBRUARY 24—I sometimes wonder how the people who are so impressed by my energy can fail to realize that any woman with a family who does all of her own work is doing in the course of a day twice as much as I ever think of doing. Just getting the meals and cleaning the house and doing the laundry, not to speak of taking care of several children, who in winter are bound to have the ailments that come the way of all children, will fill up more time and demand a more active life than I live at any time. In the few concentrated periods when I go on trips I may be nearly as active as the normal housewife, and then only because I follow the schedules which other people map out for me.

There is only one thing which I find is a real strain, and that is purely emotional, which anyone who reads about as many personal problems and tragedies as I do in the course of every 24 hours would naturally feel. Many of these problems are particularly baffling because there is nothing one can do about them. You can find out what people think, you can obtain investigations of situations which might otherwise be overlooked; you can sometimes get some material help where material help is an issue, or you may be able to make some suggestions about the proper procedure. But by and large, it seems that so often the only thing one can do is to try to understand the problems and convey in words one's sympathy and desire to help.

～

Mrs. Roosevelt and her secretary-companion Malvina Thompson were the first American women to visit the Galápagos islands off the coast of Chile.

WASHINGTON, APRIL 4—When I look back on my visit to Galápagos, I know why every man there calls it "The Rock." To a geologist, I'm sure it would furnish several years of absorbing work, but to men establishing gun positions and defenses, building airfields and trying to find level space for a recreation field, it must be one of the most discouraging spots in the world. It is as though the earth had spewed forth rocks of every size and shape and, as one man said: "You remove one rock, only to find two more underneath."

In between the rocks there is deep red dust, which permeates everything. A few cactus plants grow and also a few trees, which are easily blown over because they have no earth to root in.

All the water is either distilled from salt water or is brought in on a tank ship from another island. On the whole island, there are just two places with running water. Otherwise, tin basins or helmets are used for washing, and the regular set-up that men have at the front for showers is the order of the day. No luxurious living there! One boy in the dispensary, Corporal Edward Shwing, had spent much time putting up very good battle maps, covering every front, with colored pins showing the various activities. He told me that many boys came in to watch the pins change!

Galápagos is one of those places where "going native" would be very easy. For that reason, during the day, men at work may wear as few clothes as they choose, but for evening inspection, every man must be in uniform. The Navy bars whites because they cannot be kept clean.

One of the most attractive places on the island is the Bluejackets Club, which the men have created themselves. Every bit of furniture and every decoration is their own handiwork. On the door of the club hangs a sign which reads: "Bluejackets Club—women invited." The joke is that there are no women there! American women in Ecuador have sent a few things like curtains and Ecuadorian straw mats to various service clubs on the island, but every day room and post exchange represents much work by the men themselves.

Commander Huffman has some pets—two goats, Blackie and Ruth, each with a painted green and red horn. And, in a little enclosure outside, are two prehistoric-looking iguanas. He was disappointed because I found these native pets interesting but not attractive!

The American man's sense of humor was evident everywhere. They held a competition at the Navy base for the naming and the general appearance of the various quarters. The doctors' quarters were labeled "Rock's Docs." That won the prize.

You have to be deeply convinced that your job is an essential one in order to keep your balance and cheerfulness in these surroundings. I think perhaps it takes more fortitude and character to stand the loneliness and hardship of this kind of service without much excitement than the more active kind of service, though many women at home are probably happier with the knowledge that their men are not being sniped at by the enemy.

~

The date was June 6, destined to be remembered as D-Day, when the Allies invaded Normandy. The massive invasion—4,600 ships, 10,000 planes, and

176,000 infantryman—badly shook the Germans. The banner headline of the New York Times *gave good cause for celebration:* ALLIED ARMIES LAND IN FRANCE IN THE HAVRE-CHERBOURG AREA: GREAT INVASION IS UNDERWAY.

Reflecting on the impact of the momentous day, Mrs. Roosevelt was quick to remind American workers and employers that a massive home-front push was also needed to finish the war.

WASHINGTON, JUNE 7—So at last we have come to D-Day, or rather, the news of it reached us over the radio in the early hours of the morning on June the 6th. The first people I saw seemed very much excited. Curiously enough, I have no sense of excitement whatsoever. It seems as though we have been waiting for this day for weeks, and dreading it, and now all emotion is drained away.

All the preparation that has gone on, the endless photographing, the end-less air raids, the constant practice of the men in landing or in whatever their specialty may be—this is now ended. The fact that boys you know have been waiting with an almost desperate feeling for this day, when all their training would be tested, made you dread it and yet hope for it.

The time is here, and in this country we live in safety and comfort and wait for victory. It is difficult to make life seem real. It is hard to believe that the beaches of France which we once knew are now places from which, in days to come, boys in hospitals over here will tell us that they have returned. They may never go beyond the water or the beach, but all their lives, perhaps, they will bear the marks of this day. At that, they will be fortunate, for many others won't return.

This is the beginning of a long, hard fight, a fight for ports where heavy materials of war must be landed, a fight for airfields in the countries in which we must operate. Day by day, miles of country may be taken, lost and retaken. That is what we have to face, what the boys who are over there have been preparing for and what must be done before the day of victory. That day is coming surely. It will be a happy and glorious day. How can we hasten it?

The best way in which we can help is by doing our jobs here better than ever before, no matter what these jobs may be. Every unauthorized and unwarranted strike is an added danger to the boys over there, and a man or woman leaving a war plant today adds to some soldier's load. But on the other hand, we should remember that every employer who forces his employees into a position from which they see no way out except to strike is as guilty as the strikers. Therefore the responsibility for whatever hap-pens today which slows up production, which we need so desperately in every theater of the war, does not lie with one group alone.

~

In April 1943, more than 50,000 surviving Jews in the Warsaw ghetto made a heroic, though ultimately futile, last stand against their Nazi oppressors. Documentation of this human disaster produced a disturbing photographic work, "The Black Book of Polish Jewry," which Mrs. Roosevelt saw at the Capitol.

After D-Day, President Roosevelt offered a unifying prayer to the nation: "Almighty God: Our sons ... this day have set upon a mighty endeavor, a struggle to preserve our Republic, our religion and our civilization, and to set free a suffering humanity. ... They fight not for the lust of conquest. ... They fight to liberate ... They yearn but for the end of battle, for their return to the haven of home. Some will never return. Embrace these, Father, and receive them, thy heroic servants, into Thy Kingdom."

WASHINGTON, JUNE 8—Like everybody else, I am spending more time than usual reading the papers and listening to the radio these days, which is really not conducive to accomplishing much work.

I did, however, go up to the Senate yesterday afternoon when the Committee appointed to write the account of what had happened to the Jews in Poland presented "The Black Book of Polish Jewry" to New York's Senator Robert Wagner, Representative Sol Bloom, Representative Emanuel Celler and Mr. Michael W. Straus, first assistant secretary of the Interior Department.

I hope that many people will see this book. The pictures speak more vividly than the written word. It is a horrible book, a book which explains the terrible statistics of the martyrdom of the Jews in Warsaw and makes one ashamed that a civilized race anywhere in the world could treat other human beings in such a manner.

In the evening my daughter, her husband and I were with the President when he read the prayer in which he hoped the nation would join him. It is a good prayer to read and reread in these coming days, and I think he is right in saying that instead of one day of prayer, we must keep on praying day by day until the long march to Berlin has been accomplished.

~

Even though the war was not yet over, Mrs. Roosevelt and many other Americans wondered if the draft should extend into peacetime. In her August 21 column, Mrs. Roosevelt explained that immediately after the war, drafted young men might still be needed as a police force, as occupation troops, or as replacements for discharged veterans. She also thought a year in the service didn't provide enough time to teach specialized tasks but would accommodate basic military training. The rest of the mandatory service period, Mrs. Roosevelt thought, should be devoted to community work and lessons in democratic citizenship. Here she argues for national service, adding her ideas to a debate still under way today.

HYDE PARK, AUGUST 22—There are many arguments in favor of a year of national service.

Many things would be accomplished if it were just a year of military service. For instance, the nations of the world would know that we were never again going to be caught unprepared—that at all times the young manhood of our country was in condition, with sufficient training to protect the nation and to prevent any surprise attacks. Our equipment would be modernized and adequate.

There would also be the advantage, under any circumstances, that young men from all the different groups which make up the citizenship of the nation would be thrown together at an early and impressionable age. They would know each other, and the differences in background and environment would melt away before the stark realities which close association soon brings out. Only a man's character is the real criterion of worth. There is also the possibility of teaching young men how to take care of themselves in the open, if they have not had that opportunity in civilian life. There is the added opportunity of seeing something of a great nation, which they might not do except at the expense of the government.

I believe, however, that it is worth thinking of the possibility of giving young men a new conception, adding to the one that all men have had since time immemorial. Every man in every nation has always felt that, in time of war, it was his duty to protect his country; and the man who did not feel this obligation was usually looked down upon by his compatriots. But many people in our country, as well as in other countries, have grown up with far less sense of obligation toward their peacetime citizenship. The statistics on voting alone prove this. The fact that over and over again you can ask a group of people to name their representative in Congress and get no reply shows that we, as citizens, are not aware of the same passionate patriotism which must be devoted to peace as it has been to war.

～

Mrs. Roosevelt felt that young women should also devote a year to national service, though she imagined their duties would probably be far different from those given to young men.

HYDE PARK, AUGUST 23—One of the clippings which has been sent me starts with the following paragraph:

> "As she ages, the feminine part of the Roosevelt presidency becomes wilder in her attempts to force American youths to follow the pattern of life she wants to dictate to them. Now she is starting to campaign for compulsory military training after the war for our boys and girls of 18 years of age. She says 'Our youngsters must get it into their minds that they have a responsibility to their country.'"

In the last two days, I have tried to express clearly why we should perhaps call on some new methods to help us all to be better citizens in our great democracy.

But one thing I hope I have made very clear, and that is that everything which I say is only in the form of suggestions. These are made in order to interest people and bring about discussion. When some concrete plans are actually suggested by those who properly have the responsibility for such suggestions, there will then be among us all an awakened interest and a background of thought and discussion.

And now to this terrifying subject of what part girls might play in a program of national service. No one is more conscious than I am that many a girl, when she finishes high school, will not want to leave home, and that her family, as well, will not want her to go from under their direct supervision.

It is possible, however, that a girl might give a year of service in her own community. Such service might well prove of value to the hospitals, or to some government agencies, or to some civic or charitable activity, dealing with child care or recreation, which needed personnel.

In any of these activities, a girl might learn many things which would be a help to her in her future life, either in her home or in work which she may undertake. Quite obviously, it would be useful to any woman to have a knowledge of local conditions, a better knowledge of nutrition or of sanitation, as well as some of the first principles of hygiene or nursing. Some girls might feel that they wanted to see something of their own country beyond their immediate surroundings; but this, after all, could perhaps be offered on a voluntary basis.

The essential thing, as I see it, is that we should think out ways to increase our participation in government.

1945

*J*ust before her husband won his fourth bid for the presidency, Eleanor Roosevelt turned sixty. "I feel that I have a great deal of variety left—at least five more years of active working life, and nothing would give me greater pleasure than to spend it in a job of my own."

After the victory celebrations on election night, the First Lady was involved with holiday preparations, the receptions that would accompany her husband's fourth inauguration, and the traditional round of Birthday Balls to raise funds for the National Foundation for Infantile Paralysis.

The disciplined First Lady met the rigors of her official role, but she was not looking forward to another four years in the midst of Washington politics. President Roosevelt left her alone on reception lines to accept greetings from his well-wishers, and Mrs. Roosevelt considered Washington to be a lonely place in 1945. Henry Wallace and Aubrey Williams—men who had helped set the New Deal in motion—no longer seemed welcome in Washington. Although FDR had named Archibald MacLeish, the poet and Librarian of Congress as undersecretary of state, the department was now dominated by conservatives, headed by the new secretary of state, Edward Stettinius, Jr.

The President was preoccupied by the business of war, which often meant making concessions and cutting back on liberal domestic programs. Mrs. Roosevelt was dismayed that her husband was usually offered a one-sided opinion. There was no one willing to debate an issue—except her. Eleanor Roosevelt's role as ombudsman was diminishing.

Claiming that the First Lady's presence would be distracting, the President ruled against her accompanying him to the war strategy session in Yalta. Instead, FDR traveled with their daughter Anna. The First Lady took comfort in the fact that she would go with the President to San

Francisco, to welcome the United Nations delegates to the first official conference. Witnessing the creation of the United Nations fulfilled one of the Roosevelts' most heartfelt goals.

FDR returned from Yalta exhausted and couldn't shake what appeared to be another bout of the flu. A specialist soon revised the diagnosis: FDR had bronchitis, hypertension, and congestive heart failure. The President made a pilgrimage for recuperation to his Little White House in Warm Springs, Georgia, on March 29.

Franklin Delano Roosevelt had taken the oath of office for President in 1932 as the country reeled from the shock of economic collapse. When he died on April 12, 1945, of a cerebral hemorrhage, the nation still had not had the chance to recover fully from the economic trials of the thirties. The trauma of World War II occupied the President's attention day in and day out after the conflict broke out in Europe in 1939. Through all of this—the struggle to bring the country back to economic health with the New Deal and the struggle to win the war—Eleanor Roosevelt stood steadfastly by her husband's side.

She was not, by training or personality, a woman to wallow in grief. Allowing herself only a few days' rest after the President's death, Mrs. Roosevelt resumed writing "My Day." (It did not appear from April 12 to April 16.) At first she wrote of her activities in the transition from wife to widow, from First Lady to private citizen. But soon the great unresolved issues of the war, impending economic recovery, and the future of hundreds of thousands of refugees and displaced persons and homeward-bound servicemen and -women began to occupy Eleanor Roosevelt's attention.

The First Lady broke the news of President Roosevelt's death to new Vice President Harry S. Truman. A shocked Truman soon asked if there was anything he could do for Mrs. Roosevelt. "Is there anything we can do for you?" she replied. "You are the one in trouble now."

Truman took up the cause where FDR left off. Within days after FDR's death, Truman addressed Congress and the people to assure a smooth continuance of the dead President's military and economic policies. By late April, U.S. and Soviet troops, fighting as allies, met for the first time in Germany. In San Francisco, representatives of fifty nations gathered to work out a document that would soon become the Charter of the United Nations, an organization whose peaceful principles symbolized a ray of hope for a war-weary civilization. On May 7, Germany surrendered to the Allied command at Reims, France; Gen. Dwight D. Eisenhower accepted on behalf of the victorious Allies. President Truman declared the following day V-E Day, and the country rejoiced.

War in the Pacific Theater dragged on, however, with the Japanese still resolute. While the Big Four (United States, Britain, France, Soviet Union) met to divide Berlin and Germany into spheres of control (laying the groundwork for Cold War tensions), Allied troops in the Pacific scored numerous victories but lost thousands of lives as well. Japan surrendered Okinawa by the end of June, and Gen. Douglas MacArthur recaptured the Philippines one week later. With no comprehensive surrender by the Japanese in sight, the United States proceeded to test a new weapon: On July 16, 1945, the first atomic bomb was successfully exploded in the New Mexico desert, and the nuclear age began.

Eager to bring the war in the East to an end, and convinced there were no other more humane alternatives, President Truman approved dropping atomic bombs on Hiroshima and then Nagasaki on August 6 and 9. The extent of material destruction and loss of human life surprised even scientists who developed the bomb. On September 2, Japan surrendered unconditionally, bringing World War II to a bloody, costly end.

The work of adjusting the world to postwar life began. The Allies divided Korea at the 38th Parallel, with Soviet troops occupying the north and American troops the south, setting the stage for later conflict. President Truman urged the British, now in control of Palestine, to accept 100,000 Soviet Jewish refugees. At home, Truman and Congress began dismantling wartime economic controls. Among the first commodities from which rationing was lifted were shoes, electricity, meat, butter, and tires.

There were signs of new political life in America, too. The President proposed compulsory national health insurance for the first time in November 1945, initiating a contest of opinions among interest groups, politicians, and patients. Gen. Dwight Eisenhower, considered by many the greatest American hero of the war, was named army chief of staff, a step on his own climb toward the presidency. A major, protracted labor-management dispute began when the United Auto Workers went on strike in late November.

The last eight months of 1945 were a roller coaster for Americans, with rapid, disorienting changes. What Eleanor Roosevelt said about each of the great issues of the time touched the lives and influenced the thinking of thousands of "My Day" readers.

Eleanor Roosevelt considered the White House as private as a goldfish bowl. "The longer I stay there, the more I feel the White House for whatever family or individuals happen to be installed there is a different plan to be lived.

One's personal program must always be subordinated to the demands of official life. That rule is never to be broken."

Before Election Day 1944, Mrs. Roosevelt told the New York Times *that if her husband was not reelected, she would like a "little job." She observed that a First Lady's obligations were so varied that "I have frequently had to guess whether I was effective after all. In time you get a sense of frustration, even though here and there you can see the end result and know it worked out all right. What I would like for myself is a little job in a single category where I can see something I want to do and judge for myself what progress I am making."*

NEW YORK, FEBRUARY 10—For the first time in 12 years I have spent a full week in New York City, and I have enjoyed it more than I can possibly tell you. I like my little apartment, with the familiar things which came from my mother-in-law's house as well as ours, and the simplicity of keeping house there is a real joy.

I know quite well that I would not be happy unless I had some regular work to do every day, and I imagine that I will always feel that way no matter how old I am, unless I become completely bedridden. Even then I will probably want to use my mind as long as I retain it! That is probably because I happen to be blessed with good health!

When I come across clippings in which the writers worry about the effect upon an American family who find themselves living in the White House for many years, I always want to suggest to them that some things are a great honor, some things are very beautiful: you admire them and you appreciate the opportunities which they offer you. Never for a moment, however, no matter how long you enjoy them, do they give you the comfort and pleasure of your own home, your own things and your own personal life with which no one has a right to interfere.

～

The President's calendar for Thursday, April 12, revealed no pressing appointments. Taking a much-needed rest at the Little White House in Warm Springs, Georgia, FDR was in good spirits and looking forward to an evening barbecue.

Without warning, he muttered, "I have a terrific headache," and slumped sideways in his chair. He had fainted.

Back in Washington, the news reached Eleanor Roosevelt at the White House, but she was encouraged to attend a children's benefit. In the course of the party, she was called back to the White House. FDR's press secretary found the First Lady in her sitting room, surrounded by pictures of family

and friends, and told her that the President had died from a massive cere-
bral hemorrhage.

For the first time in her nine-year career as a columnist, Mrs. Roosevelt
arranged to take time off, and "My Day" did not appear from April 12 to
April 16.

WASHINGTON, APRIL 17—When you have lived for a long time in close contact with the loss and grief which today pervades the world, any personal sorrow seems to be lost in the general sadness of humanity. For a long time, all hearts have been heavy for every serviceman sacrificed in the war. There is only one way in which those of us who live can repay the dead who have given their utmost for the cause of liberty and justice. They died in the hope that, through their sacrifice, an enduring peace would be built and a more just world would emerge for humanity.

While my husband was in Albany and for some years after coming to Washington, his chief interest was in seeing that the average human being was given a fairer chance for "life, liberty and the pursuit of happiness." That was what made him always interested in the problems of minority groups and of any group which was at a disadvantage.

As the war clouds gathered and the inevitable involvement of this country became more evident, his objective was always to deal with the problems of the war, political and military, so that eventually an organization might be built to prevent future wars.

Any man in public life is bound, in the course of years, to create certain enmities. But when he is gone, his main objectives stand out clearly and one may hope that a spirit of unity may arouse the people and their leaders to a complete understanding of his objectives and a determination to achieve those objectives themselves.

Abraham Lincoln was taken from us before he had achieved unity within the nation, and his people failed him. This divided us as a nation for many years.

Woodrow Wilson was also stricken and, in that instance, the peoples of the world failed to carry out his vision.

Perhaps, in His wisdom, the Almighty is trying to show us that a leader may chart the way, may point out the road to lasting peace, but that many leaders and many peoples must do the building. It cannot be the work of one man, nor can the responsibility be laid upon his shoulders, and so, when the time comes for peoples to assume the burden more fully, he is given rest.

God grant that we may have the wisdom and courage to build a peaceful world with justice and opportunity for all peoples the world over.

And now I want to say one personal word of gratitude to the many people who have sent messages of affection and condolence during these last days. My children and I are deeply grateful. I want to say too that the people who waited in the stations and along the railroad to pay their last respects have my deep appreciation.

"And now there abideth these three—faith, hope, charity, but the greatest of these is charity."

~

Less than a fortnight after the President's death Mrs. Roosevelt, her immediate family, and her secretary, Malvina Thompson [Scheider], returned to Hyde Park. Many a family would have given itself a rest before diving again into the affairs of business or the sensitive issues of inheritance and distribution of memorabilia, but not the Roosevelts. Her husband had been an enthusiastic collector of everything historical from miniature books to model boats, and as President he had received scores of gifts from nations and admiring citizens around the world. Assigning presidential and private property to appropriate new homes was a monumental job.

HYDE PARK, APRIL 24—We came back to Hyde Park yesterday morning, just one week from the time we all gathered here for the committal service in our hedge-surrounded garden. My sons and I went to look at the grave. If two soldiers had not been on guard, and the beautiful orchids flown up from the South had not covered the spot where the sod had been put back so carefully, we would hardly have known that the lawn was not as it had always been.

Before very long, the simple stone which my husband described very carefully for us will be in place. But in the meantime the children and the dogs will be quite unconscious that here a short time ago a solemn military funeral was held, and they will think of it as a place where flowers grow and where the hedge protects them from the wind and makes the sun shine down more warmly. And that is as my husband would have it. He liked children and dogs and sunshine and flowers, and they are all around him now.

We drove over the boundaries of the place yesterday afternoon trying to ascertain, from the maps we had, exactly what the memorandums meant which my husband so carefully wrote out for us. If you have ever tried to reconcile a map and the actual roads through the woods with the descriptions in a memorandum, no matter how accurate it is, you will understand how difficult we found it. Many a time we stopped where two trails ran into each other and wondered just exactly where this road really was on the map.

It was a wonderful day, but very windy and much colder than when we were here two weeks ago. We have had open fires in our living rooms all the afternoon and evening. But the house as a whole is very cold, and I don't dare turn up our heat because we have a very limited amount of oil.

Miss Thompson looks with despair on three clothes-baskets filled with mail, and so, dear readers, if you don't get any answers to your letters, you will know that eventually they will all be read. Meanwhile, it is physically impossible to do more than thank you here for your kindness and your real understanding and sympathy.

Today our heavier tasks begin, as trucks arrive from Washington and things are unpacked and made available for the further business of settling an estate. I foresee that we have many long days of work in the big house before it is presentable for government visitors, and many long evenings ahead of us just opening and reading this incoming mail. Some day, however, we will actually find ourselves sitting down to read a book without that guilty feeling which weighs upon one when the job you should be doing is ignored.

~

In the wake of the death of someone close, the impulse to philosophize about the meaning of mortality is often irresistible. Eleanor Roosevelt was a person with strong though usually private spiritual instincts.

NEW YORK, MAY 7—A friend of mine has just sent me a prayer by John Oxenham, a British poet. It is a very beautiful prayer for older people, or for people who have spent themselves so greatly that they fear not to be able to give their best in their remaining years on earth:

"Lord, when Thou see'st that my work is done, Let me not linger here With failing powers, A workless worker in a world of work; But with a word, just bid me Home And I will come, Right gladly will I come, Yea— Right gladly will I come—"

I have always felt that one could have a certain sense of resignation when people die who have lived long and fruitful lives. My rebellion has always been over the deaths of young people; and that is why I think so many of us feel particularly frustrated by war, where youth so largely pays the price. It seems as though youth was so much needed to carry the burdens of peace.

A friend of mine, however, not long ago said something to me which may be comforting to many other women. In speaking of her young son, she remarked that what she wanted for him was that he should feel that he had fulfilled his mission in life; that if he had not spent himself during this war fighting for the things in which he believed, he would feel empty. If he died and was here to carry on in peacetime, she would still not rebel. She would know that to have denied him participation in the great adventure of fighting against the forces of evil, so that the forces of good might have an opportunity in the future to grow, would have left him warped and unable to carry on the battle for a better world in peace.

Of one thing I am sure: Young or old, in order to be useful we must stand for the things we feel are right, and we must work for those things wherever we find ourselves. It does very little good to believe something unless you tell your friends and associates of your beliefs. Those who fight down in the marketplace are bound to be confused now and then. Sometimes they will be deceived, and sometimes the dirt that they touch will cling to them. But if their hearts are pure and their purposes are unswerving, they will win through to the end of their mission on earth, untarnished.

~

There were ticker-tape parades, dancing in the streets; church bells ringing, factory whistles tooting all across America: War was finally over in Europe. V-E Day brought relief to a country yearning to see an end to its greatest sustained loss of life and materiel in a military conflict. Yet Mrs. Roosevelt offered a sobering perspective. As war raged on in the Far East against the third member of the Axis, Japan, she called on jubilant Americans to recognize that until this war was fully won and over, victory could not truly be declared.

New York, May 9—All day yesterday, as I went about New York City, the words "V-E Day" were on everybody's lips. Part of the time, paper fluttered through the air until the gutters of the streets were filled with it. At Times Square crowds gathered—but that first report the other night had taken the edge off this celebration. No word came through from Washington and everybody still waited for official confirmation. Today it has come.

Over the radio this morning President Truman, Prime Minister Churchill and Marshal Stalin have all spoken—the war in Europe is over. Unconditional surrender has been accepted by the Germans. I can almost hear my husband's voice make that announcement, for I heard him repeat it so often. The German leaders were not willing to accept defeat, even when they knew it was inevitable, until they had made their people drink the last dregs in the cup of complete conquest by the Allies.

Europe is in ruins and the weary work of reconstruction must now begin. There must be joy, of course, in the hearts of the peoples whom the Nazis conquered and who are now free again. Freedom without bread, however, has little meaning. My husband always said that freedom from want and freedom from aggression were twin freedoms which had to go hand in hand.

The necessity to share with our brothers, even though it means hardship for ourselves, will now face all of us who live in the fortunate countries which war has not devastated.

I cannot feel a spirit of celebration today. I am glad that our men are no longer going to be shot at and killed in Europe, but the war in the Pacific still goes on. Men are dying there, even as I write. It is far more a day of dedication for us, a day on which to promise that we will do our utmost to end war and build peace. Some of my own sons, with millions of others, are still in danger.

I can but pray that the Japanese leaders will not force their people to complete destruction too. The ultimate end is sure, but in the hands of the Japanese leaders lies the decision of how many people will have to suffer before ultimate peace comes.

What are our ultimate objectives now? Do we want our Allies in Europe, and later in the Far East, to have the opportunity to rebuild quickly? Looked at selfishly, we will probably gain materially if they do. That cannot be our only responsibility, however. The men who fought this war are entitled to a chance to build a lasting peace. What we do in the next months may give them that chance or lose it for them. If we give people bread, we may build friendship among the peoples of the world; and we will never have peace without friendship around the world. This is the time for a long look ahead. This is the time for us all to decide where we go from here.

~

At the time the U.S. Air Force dropped the first atomic bomb on Hiroshima (August 6, 1945), many people—politicians and military experts among them—did not recognize the gravity of the decisions first to develop and then to use the atomic bomb. Mrs. Roosevelt seems to have grasped almost immediately both the strategic military implications of the new weapon and its long-term political meaning.

NEW YORK, AUGUST 8—The news which came to us yesterday afternoon of the first use of the atomic bomb in the war with Japan may have surprised a good many people, but scientists—both British and American—

have been working feverishly to make this discovery before our enemies, the Germans, could make it and thereby possibly win the war.

This discovery may be of great commercial value someday. If wisely used, it may serve the purposes of peace. But for the moment we are chiefly concerned with its destructive power. That power can be multiplied indefinitely, so that not only whole cities but large areas may be destroyed at one fell swoop. If you face this possibility and realize that, having once discovered a principle, it is very easy to take further steps to magnify its power, you soon face the unpleasant fact that in the next war whole peoples may be destroyed.

The only safe counter weapon to this new power is the firm decision of mankind that it shall be used for constructive purposes only. This discovery must spell the end of war. We have been paying an ever-increasing price for indulging ourselves in this uncivilized way of settling our difficulties. We can no longer indulge in the slaughter of our young men. The price will be too high and will be paid not just by young men, but by whole populations.

In the past we have given lip service to the desire for peace. Now we meet the test of really working to achieve something basically new in the world. Religious groups have been telling us for a long time that peace could be achieved only by a basic change in the nature of man. I am inclined to think that this is true. But if we give human beings sufficient incentive, they may find good reasons for reshaping their characteristics.

Good will among men was preached by the angels as they announced to the world the birth of the child Jesus. He exemplified it in His life and preached it Himself and sent forth His disciples, who have spread that gospel of love and human understanding throughout the world ever since. Yet the minds and hearts of men seemed closed.

Now, however, an absolute need exists for facing a nonescapable situation. This new discovery cannot be ignored. We have only two alternative choices: destruction and death—or construction and life! If we desire our civilization to survive, then we must accept the responsibility of constructive work and of the wise use of a knowledge greater than any ever achieved by man before.

NEW YORK (UNDATED)—When word was flashed that peace had come to the world again, I found myself filled with very curious sensations. I had no desire to go out and celebrate. I remembered the way the people demonstrated when the last war ended, but I felt this time that the weight of suffering which has engulfed the world during so many years could not so quickly be wiped out. There is a quiet rejoicing that men are no longer bringing death to each other throughout the world. There is great happiness, too, in the knowledge that some day, soon, many of those we love will be at home again to give all they have to the rebuilding of a peaceful world.

One cannot forget, however, the many, many people to whom this day will bring only a keener sense of loss, for, as others come home, their loved ones will not return.

In every community, if we have eyes to see and hearts to feel, we will for many years see evidences of the period of war which we have been through. There will be men among us who all their lives, both physically and mentally, will carry the marks of war; and there will be women who mourn all the days of their lives. Yet there must be an undercurrent of deep joy in every human heart, and great thankfulness that we have world peace again.

These first days of peace require great statesmanship in our leaders. They are not easy days, for now we face the full results of the costs of war and must set ourselves to find the ways of building a peaceful world. The new atomic discovery has changed the whole aspect of the world in which we live. It has been primarily thought of in the light of its destructive power. Now we have to think of it in terms of how it may serve mankind in the days of peace.

This great discovery was not found by men of any one race or any one religion and its development and control should be under international auspices. All the world has a right to share in the beneficence which may grow from its proper development.

Great Britain and Canada and ourselves hold the secret today and quite rightly, since we used its destructive force to bring the war to an end. But if we allow ourselves to think that any nations or any group of commercial interests should profit by something so great, we will eventually be the sufferers. God has shown great confidence in mankind when he allowed them wisdom and intelligence to discover this new secret. It is a challenge to us—the peoples who control the discovery—for unless we develop spiritual greatness commensurate with this new gift, we may bring economic war into the world and chaos instead of peace.

The greatest opportunity the world has ever had lies before us. God grant we have enough understanding of the divine love to live in the future as "one world" and "one people."

~

Conservation of natural resources and preservation of such national trea-sures as the White House were among Eleanor Roosevelt's favorite causes. Mrs. Roosevelt took on a formidable adversary in Robert Moses, the contro-versial New York City Parks commissioner and chairman of New York

State's Council of Parks, who wanted to remove Fort Clinton in Battery Park at Manhattan's southern tip.

Known around City Hall as a power broker, Moses used official posts (held under several mayors, 1934 to 1960) to lobby for enormous projects, many of which Eleanor Roosevelt supported. The monuments in his legacy include dozens of state and city parks, including Jones Beach on Long Island; 416 miles of highways; Whitestone, Triborough, Throgs Neck, and Verrazano–Narrows bridges; Queens Midtown Tunnel; numerous housing projects; Lincoln Center; and the United Nations complex.

Still, in the face of such power, Eleanor Roosevelt did not hesitate to speak her mind.

NEW YORK, OCTOBER 23—All over our country we destroy old historic buildings when we should preserve them, and here in New York City I understand that the war is on again between our very efficient Parks Commissioner, Robert Moses, and such people in the city as really care about preserving old landmarks. The issue this time is Fort Clinton, which was designed by John McComb, the architect of our City Hall.

The fort should be preserved as one of New York City's historic spots. Heaven knows, I am not one of the people who object to change when it is really necessary to bring about improvements. But there are very few of these old landmarks left. The walls of Fort Clinton are nine feet thick, it speaks of years gone by when forts really could defend New York, and it might serve as a landmark to teach many children the history of their city.

In 1941 the Board of Estimate authorized Mr. Moses to destroy the fort. A short time ago, President Nathan of the Borough of Manhattan moved to rescind that vote. But Mr. Moses is a powerful antagonist, and while under ordinary circumstances the Board of Estimate might be willing to let the old fort stand, and feel rather happy about it, they certainly would not be happy to antagonize Mr. Moses.

I am sure I am not the only older person in New York who has associations with this building. I have been there with my children. I have an affection for the Battery, and I can remember when a very old and charming cousin, who once danced with Lafayette, told me how the high society of her day promenaded on the Battery. I like to see it all in my mind's eye when I go back and walk there.

I don't want to give up my modern comforts and live as my ancestors did. I like central heating and running water—but that doesn't seem to enter into this controversy, since no one is going to have to live in the fort.

In Washington, I found that all young people who visited the White House seemed to be impressed by the fact that it still had the same walls which were in the original house before it was burned when the City of

Washington was captured in the War of 1812. For that reason, I think in a completely reconditioned Battery Park with all of the old landmarks removed there will be nothing to tie the imagination to the history of the past.

Down at Williamsburg, Virginia, much money and research and architectural skill have been put into rebuilding many buildings that had almost disappeared, so that we can see how people once lived and how they carried on their local government in the earliest days of our country. Thousands of people go there to see a reconstructed town. Why, then, do we have to destroy such things as we have still intact from the past?

~

As the year ended and the evidence of Eleanor Roosevelt's value to the country grew, President Truman made an astute political move. Choosing the former First Lady as an official delegate to the United Nations General Assembly, he accomplished several things at one stroke. He reinforced an already known fact: Eleanor Roosevelt was not about to retire. He gave a huge vote of confidence to women as national spokespeople and leaders. He secured for America's benefit an absolutely untiring worker in the UN cause. In October 1945 Mrs. Roosevelt turned sixty-one, and a decision to seclude herself at Hyde Park, attending to social life and her knitting, would have been understood by the nation. Instead, with this artful push from Harry Truman, Eleanor Roosevelt launched into harder work than ever before.

NEW YORK, DECEMBER 22—Now that I have been confirmed by the Senate, I can say how deeply honored I feel that President Truman has named me one of the delegates to the General Assembly of the United Nations Organization. It is an honor, but also a very great responsibility. I know it has come to me largely because my husband laid the foundation for this Organization through which we all hope to build world peace.

In many ways I am sure I will find much to learn; but all of life is a constant education. Some things I can take to this first meeting—a sincere desire to understand the problems of the rest of the world and our relationship to them; a real good will for all peoples throughout the world; a hope that I shall be able to build a sense of personal trust and friendship with my co-workers, for without that type of understanding our work would be doubly difficult.

This first meeting, I imagine, will be largely concerned with organization and the choice of a site within this country as a permanent home.

Being the only woman delegate from this country, I feel a great responsibility, also, to the women of my own country. In other lands women have gone with their men into the fighting forces. Here we have more nearly followed the traditional pattern of working and waiting at home.

1946–1952

Building
the Peace

1946

merica entered World War II reluctantly (not until after the Japanese attack on Pearl Harbor) and struggled alongside its allies until a decisive ending was achieved. How would the United States react to the outbreak of peace? If the signs were unclear in late 1945, the new year would provide answers. While muddling through the economic complications of converting the domestic economy back to peacetime activity, the country began quickly to assert itself as a confident global power, aware of its new responsibility to take the lead in worldwide reconstruction.

The United Nations held its first formal meetings in 1946, in London and then in New York—where philanthropist John D. Rockefeller, Jr., provided $8.5 million to buy a Manhattan building site for its yet-to-be-designed headquarters. It created UNESCO (United Nations Educational, Scientific, and Cultural Organization), which the United States joined at midyear. The General Assembly also set up the UN Atomic Energy Commission to steer atomic power into civilian control rather than military. The United States followed suit, establishing a few months later its own Atomic Energy Commission. Never shy of contradictions in policy, the Truman White House authorized more military testing of the bomb on Bikini atoll in the Pacific's Marshall Islands.

July 4, 1946, saw President Truman declare the Philippines a republic; August saw Congress pass the Fulbright Act, creating a structure for the exchange of international students and professors on the assumption that the better we know our global neighbors, the better our trade and political relations will become.

Contrasting with such bright spots in foreign policy were distinctly foreboding statements, the first by Winston Churchill who coined the term *iron curtain* to describe the way "police governments" were taking control of and closing off Eastern Europe. And Undersecretary of State Dean Acheson asserted unequivocally that the United States would not leave Korea until that nation was reunited and politically free.

Domestically, the country clamored for relief from wartime economic controls, but Mrs. Roosevelt urged caution. Early in the year the President appointed Chester Bowles (an Eleanor Roosevelt favorite) director of the new Office of Economic Stabilization. By year's end most price controls on consumer goods were lifted. Farm prices reached a twenty-five-year high in April. But wages were the central issue: 1946 witnessed a rash of strikes, some wildcat, many well-planned and of long duration, as pent-up frustration over wartime wage controls erupted. Telephone mechanics, steelworkers, autoworkers, railroad men, and many other unions went on strike. John L. Lewis, vice president of the American Federation of Labor, steadily gained power in organized labor and hence in the economy, a fact that brought no cheer to Mrs. Roosevelt.

The Republicans swept both houses of Congress in November's elections, but Truman forged ahead confidently, shaping his postwar program, the Fair Deal. Mrs. Roosevelt gave him respectful support. Recognition of women's growing social power came in 1946 when Emily Green Balch, head of the Women's International League for Peace and Freedom, won the Nobel Peace Prize. And a happy publishing event caught the attention of thousands of expectant and new parents: Dr. Benjamin Spock's *The Commonsense Book of Baby and Child Care,* destined to become the nation's bible in the crib room, was born.

Reeducating the German people for participation in a democratic government based on acceptance of all races and religions was a high priority for Eleanor Roosevelt. She believed reeducation was the only way to ensure that the appeal of racist totalitarianism would be eradicated from German consciousness forever. Here Mrs. Roosevelt combines her idealistic faith in the power of education and a free press to reshape national character with her virulent disapproval of Nazism.

NEW YORK, FEBRUARY 27—I want to tell you a little today about one branch of the work our Army is doing in Germany which I think we know little about over here. In the American zone, Brigadier General Robert A. McClure, a Regular Army officer, is in charge of the policies and operations of the information-control division of our Military Government. He seems to be fully aware of the issues at stake and very well qualified for his job. I talked to a number of the men working under him and gained an in-

LEFT: Eleanor Roosevelt with her infant son John and Franklin Jr. in 1916. In 1909 the first Franklin Jr. died in infancy.
(FDR Library)

BELOW: The Roosevelts summered at Campobello Island. This family portrait was taken in 1920, a year before FDR contracted polio. Mrs. Sara Delano Roosevelt sits between Franklin and Eleanor. The children (from left to right) are Elliott, Franklin Jr., John, Anna, and James.
(FDR Library)

LEFT: Arthurdale, West Virginia, a rejuvenated Appalachian community, was one of Mrs. Roosevelt's favorite New Deal projects. Through the Subsistence Homestead Act and supplemental funds raised by the First Lady, residents ran co-operative farms and small factories and built new housing and a progressive school. Here Mrs. Roosevelt visits Arthurdale in 1933. *(FDR Library)*

RIGHT: Eleanor Roosevelt liked to have a morning ride on her horse, Dot. Her close friend Elinor Morgenthau, wife of the secretary of the treasury, was often her riding companion. *(FDR Library)*

ABOVE: In "My Day," Mrs. Roosevelt reported how the Works Project Administration (WPA) enabled many Americans to find steady employment once again. Mrs. Roosevelt visited a Des Moines, Iowa, WPA project in 1936, where a city dump was transformed into a waterfront park. *(FDR Library)*

RIGHT: Springwood, a Georgian mansion built in the early 1800's, was FDR's lifelong home. The residence, in Hyde Park, New York, is now part of the 300-acre Franklin D. Roosevelt National Historic Site. *(FDR Library)*

LEFT: People wondered how the First Lady got so much accomplished. Mrs. Roosevelt knew that her own energy and determination went only so far: She often credited secretary Malvina Thompson as "the person who makes my life possible." *(FDR Library)*

LEFT: For decades, Mrs. Roosevelt spoke out against racial inequities and championed the struggle for civil rights. Here Mary McLeod Bethune, director of the Division of Negro Affairs in the National Youth Administration, looks on as Mrs. Roosevelt addresses the National Conference on Negro Youth in January 1939. *(Wide World)*

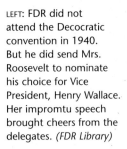

LEFT: FDR did not attend the Decocratic convention in 1940. But he did send Mrs. Roosevelt to nominate his choice for Vice President, Henry Wallace. Her impromtu speech brought cheers from the delegates. *(FDR Library)*

RIGHT: Eleanor Roosevelt loved picnicking at Val-Kill, her own house in Hyde Park. Hot dogs were a favored dish, whether the guests were relatives, students, or British royalty. *(FDR Library)*

ABOVE: When the U. S. began to prepare for war in 1941, New York City's Mayor Fiorello LaGuardia became director of the Office of Civil Defense. He chose as his associate the nation's best-known volunteer, Mrs. Roosevelt. Eventually, the two would find that they had to defend themselves from attacks by the press and politicians. *(FDR Library)*

The labor movement had few more staunch supporters than Eleanor Roosevelt. Although she could be critical of labor leaders whose vanity made them grab at unjustified power and critical of unionized public service workers who wanted to strike, she used her "My Day" column repeatedly to explain rank-and-file viewpoints to a not-always-sympathetic public. In 1942, Mrs. Roosevelt spoke to union members at the Hudson Shore Labor School in West Park, New York. *(FDR Library)*

Trying to talk to as many enlisted men as possible, Mrs. Roosevelt often ate with soldiers in the mess hall and spent hours visiting the wounded. Here she visits U.S. troops in Australia in September 1943. *(FDR Library)*

BELOW: At the funeral service for FDR, the First Lady asked the priest to include the words with which the late president inspired the country at his first inauguration: "The only thing we have to fear is fear itself." Dignitaries from around the world accompanied Eleanor, Anna, and Elliott Roosevelt to the rose garden at FDR's Hyde Park mansion for the burial. (FDR Library)

RIGHT: The initial delegation of the United States to the United Nations was as bipartisan as any that America would ever send there. In this 1946 photo, Mrs. Roosevelt huddles with John Foster Dulles (left), a conservative who, under Republican President Eisenhower, became a primary architect of U.S. foreign policy in the cold war; and with Adlai Stevenson (center), a liberal who twice ran unsuccessfully for President as a Democrat. (FDR Library)

LEFT: Mrs. Roosevelt's acquaintance with Winston Churchill had grown over the years from the many meetings and formal banquets the British Prime Minister attended as a guest of FDR at the White House. In 1946, a year after FDR died, Churchill, his wife, and Mrs. Roosevelt visited the late president's grave at Hyde Park. *(National Park Service)*

RIGHT: A young, famous, and hugely successful Frank Sinatra was Mrs. Roosevelt's dinner companion in Los Angeles on June 5, 1947 at a ceremony commemorating Jackson Day. FDR had already begun to pass into the realm of legend, as the miniature sculpture in the singer's hands suggests. *(FDR Library)*

LEFT: If ever there was a "First Dog" in the White House, the Roosevelt's Fala was it. For years after Mrs. Roosevelt left Washington, the public remained charmed by the famous scottie's adventures, frequently reported in "My Day." Here, in 1947, Mrs. Roosevelt and Fala are out for a walk at Val-Kill. *(FDR Library)*

RIGHT: It was one of the greatest triumphs of her life even after a host of painful compromises: the United Nations "Universal Declaration of Human Rights." As Chairman of the UN Commission that drafted the document, all of Mrs. Roosevelt's diverse diplomatic skills were fully utilized, including her patience and sense of humor. *(FDR Library)*

ABOVE: Biographer Joseph Lash portrays Mrs. Roosevelt's friendship with the considerably younger Dr. David Gurewitsch as an affair of the heart that began in the late 1940s and lasted until she died in 1962. They carried on an extensive, often intimate correspondence. Dr. Gurewitsch accompanied Mrs. Roosevelt on her trip to India in February 1952. *(FDR Library)*

sight into some of their problems. Hitler and Goebbels did a wonderful job, from their own point of view, on the thinking processes of the German people!

We began, of course, in the period of psychological warfare, to study the warped German mentality and the propaganda techniques used by the Nazis to bring it about. We are now carrying on a re-education and a re-orientation program. This must not be relaxed for a minute or the consequences will be very serious, for the Nazi poison has gone deep into the hearts and minds of young and old in Germany.

Their Führer gave them some material things which they could appreciate—full employment (even if it was in preparation for war), better houses, radios, the little three-wheeled cars. They closed their eyes to the concentration camp which lay over the hill and which, as human beings, they had to forget in order to be able to enjoy life. The job before us is a long-term job.

One of the things going on now is an effort to re-establish a free press. None has existed in Germany for many years. It is not wholly free today, for it is not allowed to criticize the Military Government or Allied policy. However, the papers are staffed by German editors and German reporters, and are subject only to post publication scrutiny. They are being encouraged to develop high modern standards based on the high ideals of American journalism, but they may not propagate ideas of racism, Nazism or militarism. The same general policy applies to radio news.

This is one of the most important undertakings by our Military Government, and everyone should be watching it with interest and should insist that it be carried on until the roots of Nazism are wiped out.

~

A steady stream of mail, sometimes a near tidal wave of correspondence, came to Eleanor Roosevelt from all across the country. Through "My Day" and other journalism she invited the public to tell her about social and personal problems that might be of interest to others. The contents of someone's letter to Mrs. Roosevelt could become the text of her newspaper column if the point it brought out was general enough. Offensive instances of ethnic discrimination always caught Mrs. Roosevelt's attention.

NEW YORK, MARCH 8—I had a sad letter the other day—one which points out one of the big problems that the people of the United States are facing today. I am quoting from it for that reason:

"In 1944, I married a young Chinese woman who had come to the United States in 1938 with her A.B. from Yenching University seeking higher education. She received her M.A. from Mills College in 1940, and it was in the fall of that year that I met her when she came to the University of California to work for a Ph.D. in educational psychology. She is a most beautiful young woman, beloved by all who know her. After a great deal of soul-searching, we were finally married—while I was a junior medical student.

". . . When we were married, we were entirely conscious of the shape of general social reaction in the United States, most particularly in the West, against mixed marriages. Indeed, California has a statute against miscegenation which made it necessary for us to be married in Washington. Nevertheless, until recently, we have not encountered any direct evidence of this traditional hostility.

"Our recent encounter has been in the field of housing accommodations. Recently I have taken a position in the Donner Laboratory of Medical Physics at this university. . . . In order to function effectively in this new job, it was necessary for us to move to Berkeley. I arranged for an exchange of apartments from San Francisco to Berkeley, and we moved in.

"I did not tell the manager that my wife was Chinese. I did not and do not feel that I had any moral obligation to give such information. By present rental and housing rules of the OPA, we are quite secure in our new home. The unpleasant experience that precipitates my writing was a conversation with the manager and his wife, just held after a month's tenancy, in which I was reproached for not informing them of the fact of my wife's nationality.

". . . I am writing for my many Oriental friends, whom I know through my marriage and through residence at the Berkeley International House, where I met my wife, for my Negro friends, for my Filipino and Mexican friends, and for the host of all these races whom I can only know as they are symbolized in my friends."

If this sort of prejudice exists in our land, it seems to me that we deny the spirit of the various religions to which we all belong, for all religions recognize the equality of human beings before God. We deny the spirit of our Constitution and Government which our forefathers fought to establish. We make future good will and peace an impossibility, for no United Nations organization can succeed when peoples of one race approach those of other races in a spirit of contempt.

~

Harry Hopkins was crucial to the Roosevelt presidency. Head of the Federal Emergency Relief Administration (1933) and the Works Projects Administration (1935–1938), Hopkins oversaw distribution of $8.5 billion toward *unemployment relief. Secretary of Commerce (1938–1940), head of the Lend-Lease Administration (1941), the President's personal envoy to Russia and Britain, and a member of the War Production Board (1942), Hopkins also served as Special Assistant to the President (1942–1945). He was only fifty-six when he died.*

NEW YORK, MAY 22—In Washington tomorrow, May 22nd, there will be held a memorial service for Harry Hopkins. Those of his friends who are able to attend will be grateful for an opportunity to think of him and to talk about him to others who still keenly feel his death.

In the last years of my husband's life, Harry Hopkins was probably his closest and most trusted co-worker. He went on missions that required tact and courage, and he met the great men of the world face to face. I cannot remember the time when he looked really strong and, as the years went by, he became more and more delicate. Yet he seemed to be able to rise above his bodily weakness and meet every great emergency. Perhaps it was this quality of indomitable spirit which first drew my husband and Harry Hopkins together.

They met and worked together in New York State while my husband was Governor and Mr. Hopkins had charge of the State unemployment relief program. They got on well then, and when Mr. Hopkins came to Washington to take over the much larger and more serious relief job that faced the nation, my husband felt he was dealing with someone he already knew and on whom he could count. It was not, however, until domestic issues began to be secondary and the war seemed to be growing daily closer to us that the two men really began to work on the whole world picture together.

My husband recognized the weaknesses as well as the strength of the people with whom he worked, and I often heard him take Harry Hopkins to task because, in spite of repeated warnings, he would do the things which he enjoyed doing and then his health would suffer. However, my husband understood the impatience with bodily handicaps which made Mr. Hopkins such a poor patient.

To a man who was handicapped physically in the way my husband was, it was almost essential that he have a few people whom he could trust absolutely and whom he could use as messengers. He had to have the knowledge that his messages would be delivered accurately and that his ideas would be conveyed in the way he wished them conveyed. True, he expected everyone who worked for him to use their own initiative and their own judgment whenever the need arose, but when they were carrying a message, or getting a plan across, any initiative must bear on the ultimate accomplishment, and the personality of the individual must not in any way obscure the job that had to be done.

Harry Hopkins was in himself a very big person. I think it was because of this that he was willing to subordinate himself and to accept the fact that the objects for which he and my husband worked together were more important than any kudos which he might acquire for himself.

In some ways, the comforts and luxuries of this world were matters of complete insignificance to Mr. Hopkins, and yet there was another side to his character. There were times when he felt he wanted to enjoy them all. But always his tongue was in his cheek, and you felt that a little imp sat on his shoulder and said: "Go ahead and have a good time, but you know it has no real value." His was a life spent too fast, and yet it was well spent. Few people have left a greater record of accomplishment to spur their children and future generations of mankind to achievement.

~

Model communities, set up by New Deal legislation, fostered by private en-terprise and government ownership, were among the Roosevelts' pet proj-ects. Mrs. Roosevelt was particularly pleased when she could report on the successful evolution of such a community to the stage of financial indepen-dence. But the Roosevelts and their supporters incurred the wrath of critics who believed government intervention in the financial side of private lives was unconscionable. Mrs. Roosevelt never tired of pressing her side of the argument.

The best-known of the New Deal communities created under FDR's Sub-sistence Homestead Act was Arthurdale, an extremely poor Appalachian town near Morgantown, West Virginia. When Mrs. Roosevelt visited Arthurdale in 1936, she found living conditions shocking. Her report to the President put in motion the legislation providing federal assistance to these financially hopeless Americans. Though Arthurdale developed nicely into a self-sufficient community, with families living for the first time in houses with refrigerators and indoor plumbing, the project upset critics who be-lieved government should leave people to fend for themselves.

Here, Mrs. Roosevelt reports on another similarly successful New Deal community.

HYDE PARK, JUNE 29—I was very much interested the other day to receive an article sent to me from "Pageant Magazine" on a New Jersey commu-nity which has changed its name from Jersey Homesteads to Roosevelt. This is one of the homesteads started in the days of the Depression, and it has had a hard and discouraging career.

A small group of New York City garment workers originally moved out there from the slum areas of the city. Each contributed a small amount of money, and their plan was to run their own factory, live on small garden or farm plots, and have the stores municipally owned. It didn't work, partly because the experience was not there to run this type of community.

Today things are privately owned and run, but I judge from this article that a spirit of cooperation still exists and the community is politically active. They have a high rate of actual voters in elections. The borough council meetings are open to the public, and public issues are discussed there and at specially called town meetings in which the citizens take part.

I was very glad to see this article because so often we are told that these experiments of the Depression years have produced nothing but loss to the taxpayers. The other day, for instance, I received a long letter from the minister at Arthurdale, West Virginia, who runs the community church. It is an encouraging report on the success of the people in the community. Yet I had just read, rather sadly, a diatribe in some paper quoting the cost of the original experiment and stating that the people had not liked the paternalism of Government control, that the Government had now sold the community and only recovered about 5 percent of the original expenditure.

All this may be true, even the part about the people not liking to be helped, and yet I can hardly believe that this was universal when I remember the conditions from which those people came. If at that time some kind of Government help had not come, they and their children today might be costing the taxpayers far more than the loss on that investment in the Arthurdale community.

Children brought up in utter misery, with scant food, children whose parents are too worried to really do anything constructive for them, are the ones we find today in reformatories and later in prisons, or in state hospitals. All of these institutions are supported by the taxpayers, and the greater the number of inmates, the greater the cost.

I am glad that the Arthurdale experiment, like the Jersey homesteads, is now owned by the people; that a private company has taken over the factory buildings; that the school buildings are run by the school system of West Virginia. I cannot help believing that the people who now own those houses and live in those communities have healthier, happier children, and that these children have grown in the past fourteen years to better citizenship than they could have achieved if there had been no Jersey Homesteads and no Arthurdale, or the equivalent in various parts of our nation.

As Eleanor Roosevelt tended her vegetable garden, appreciating its bounty, she thought of America's surplus and other nations' needs. (The Mrs. Byrnes mentioned below was the wife of James F. Byrnes, Secretary of State from 1945 through 1947. Mrs. Nimitz was married to the commander in chief of the U.S. Pacific fleet during the war; he was chief of naval operations at the time this was written.)

NEW YORK, JULY 23—In the papers last week, there was a nice photograph of Mrs. James F. Byrnes and Mrs. Chester W. Nimitz busily canning. I hope it reminded a great many people that one of the best ways to help the food situation throughout the world is for everyone who can do so to have a garden, and to put up anything they can't eat now, so they can enjoy it next winter.

Of course, if you happen to have a deep freeze, you already know the joys of taking out your vegetables or your fruits and using them all through the winter and spring. Many things are far better put into the freezer than preserved in any other way, particularly now when there is such a shortage of sugar, for one can do so much better in the deep freeze with less sugar.

I have only just finished using up peaches which I put into the deep freeze last summer. I can vouch for the fact that they made very good peach shortcake! The things, however, which give me real joy are those which I have grown myself. I find that peas and beans, beets and carrots, put straight from the garden into the deep freeze, come out just like fresh vegetables. During these two or three weeks while I am away from Hyde Park, everything possible is going into my deep freeze, since l cannot be home to eat part of it now.

～

The annual trek to Campobello Island off the Maine coast would have been sad for Mrs. Roosevelt in 1946, the first time in decades she had visited the Roosevelt summer home without the President. Yet she had the practical wisdom to find pleasure in the delicious details of small things like fresh strawberries.

EN ROUTE TO CAMPOBELLO, JULY 31—After stopping overnight in Portland, Maine, I have driven on up the coast, looking for familiar landmarks as I went. Where was that nut shop or that place where, in the past, I stopped to buy jellies or jams? On the way up to Campobello Island, I used to make acquisitions which my family enjoyed, since it is not very easy on the island to get a variety of food. Gardens are late, but fish is always plentiful there.

I may be in time for the late strawberries, because they ripen slowly. They have a wonderful flavor, somewhat like the ones grown on the Ile d'Orleans, in the St. Lawrence River, near Quebec. These are famous for their delicious flavor. It used to be easy, when we had a boat, to go and come to the mainland, but a storm destroyed our boathouse and our boat last winter.

On August 1, a monument will be unveiled in the little village of Welch-pool, Campobello Island, N.B., in memory of my husband, who went there so often in his boyhood and early manhood and loved not only the island itself but the waters all around it. He knew the coast of New Brunswick and of Nova Scotia and was as good a sailorman thereabouts as many of the natives. They asked me particularly to try to be in Campobello on August 1, so I am glad that, with my son Elliott and his family, I will be there. Soon afterward, we will start for home.

~

Henry A. Wallace was a colorful character in American politics in the 1930s and 1940s. After distinguishing himself as a plant geneticist and as editor of a farmers' journal founded by his father in 1895 in Iowa, Wallace was chosen by FDR as Secretary of Agriculture and served from 1933 until 1940. Idealistic, hardworking, a conservative Christian, and an outspoken political liberal, Wallace earned FDR's confidence and let his own ambitions rise. He served as Vice President under FDR during the President's third term, 1941–1945. But aloofness and disdain for the necessary compromises of political life alienated Wallace from most party leaders and made him ineffective. Harry Truman replaced him on the ticket in 1945.

The consolation prize for Wallace was the Commerce Secretary's post, where he frequently held forth on a broad range of issues, particularly international affairs. Believing himself the true flag bearer of the faltering New Deal after FDR's death, Wallace must have found it hard to swallow Mrs. Roosevelt's criticism.

Eleanor Roosevelt's idealism colored her vision of the postwar world under the presumed beneficence of the newly organized United Nations. Though she was wary of the consequences of allowing the atomic bomb to get into irresponsible hands, she nonetheless believed the UN—if equipped with means of forceful control (an idea she never defined)— would keep the peace. Mrs. Roosevelt does not yet appear to have recognized the dark implications of the political wall between East and West that was rapidly being created by expanding Soviet Communist influence in Eastern Europe.

NEW YORK, SEPTEMBER 20—The "spheres of influence" section of Secretary of Commerce Henry Wallace's speech last week seems to me to have been written without proper explanation. Because Russia has gained a predominant military and political interest in certain countries along her borders, and because Great Britain has always shown the same type of interest in countries along what are known as her "lifelines," and because we in this hemisphere find that we have similar interests with our neighbors, many people feel that we must of necessity accept the fact that there will be spheres of influence in the future. However, I really think this matter requires a little more thinking through.

Within its sphere of interest, each great power is required, by its acceptance of the principles laid down in the Atlantic Charter and in the United Nations Charter, to give freedom of action to the peoples of the various nations in that sphere. And if their interests should clash, the great power, under these agreements, would have to accept whatever differences a smaller nation might choose in religion, politics or economics. Spheres of interest, in other words, can only be held together by mutual agreement, and there is no reason why this concept should prevent our trying to keep the world "One World" and to achieve the basic principles which concern us all.

This can only be done through the United Nations and the organs established under the United Nations. To preserve peace in the future, I count as most important world cooperation through the UN Food and Agriculture Organization, through the UN health and labor organizations, and through UNESCO, which will develop cultural and scientific cooperation among the different nations. The Economic and Social Council, with its various commissions, is designed specifically to prevent friction. When questions reach the Security Council, we must have an organization to enforce its decisions.

Until a decision is made on control of the atomic bomb, our method of joint enforcement is held up. But as soon as possible, a method should be decided upon because, as long as force rules anywhere in the world, we have no choice but to make it a collective force if we do not wish to see the big nations enter into an armament race. And such a race, as Secretary Wallace pointed out in his letter to the President, would lead to war.

President Truman, some months ago, stated that the foreign policy of the United States was his foreign policy, and that Secretary of State Byrnes was negotiating and making the fight for peace treaties as a representative of the President of the United States. These negotiations are bound to develop friction.

The men concerned are representing their governments to the best of their abilities, and are trying to obtain the things which they feel their people, as represented by their home governments, really want. Our representatives are probably more conscious of the thinking of the people at home than are those of other nations. For that reason we have able members of our Senate, representing both political parties, advising the Secretary of State.

~

Unionization and the right to strike could easily turn ineffective and illegitimate in Mrs. Roosevelt's view. Staunch as she was in her defense of labor, she placed the broader national and international needs of working people above the immediate concerns of specific labor unions. John L. Lewis, head of the United Mine Workers, provoked Mrs. Roosevelt's ire when she suspected he used union support for his own political ambitions. And what could be worse, from a New Dealer's viewpoint, than a labor leader apparently pandering to the Republicans?

NEW YORK, NOVEMBER 19—For several days now the chief headlines in the papers have been held by John L. Lewis and his threats against the Government. Curiously enough, what he says rarely stresses the one point which I think is important—namely, that the conditions under which the miners today are working may need to be changed. He insists that there must be a strike, but one has the feeling that it is not because every effort to better the miners' condition has failed, but because Mr. Lewis wishes to show his power.

There was a time, a long while ago, when I thought Mr. Lewis one of the best labor leaders in the country. I thought he cared about the men in the mines. I know that the reason he has kept his hold over them is that they thought he cared. They knew that, at the time when they needed help, he was the only person who got them even the slightest consideration. I remember what conditions for the miners were at their worst. I remember what they were in the early '30s, in the black days of the Depression. I have always had respect for the work they do and a desire to see all possible improvements made in their working and living conditions.

The miners still trust Mr. Lewis, and the long-distant past would justify that trust. But a nearer view makes one begin to wonder. For a long time now, it has seemed that John L. Lewis and those immediately around him feel that they rule an empire. The people who make up that empire seem to be there mainly to serve a lust for power which seems practically insatiable. No one could read Mr. Lewis' last letter without being struck by its arrogance.

A strike in the coal mines will mean the stopping of hundreds of industries—industries which are necessary to the rebuilding of the economy in our own country and in the world.

I cannot help wondering which of two things Mr. Lewis is trying to achieve. Number one—is he expecting recognition from the Republican Party if they should win in 1948? Has he entered into an understanding with the owners of the mines whereby, if he breaks the contract with the Government, he hopes to force the return of the mines to the owners and then to make a better contract with the owners? This would make him a great figure in labor. The Republican Party and the industrial leaders might feel that they had someone whom they could safely place in power, because he would be amenable to their interests in the long run, even though he might ask enough for labor to hold his power over them. That power the practical Republican leadership knows is essential.

The only other alternative, of course, is that he does not realize how much resentment a strike in an essential industry is going to cause on top of the other strikes which have only just been settled. It is just possible that what he is doing now may lead to a demand in our country for the nationalization of the coal industry as a basic utility which the people themselves must control.

I would be sympathetic with a plea for better conditions, but I cannot help believing that, at the moment, we have to subordinate ourselves to the paramount interest of getting our economy running full blast. How can the people of devastated countries hope to succeed in this if we don't succeed?

1947

arry Truman put his own stamp on the presidency in 1947. He appointed retired Army Chief of Staff General George Marshall secretary of state. Together, Truman and Marshall would quickly evolve the European Recovery Program known as the Marshall Plan, providing economic and political aid in the billions of dollars. The first step was an aid package of some $400 million for Greece and Turkey aimed specifically at helping those countries resist Russian Communist influence, a policy immediately dubbed the Truman Doctrine. The Cold War, as yet unnamed but gaining in recognition as a foreign policy fact of life, intensified.

Eleanor Roosevelt participated fiercely in the political battles of the day, and not only in her capacity at the United Nations. She was among the first to question Truman's notorious Executive Order 9835 (March 1947) establishing a Loyalty Program in the federal government requiring investigation of employees and job applicants and reflecting the growing fear of Communist subversion. By autumn this fear, which Mrs. Roosevelt generally saw as paranoia, led the House Un-American Activities Committee to open an investigation of suspected Communist infiltration of the movie industry. The stage was set for the witch-hunts of Senator Joseph McCarthy, the rabid anti-Communist, in the 1950s.

Americans rejoiced over the lifting of sugar rationing in June, after five years of deprivation. The bitterness in labor-management relations in the immediate postwar years culminated in passage by the Congress over the President's veto of the Taft-Hartley bill, which substantially strengthened employers' hands in their dealings with the unions. Mrs. Roosevelt, a frequent commentator on labor-management disputes, always looked for ways to reconcile workers' demands with national needs.

Perhaps reflecting the country's recognition that too much of an apparently good thing might be bad after all (in this case FDR's four-term presidency and the New Deal), the Twenty-second Amendment was proposed, limiting any subsequent President to two terms. Revision of the Presidential Succession Act made the Speaker of the House of Representatives next in line after the Vice President.

Harry Truman took his first major foreign policy crisis—divided, occupied Korea—to the United Nations, which responded with a resolution calling for a united, free country. In 1947 the President also became the first world leader to address his nation on television. As tensions worsened in the Middle East, the White House gave its support to a UN proposal for autonomous Jewish and Arab states in Palestine. Eager to streamline the executive branch, the incumbent Democratic President appointed former Republican President Herbert Hoover to head a commission of inquiry. Another presidential commission, on civil rights, set in motion one of the few truly noble reform efforts of the time, a campaign for justice that occupied much of Mrs. Roosevelt's time and thought.

The year 1947 witnessed the first supersonic flight, by Air Force test pilot Charles (Chuck) Yeager, and the first black major-league baseball player, Jackie Robinson, signed with the Brooklyn Dodgers. Two great new dramatic characters appeared on the American stage. Tennessee Williams's *A Streetcar Named Desire* opened in New Orleans, bringing the brutal Stanley Kowalski and the fragile Blanche Dubois to life.

Harry Truman found himself in a real race for reelection when Republican Senator Robert Taft (Ohio) and former Vice President Henry Wallace, now running on a third-party (Progressive) ticket, opposed him. Try as she might, Mrs. Roosevelt could not keep clear of the acid debate that ensued.

Did Mrs. Roosevelt's suffer from "Germanophobia"? Twenty-first-century Americans may find it difficult to comprehend the anxiety anything German could elicit in those who had lived through two world wars. Even an intelligent international observer like Eleanor Roosevelt, who knew the subtleties of how nations deliberately and inadvertently conspired to bring about these wars, could nonetheless fixate on one all-purpose enemy. In "My Day" we rarely hear Mrs. Roosevelt rail against the Japanese or the Italian and Spanish Fascists. Whether right or wrong in her unwavering opinion about Germany, she consistently articulated its implications, despite angering some people, as with the American soldiers mentioned here.

Hyde Park, January 3—I have received a letter which voices a strong protest against some of our policies in regard to the Germans.

The nine signers of the letter are worried, first, about the relaxing of many controls in our zone of occupation in Germany, which tends to allow the Germans to run their own country. In answer to this, I would say that the Germans eventually will have to run their own country, and we have to prepare them for the time when they will be left without an army of occupation,

Our safeguard in Germany should be the insistence that there shall be no rebuilding of heavy industry of the kind which would permit Germany again to become a great industrial nation and rebuild a war machine. Small industries needed for export purposes and for the daily life of the people should, of course, be permitted. The one thing to be viewed with alarm is any policy on the part of the United States or Great Britain, no matter what the reason, which would allow Germany again to become a potential war breeder.

The second protest is against granting licenses to GIs to marry German girls and allowing them to bring their wives to this country. I was asked about this question when I was in Germany last year. I said then that I felt that any boy in love with a girl over there should not be allowed to marry until he came home and had sufficient time to be quite sure that his love was not born of loneliness and propinquity in a strange country. Many young soldiers were annoyed with me, but they saw the point. And I still believe that a rule requiring a boy to be home for at least four months before he could bring over the girl he wished to marry would be a safeguard to our present young army in Germany.

These boys are not the boys who fought the war. Many of them have no real feeling against the Germans and do not understand the background of the two World Wars. And as the German girls are quite ready to be friendly, the soldiers are apt to be carried away.

There are exceptions, of course. One boy told me he had been engaged to a girl for years and she had gone to Germany before the war to visit members of her family. Then the war broke out, preventing her return to this country. Now, he had finally found her again in Germany. Naturally, he wanted to marry her, but the wartime rule prevented it. He stuck to his purpose and succeeded. In that case, the boy was right.

The third protest of my correspondents is against the bringing of German scientists and their families to this country. I am trying to find out the reason for this. I thought we were bringing over certain scientists who never were Nazis, but I do not really understand the reasons for doing this.

My correspondents fear that we are building up "a strong nucleus" of Nazi spies in this country and are "strengthening the Nazi cause all over the world." This is a consideration which should not be taken lightly. I think there is no question but that any Germans coming into this country should be very carefully screened. Their background should be examined and tested in every possible way.

~

Mrs. Roosevelt's automobile accident caused no harm to anyone, although her own car and the one she mistakenly hit while "motoring" through the upstate New York countryside were slightly damaged. She explained confessionally in other columns that she had indeed had a lapse of attention while at the wheel and couldn't blame anyone else. Awkward though it was to go without a license for a time, Eleanor Roosevelt had a chauffeur when she needed him, and there were plenty of sympathetic friends and family to ferry her about. At the time of the accident she was sixty-two.

NEW YORK, JANUARY 16—Today I received the notice of the cancellation of my driving license for reckless driving in connection with the accident I had last summer. I am a little sad about this, since it takes away one of the things that I enjoy, but I recognize fully the justice of punishment for endangering other people. And while I hope that some day the license may be restored to me, I shall certainly not ask for any special consideration. I can only be deeply grateful that no one was permanently injured in the accident.

Perhaps at my age, in any case, it is wise to curtail one's activities. One thing is sure—that if you give up any activity, it is much more difficult to start in again. And since the accident, I have done no long-distance driving, not even from Hyde Park to New York City. It will be distinctly awkward to have to walk everywhere around the Hyde Park place, instead of driving. However, at all times and as long as one lives, life administers disciplines, and it is in accepting and obeying them that one learns.

~

Though the Roosevelt family homestead at Hyde Park had always been a working farm, which meant serious business, there was still room for fun and the old-fashioned pleasures (like homemade butter) that took inordinate amounts of work but seemed well worth the effort.

HYDE PARK, MAY 6—About a month ago, our farmer told us and proved to us that it was highly uneconomical to make butter on a dairy farm; that we could sell our whole milk and make more cash; that the cost of the cream and the time consumed in making butter, even though we had an electric churn, was pure waste.

I remembered that, when I was a little girl, my grandmother made butter in a little glass churn on the dining-room table. It was completely sweet, fresh butter, and we thought it the greatest possible luxury. And my mother-in-law always boasted of having her own butter. It seemed somewhat of a wrench to me to give this up, so I loftily said to our farmer, "I will take the churn, and in our cellar we will make enough butter to last both my son's house and mine for several weeks. It can be stored in the deep freeze."

Last Friday, the farmer brought the churn. Our superintendent was on hand. So was I, assisted by Miss Thompson and the cook. We all stood around, prepared for our first lesson.

The farmer first showed us how to wash the churn and the implements. Then, firmly telling me the cost of the cream which he was pouring in, he poured it in, adjusted the cover of the churn, and started it. All of us were spattered with cream. He stopped the churn, looked at the cork in the bottom, adjusted the top, and started the churn again.

Then the five of us watched with pride for fifteen minutes while the electricity did its work. Finally, I inquired how long it took. The farmer said "Anywhere from twenty minutes to four hours. It depends on the temperature." I thought he meant the outdoor temperature and did not realize he meant the temperature of the cream, which in our haste we had forgotten to take.

Time wore on. Miss Thompson decided she had to go back to being a secretary. The two men decided they had to go and eat dinner and attend to a few chores. The cook decided she had to go and prepare lunch. So we left the churning!

Three hours later, I returned. Still no butter. The men tried putting in ice cubes, which spoiled the buttermilk. It came time for the men to do the afternoon chores, and so they said, "Leave it overnight and turn it on in the morning and the butter may come."

The next morning, around 11 o'clock, the cook and I finally finished our lesson and at last the men could go back to their work on the farm. We had learned how to use the electric churn, how to work the butter afterwards, and how to do it up neatly in half-pound packages. For all of that time and all of that labor, we had $13\frac{1}{2}$ pounds of butter!

I am quite sure now that our farmer's economics are correct, but I had fun and I think the cook and I will try it again. It may be a waste of both time and money, but I am still old-fashioned enough to like the idea of having my own butter. I am rather glad, however, that the churn is electric. I think that if I had had to churn by hand for all of that time, I would not be writing about it today!

~

Campobello Island offered extraordinary beauty, wonderfully fresh food, and a blessed escape from everyday business. Nonetheless, some work went forward while Mrs. Roosevelt was at Campobello, including the last stages of an autobiography, her regular columns, and continued thinking about serious political matters. Though far removed from Washington on this midsummer holiday, she was moved to argue against former Vice President Henry Wallace's plans to run for President as a third-party (Progressive) candidate and to lambaste the House Un-American Activities Committee for its insinuations that anyone in a third party must be a Communist.

CAMPOBELLO ISLAND, N.B., JULY 24—I begin this column by saying that I do not believe there should be any third party in 1948, no matter who headed it. I had planned to say nothing on this subject but an article which I saw in one of the Maine papers this morning moves me to make certain remarks.

It stated that the Un-American Activities Committee was going to examine Henry Wallace and anyone suggesting his nomination as leader of a third party because, forsooth, they heard that the people backing a third party were all Communists. This is really too idiotic. Naturally the Communists in this country are going to back a third party—they are a disruptive force and a third party would be something which they would back. But to label all liberals as Communists just because you or I think them foolish to consider a third party is just plain arrogance. When will our sense of humor reassert itself and dominate our foolish fears?

There are in both our major political parties a certain number of liberals. On the whole in the past, I feel that the Democratic Party has had more liberals than the Republican Party. And in general, I think it might be said that the great moneyed interests keep in closer touch with the Republican leaders and their policies than they do with the Democratic leaders and their policies. On the whole I think that it is harder for special interests to ride the Democratic Party and that this party has been the rallying ground for more people who had the general interest at heart. However, it has its conservative group, which we can identify in many votes which have been taken in Congress.

If the liberals of this country want to accomplish anything in the next ten years, they had better work to make one or the other major political party, or both parties, responsive to their ideas. They can do this by making it plain where they stand on certain policies, they can vote for men who stand four-square on these policies, and they can go into the primary campaigns and work wherever they see that good men have a chance of nomination.

The independents, if they have a program and are well enough organized, can elect almost any candidate in any election. The organization of a third party would only mean that the liberals would gain nothing and the conservatives would have every opportunity of carrying their candidates into office.

~

Always a politician, never an officeholder. Probably no one in American political life ever wielded more power without holding office than Eleanor Roosevelt. With access to the media through press conferences as First Lady, through her "My Day" column, and through much magazine journalism, Mrs. Roosevelt never lacked outlets for her opinions. Such exposure would have been the envy of her most resolute opponents. In her one administrative stint, in 1941 when she shared with New York City's former mayor, Fiorello LaGuardia, the job of directing the Office of Civilian Defense, neither the mayor nor the First Lady could keep their colorful opinions under wraps. Mrs. Roosevelt eventually resigned, after stirring up enough controversy for even the President to be unhappy.

NEW YORK, SEPTEMBER 13—I have received several letters lately stating how pleased the writers are to hear that I am going to "run for the Senate," and offering me help and support. So far those who would be against me have not written to me in great number. But to all alike I have to reply that I am not going to run for any office! What I have often repeated in the past makes no dent, but one of our prophetic commentators, who never bothers to find out from me whether his statements and prophecies concerning me are correct, is believed without question!

Here I am, therefore, forced again to state—as I did when rumors flew about in 1945 and in 1946—that I not only have no political aspirations, but under no circumstances whatsoever would I run for any political office.

I can hear people say "Why, then, do you accept work with the United Nations?" I accept for the simple reason that it seems to me that there I may make a contribution, both as an individual and as my husband's widow. I think the arguments within our nation as to how we shall achieve this or that should be settled by younger people. In a short time I shall be 63 years old; and if, in the course of the years, I have gained any wisdom whatsoever, it is the wisdom to know that the Kingdom of God must come on earth through the efforts of human beings and that war in the atomic age will simply mean annihilation, certainly not evolution. With age has come also a capacity for patience; rooted beliefs in certain fundamental things, but an ability to try to understand the motivations of other people; and a kind of interest in human beings which allows for no bitterness toward any person.

~

NEW YORK, NOVEMBER 29—There is always a little excitement about going off to a new job, but as I grow older I find that I regret the things I leave behind. The lovely pink light in the sunrise sky as I awake on my porch at Hyde Park, the morning walks in the woods with a little black dog cavorting happily beside me or dashing off after the squirrels, the beautiful bluebird I saw unexpectedly take wing across my brook the other day, the family and friends I like to have around me, the Christmas preparation which I enjoy—all these are hard to leave. Only the sense of something tangible accomplished, that may be of value in the future, will seem to me to make this trip worthwhile.

~

She could be royally gracious or pugnaciously blunt; it depended on how one rubbed her. Henry Wallace rubbed Mrs. Roosevelt the wrong way. Behind the almost vitriolic put-down here of Wallace's plan to run for President in 1948 as a third-party candidate was Eleanor's residual loyalty to FDR. She believed Wallace (FDR's own Vice President) had criticized the President's policies too often, had essentially abandoned the White House by becoming too radical. The criticism leveled here at Wallace does not reflect well on FDR's political savvy in choosing Wallace as his running mate in the first place. In this New Year's Eve column, Mrs. Roosevelt goes out, like the year, with a bang.

HYDE PARK, DECEMBER 31—So Henry Wallace is really going to head a third party and run for President in 1948! What strange things the desire to be President makes men do!

He has probably forgotten, but I remember his coming to see me in the summer of 1945 in Washington. At that time, I felt very strongly that it would be good for the country if Henry Wallace, whom we all believed in and admired, would leave active politics and become the leader of the independents of the country. Their vote had increased greatly in the years between 1929 and 1945, but they needed leadership and organization.

They were neither Republicans nor Democrats. They were primarily interested in getting the kind of leadership which would keep them free of economic depressions. And they wanted to continue what had been a peaceful but steady revolutionary movement which had given us, over the years, a greater number of people in the middle-income brackets and fewer people in the millionaire group or in the substandard-income groups.

This had been accomplished in smaller countries like Norway, Sweden and Denmark, but it was a little more complicated in a country the size of ours and had to come more gradually. It could be done under our capitalistic system with proper regulation and was being done, but the independent vote of the country was very largely responsible for the way our economy and social thinking was developing.

I felt that out of politics Henry Wallace could do a tremendously valuable piece of work to keep both of our political parties on their toes; to make both of them less prone to act for purely political reasons; to make both of them realize that to win any election this independent liberal vote was essential and must be courted by deeds, not words.

The women of the country belong largely in this group. They are not hidebound and they are very practical. They know that well-being spread over a great number of people is a safeguard and the best defense of one of our most important freedoms—freedom from want. The young people of the country needed leadership to be in this group; and to feel that they had with them an older man of complete integrity would have been a tremendous inspiration.

At that time, Henry Wallace told me he believed it was his duty to stay and work in the Democratic Party. I knew then, as I know now, that he was doing what he thought was right. But he never has been a good politician, he never has been able to gauge public opinion, and he never has picked his advisers wisely.

All of these things might have been less important if he had been a disinterested, nonpolitical leader of liberal thought, but as a leader of a third party he will accomplish nothing. He will merely destroy the very things he wishes to achieve. I am sorry that he has listened to people as inept politically as he is himself.

1948

year of escalating conflicts. In January the Supreme Court declared discrimination on the basis of race, concerning admission of a law school applicant, was unconstitutional, establishing a precedent for subsequent school desegregation rulings. The next month the President introduced civil rights legislation, calling for an end to all school segregation. In March the high court ruled that religious training in the public schools was unconstitutional. Mrs. Roosevelt was outspoken on civil rights issues. She supported Truman's initiatives, gave the high court praise, and through her column brought particularly offensive examples of racial discrimination to light.

When the national party conventions rolled around in July, Democrats nominated Truman, with Kentucky's Alben Barkley as his running mate, then adopted a civil rights platform. Outraged Southern conservatives—the Dixiecrats—walked out, regrouping just days later to form the States Rights Party with Strom Thurmond of South Carolina at the helm and a platform urging continued racial segregation. Dissident liberal Democrats organized the Progressive Party, under former Vice President Henry Wallace. The GOP chose two governors as nominees: Dewey of New York for President and Warren of California for Vice President.

Truman called a summer session of Congress to deal with civil rights and problematic labor legislation, but he came up short, with none of the bills he desired. Only an all-out 10,000-mile whistle-stop campaign across the country by the President saved him in the November election, where he narrowly beat Dewey. (The race was so tight that some major newspapers infamously printed DEWEY DEFEATS TRUMAN headlines—which the President showed off with glee the moment his own victory was clear.) Dixiecrats garnered thirty-nine electoral votes, but Progressives didn't win any. Each of the two minor parties nevertheless collected about a million popular votes. Eleanor Roosevelt backed Harry Truman and several times criticized Henry Wallace in "My Day" but unfortunately could not give undivided attention to the campaign; her status as a UN delegate demanded too much of her time.

Strikes continued to disrupt the economy or to advance the cause of labor, depending on one's viewpoint. In May, when a national railroad workers' strike crippled transportation, President Truman called out the Army to run the railroads. The White House had failed earlier in the year to avert a coal miners' strike by 200,000 workers that lasted almost a month. Although the compromises that settled the dispute were partially negotiated by UMW President John L. Lewis, he was nonetheless fined $20,000 under Taft-Hartley and his union was assessed $1.25 million for contempt of court. When Eleanor Roosevelt addressed the labor-management dispute in "My Day," she didn't mince words, labeling Lewis a suspiciously self-serving union leader. However, she showed sympathy for the workers, as long as their strikes didn't threaten the overall economy. When work stoppages did pose such a danger, Mrs. Roosevelt called for a quick resolution of the issues—for the good of the nation.

Tensions increased on the foreign-policy front as well. The Soviets barred a UN commission, charged with overseeing elections in Korea, from entering North Korea. In June the Soviets blocked access to Western-held sectors of Berlin; Truman ordered American military planes in Europe to fly in food and fuel. By fall two independent competing republics had been declared in Korea, a recipe for inevitable conflict between Soviet and American policies there.

But certain happier notes in foreign affairs also emerged in 1948. The Organization of American States held its first meetings in Bogota. When Israel declared independence in May, the U.S. was first to recognize her, and Eleanor Roosevelt applauded. The United States won the team competition at the London Olympics, the first since 1936. But a wise old man of American politics, Bernard Baruch, coined a term in 1949—*cold war*—evoking the dark undercurrent of international developments.

The Communist scare in America intensified, with Representative Richard Nixon sponsoring a bill requiring all Communists to register with the government. (The Senate never passed it.) Repeatedly Mrs. Roosevelt called for cool reason in an increasingly hot emotional climate. The Whittaker Chambers–Alger Hiss case, concerning alleged Communist activities, occupied the public's attention for weeks because of its witch-hunt drama.

Rounding out the year, T. S. Eliot (claimed by both America and England as a national poet) won the Nobel Prize for Literature; Columbia

Records introduced long-playing records (LPs); and another Columbia, the university in New York, got a new president, Dwight Eisenhower, for whom even bigger things were in store.

Albert Einstein and other scientists and foreign-policy planners who worked on the Manhattan Project to create the atomic bomb in 1945 later became advocates for the peaceful use of atomic energy and for the establishment of one world government. Einstein in particular had a nightmare vision of the next world war: nuclear weapons wreaking havoc across all civilizations. To him, nationalism was the central problem, its fierce pride and territoriality making war "once in every generation" a near certainty. Only through the abolition of nationhood and the substitution of a single world government could civilization survive, went the argument. Many writers joined the campaign, among them New Yorker *columnist and children's book author E. B. White. The usually idealistic Eleanor Roosevelt struck a cautionary note.*

HYDE PARK, JANUARY 29—A bulletin of the atomic scientists is accompanied by a letter in which Prof. Albert Einstein states that only a world government can keep the world safe from destruction.

The scientists who made the atomic discoveries, which have such great potentialities both for destruction and for improvement in the conditions under which people live, naturally feel a great sense of responsibility and desire to see their discoveries used for the good of humanity. Apparently, by the proper use of atomic energy, we could revolutionize many things related to the basic needs of people—power, production and soil conservation. The scientists therefore feel that it is very wasteful for us to concern ourselves with the production of bombs when there is so much to be done on the constructive side.

I can quite understand why men like Prof. Einstein feel that a world government would answer the problem, but any of us who have worked in the United Nations realize that we will have to learn to crawl before we learn to walk. If the great nations find it so hard to agree on the minor points at issue today, how do any of these hopeful people think that a world government could be made to work? People have to want to get on together and to do away with force, but so far there are many throughout the world who have not advanced to the point of really wanting to do this.

～

As Eleanor Roosevelt watched the Red scare of the late 1940s heat up into a genuine witch-hunt for Communists in all walks of life, she strained for a way to educate the public and certain legislators about the stark difference between theoretical communism as an ideology and practical communism as a political strategy that might advocate the violent overthrow of the status quo to achieve its aims. Hindsight shows that Mrs. Roosevelt was a dreamer in her belief that education could quell the anxieties and hatreds harbored by the Communist-hunters.

HYDE PARK, FEBRUARY 24—I think the thing that needs to be settled today is whether a statement that you believe in certain economic and political theories known as Communism implies that you also believe in the overthrow of your government by force. Once that point is established, then this whole situation which bothers so many would be cleared up, I think. A belief in the principles of Communism, provided you did not intend to work to bring this form of government into being through violence, would not be any more dangerous than a belief in Socialism, which has been preached in this country for many years without marked advance.

You hear people say they want to outlaw the Communist Party, forbid its existence in our country, deport citizens who are Communists. It seems to me that this attitude is valid only if it is proved that being a Communist means that you believe in the use of force against the existing government.

~

What would Mrs. Roosevelt think fifty years later about the scandalous rise in homelessness among the urban poor, and about the scourge of drug and alcohol addiction that puts so many people more or less permanently on the street? In this column she says "I don't think I like the way we live these days," and one can only suspect that were she to see New York at the turn of the twenty-first century rather than in the middle of the twentieth, her sense of outrage might be even deeper.

NEW YORK, MAY 15—A curious thing happened to me the other night. I came out of my apartment house and walked toward Eighth Street to attend a lecture given by Eugene O'Neill, Jr., at the New School for Social Research. Suddenly, I saw on the sidewalk the figure of a man. He lay there drunk or ill or asleep—very thin and very poor-looking. People glanced at him and hurried by. Some of us made sure that he was breathing. But here in a big city, what did one do with a stranger who lay senseless and helpless on the sidewalk?

What we did was to report him to the first policemen we met which I suppose was the proper thing to do—but it left me feeling very odd. The story of the Good Samaritan kept running through my head, and I wondered whether it was possible in a big city to feel the same responsibility for your fellow man as you would feel on a country road.

I don't suppose the man was worthy, and I doubt if you can take a man you see lying on the street and have him carried into an apartment house. But leaving him there seemed heartless and senseless and inhuman, and I don't think I like the way we live in these days.

I had no further responsibility after we found the policeman, but the incident haunted me all through Mr. O'Neill's lecture about my husband as a man of ideas and a man of letters. And the next day, at Lake Success [where her UN committee on human rights was meeting], as we argued about human rights at a committee meeting, I wondered how many human rights that poor man had. At heart I imagine I am really a country bumpkin—I like to know my neighbors and to have some sense of responsibility for them.

~

The Red scare of the 1940s and 1950s had at its heart the scurrilous tendency to brand entire ethnic groups as suspect. The "DPs" Mrs. Roosevelt refers to here are displaced persons, people uprooted from their homes and, often, from their homelands during the war, who now, under the political circumstances of postwar Europe, either could not go home or would not want to for fear of persecution. Many DPs were Eastern European Jews; some were lower-class Catholics from the Latin countries. Certain congressmen in the United States habitually labeled all DPs "bums and loafers," and on the basis of such prejudice made immigration law block or discourage passage to America and a chance at a new life for these hapless victims of the war.

NEW YORK, JUNE 12—I am sorry to see that in the debate in the House on the bill to admit 200,000 Displaced Persons into the United States, Representative E. E. Cox (Democrat, Georgia) opposed the bill on the grounds that the inhabitants of DP camps are "the scum of all Europe—an aggregation of loafers. As a whole these camps are the hotbeds of revolutionists and if these people come here they will join those who are gnawing away at the foundation of our constitutional government."

He was joined by Representative Edward Gossett, a Democrat of Texas.

All one can say about these gentlemen is that they never visited these DP camps or they visited them with an amount of prejudice and ignorance that prevented them from seeing the most self-evident truths.

The people in the camps are certainly not revolutionists. They would naturally not be in favor of a regime that condemns any human being to spending an indeterminate number of years in camps scattered throughout Europe. Most of these people have skills and are anxious to work, and some of them have professions and were men of note in those professions before they were forced to leave their homes.

The record of similar people who have been allowed to come into our country has been remarkably good. They make successful American citizens and it is un-Christian and uncharitable to brand people as "bums and loafers" when they are the victims of circumstances beyond their control.

~

When an alliance recently tested by the cruel challenges of war unravels, it is inevitably disturbing, particularly to the party who wants it to continue peacefully. Mrs. Roosevelt was among the earliest to acknowledge that the Russians were no longer trustworthy allies. The Soviet actions temporarily blocking access to U.S.- and British-controlled sectors of Berlin were the last straw. After that, Mrs. Roosevelt knew when she was debating with her Russian colleagues in the UN that she could no longer consider them reliable friends.

New York, June 17—Last night I read in the evening papers that the Russians have taken again to their irritating tactics in Berlin and have prevented 140 coal-carrying railway cars from entering Berlin from the Western zone in the last few days and have shut off the auto bridges over the Elbe. This was reported by Allied authorities, and by that is meant the Western Allies. British authorities stated that only trains bound for the Western sectors of Berlin were halted. Those destined for the Russian sector went through unmolested.

An excuse was given, of course, but these tactics explain why we no longer seem to consider that the Russians are our Allies. This is a shock and makes one look backward and wonder where this point of division began. Somewhere the Soviet Union, Great Britain and the United States got off the track. Instead of agreeing together, as under the United Nations Charter the great nations were supposed to do, they started to disagree and the disagreement has grown greater and greater until now it is almost difficult to find any point at which we can agree.

~

Happy days in the country at Hyde Park seemed to Mrs. Roosevelt well-earned respites from the swirl of UN meetings on Long Island, and the social appointments and speaking engagements that ordinarily kept her moving at a rapid clip in the city. Eleanor Roosevelt was probably never happier than when her house was full of children. From the kids' viewpoint, the fun of summering at Mrs. Roosevelt's Val-Kill Cottage was inexhaustible: fields and woods to roam, a swimming pool, and a bottomless well of good food and goodwill.

The granddaughter to be married in Phoenix is Anna Roosevelt's first child, Anna Eleanor Dall, whose nickname was "Sistie."

PHOENIX, ARIZ., JULY 8—This is working out as a very successful summer. But to most people it might seem as if we were running a children's camp at Hyde Park, for we have had an average of nine children steadily since early June! When one or two leave, others arrive. However, they all fall into the routine very quickly, and it seems to be enjoyable for them. At least I have heard no complaints.

One of Elliott's sons likes working on the farm. He has a friend with him who seems quite willing to go along with whatever he does, whether it is helping with the cows or mowing the lawn, and he must be enjoying it for he has asked his mother to please let him stay for a longer visit.

Those who ride take care of their own horses. The littlest ones play in the sandbox and swing in the swings by the brook and swim in the pool. All the youngsters spend hours of every warm day in the pool. The two children who are not quite three years old have to wear life belts, but they go through all of the motions of swimming and evidently learn from just watching the others.

I am looking forward to having Franklin Jr.'s younger boy, Christopher, with us for ten days this month and possibly we may be able to get a longer visit from young John Boettiger, who is nine. Elliott's four children, with their friends, and my cousin, Mrs. W. Forbes Morgan, with her two children are our steady, permanent summer residents.

We picnic by the pool for luncheon every day, and that seems to be a perfect idea because the children do not have to take off their bathing suits, which always creates sadness and controversy.

We went off Sunday, the Fourth of July, for our annual picnic in a particular spot where there is a wonderful, rushing stream that has quite a deep waterfall and dark green hemlocks on either side growing out of the rocks. It is a beautiful place, and the children had a wonderful time following the stream along the rocks. They returned, dripping water from head to toe, having all fallen into a pool.

I read poetry after lunch to the six- and seven-year-olds and have found that Robert Louis Stevenson's "Poems of Childhood" are as much enjoyed by this generation as they had been by my own children a generation ago.

I was sorry to leave them all on Tuesday, but Miss Thompson and I left for Phoenix bright and early. This trip is partly business and partly pleasure. I have not been anywhere in the United States away from the East in a long time, and I think if one wants to gauge the popular feeling of the people throughout the country one has to get away from the Eastern Seaboard, if only for a day.

I am, of course, excited about my grandchild's wedding, the first in the family. I suppose this should make me feel very old, but, strangely enough, it does not seem to affect me that way at all!

~

As Chair of the United Nations Commission on Human Rights, Mrs. Roosevelt traveled to Paris for continuing discussion about human rights. She often undertook to strike at least a rhetorical blow for racial equality. The political and moral reality of South African apartheid gave her one such occasion.

PARIS, OCTOBER 9—One amendment [to the proposed Universal Declaration of Human Rights], presented by the delegate for the Union of South Africa, created a great effect upon a number of the members of the committee. I immediately asked to speak, but now I think it was fortunate—since there are many other amendments yet to be presented—that the opportunity was not given to me yesterday. I now realize I would have spoken with too much emotion and perhaps not as objectively as the conditions called for.

As far as one can judge, the present government of the Union of South Africa must live under a cloud of fear. I realize I do not know the exact numbers of the white population, and perhaps if I did it might explain to me their basic philosophy as regards all peoples of color and even extends itself to the position of women.

The fundamental human rights and freedoms that the Union of South Africa is willing to accord all peoples do not include, I gather, any social rights and I doubt whether they include equal economic rights.

It was a strange speech, and when you looked around the table where 58 nations are represented you wondered how any nation could live in the world of today and hold such a philosophy.

It was rumored the other day that the Union of South Africa wishes to withdraw from the United Nations because of their difference in point of view. But I think if they make such a decision in the world of today, in which so much of their own population cannot even be drawn into the circle of social acquaintances, they will be standing still while the rest of the world moves forward in a spirit of fraternity and equality.

~

As the work on the human rights declaration came to a close, Mrs. Roosevelt contributed whatever she could to polish the statement. But as this sardonic comment shows, she could not always get what she wanted. Later in 1948, when the UN General Assembly finally adopted the Universal Declaration of Human Rights, Mrs. Roosevelt reached the high point of her diplomatic career.

PARIS, DECEMBER 10—I would have been delighted to see in the preamble a paragraph alluding to the Supreme Power. I knew very well, however, there were many men around the table who would violently be opposed to naming God, and I did not want it put to a [roll call] because I thought for those of us who are Christians it would be rather difficult to have God defeated in a vote.

~

Dozens of family members would gather, as they did every year, at Hyde Park for Christmas—a cheerful prospect. Yet Mrs. Roosevelt still reflected seriously on the domestic, everyday lives of the French people who had been her hosts in Paris during the UN session. By way of comparison, life for the average American was better in many respects, or at least easier. The point was not to pass judgment but to show her readers the lingering effects of war, even in a country as resilient and sophisticated as France. The psychological consequences for France of having been for several years a conquered nation would be food for thought, Mrs. Roosevelt believed no doubt, for complacent Americans who might be losing patience with the demands of the European recovery program.

EN ROUTE TO NEW YORK, DECEMBER 13—The day has come to leave and I have been trying to add up my final impressions of France.

The French people are badly off. If you walk around on a Sunday or watch them going down into the Metro you very quickly realize that most of the people you see look tired and listless. This undoubtedly comes from lack of energy-giving foods, with little sugar or chocolate or butter available. There is no milk for older people. They do have a milk ration for babies and children and that is one reason, I think, why the youngsters look fairly well. But the older people uniformly look badly.

The French have done their best to receive their guests with warmth and with their customary hospitality. When we have gone to their apartments they tried to warm them up for us and to give us all kinds of food in the lavish ways of days gone by. Only now and then by a casual sentence do you realize what they have gone through. One woman said to me as we waited for the absurd little elevator that graces the stairwells in all large French apartment houses, "It is wonderful to have the lift running again. All these flights of stairs when you carried home your potatoes and vegetables from market—that was really hard. The sacks of potatoes are heavy." Electricity is still rationed and often cut off for hours.

France is not moribund. It is just very tired and it cannot revive until the physical body has been somewhat built up. One must eat. Particularly the French people must eat, because to them it is also a necessary ritual. No businessman or woman here dashes hastily into a corner drug store and gets a sandwich and a cup of coffee for lunch. That would be a sacrilege. The French go home and sit down with their families to a complete meal. They may lose a couple of hours away from business by doing it, but they are no worse off than other businesspeople because everyone does the same thing.

France, too, was conquered. One woman, speaking of what she had been through, said she had seen the French army routed, with officers picking up their wives and children and fleeing through Paris to any place where they might find temporary safety. She said rather sadly, "It takes a long time to restore the soul of a conquered country. You are free, but you know that you have been beaten. You cringe because you have known the conqueror's touch."

1949

*E*leanor Roosevelt and many in the liberal camp, including Harry Truman, believed the New Deal set in motion an irreversible tide of social change in America that would bring justice and at least a minimum of prosperity to all the people. The war was seen by many as a tragic interruption in this tide of social change. As the country settled into peacetime routines, the White House and Congress turned their attention more frequently to domestic, rather than foreign, affairs.

In January 1949, when Truman was inaugurated to serve a full term as an elected President, he expected to secure passage of several major legislative initiatives assuring a Fair Deal to a broader cross section of Americans. But with a recalcitrant Congress dominated by conservatives, Truman ended up with only a few key ideas written into law. His frustration was shared by Mrs. Roosevelt, although she was not hesitant to criticize even the President if she thought his tactics were off base.

The Supreme Court led off the year with a ruling allowing states to ban the closed shop, giving nonunion labor a boost. Liberal Sam Rayburn of Texas was reelected Speaker of the House, a post he would hold for decades. The Justice Department successfully pressed an antitrust suit against AT&T requiring the manufacturing component of the giant communications company, Western Electric, to separate from its parent. President Truman's proposal for compulsory national health insurance continued to meet stiff resistance from the American Medical Association, which favored a voluntary plan. Mrs. Roosevelt was less concerned about which proposal for national health insurance might be adopted by Congress than she was that something be done quickly to benefit all Americans. She underestimated not only the strength of the AMA lobby but also the fear many Americans had developed since the war of government-financed social welfare programs such as those characterizing the New Deal.

Several strikes interrupted the flow of the economy but won for the workers better wages and working conditions. John L. Lewis ordered soft-coal miners to stop work for two weeks to protest the administration's appointee, Dr. James Boyd, to the post of director of the Federal Bureau of Mines. In October 500,000 steelworkers struck successfully for higher wages. Later that month Congress raised the minimum wage from forty to seventy-five cents per hour.

One central part of Truman's Fair Deal did pass Congress—the Housing Act—to alleviate the critical postwar housing shortage. Mrs. Roosevelt, an ardent supporter of the bill, received many letters from middle- and lower-class Americans, often veterans or their wives, concerning the severe shortage of affordable housing.

Secretary of State Marshall, architect of the Marshall Plan, resigned in January and Dean Acheson took the post. The Department of Defense was created in 1949, replacing the War Department. It was a year of hopeful and frightening military events. The United States sent a missile higher than ever before (250 miles). Twelve nations signed the North Atlantic Treaty, a mutual defense pact that laid the groundwork for NATO. Mrs. Roosevelt saw this as a positive development. The U.S.-occupied zone of Germany was merged with those occupied by Great Britain and France, and on May 21 the Federal Republic of Germany was born. That month the Soviets lifted their blockade of Berlin.

In late June, gambling that stability in Korea could be maintained without American military presence, U.S. troops ended their postwar occupation of South Korea. When in October the Communist government on mainland China sought international recognition, the White House refused despite the quick recognition extended to Mao Tse-tung's new government by Britain and France. The President and many in Congress were anxious about the growing worldwide strength of communism, especially in the military sphere. In September 1949 the Soviets had achieved a military breakthrough, detonating their own atomic bomb. Eleanor Roosevelt implored both nations—the U.S. and the USSR—to avoid an arms race, but her arguments were to no avail. Now America was not the only country with the dreaded atomic weapon, and the balance of power began shifting seriously again.

Mrs. Roosevelt's diverse reading habits included little if anything by the Southern gentleman William Faulkner, of Mississippi, whose work won the Nobel Prize for Literature in 1949. No doubt the proudest and most encouraging note of the entire year for Eleanor Roosevelt was the dedication, on the East Side of Manhattan, of the United Nations' new permanent headquarters. She would spend countless hours there in the years to come.

Some social problems do not go away, a fact Eleanor Roosevelt had trouble swallowing. Severe poverty in the slums of Washington, D.C.—virtually in view of congressional offices—was scandalous then as it is now. With only minor changes, this column could well be run again in today's newspapers. Without naming it, Mrs. Roosevelt alludes to the nature versus nurture debate in sociology and psychology, concluding that "nurture" (in this case social conditions) is a crucial factor in breeding crime and cross-generational poverty.

NEW YORK, APRIL 22—I hope that the recent excursion of a few Senators into the old and ancient alleys near the Capitol in Washington will have a more lasting effect than previous excursions have had.

When I first went to Washington in 1933, Mrs. Archibald Hopkins, who had worked to remove these alleys from the Washington scene ever since Woodrow Wilson was President, came to get me one day and insisted that we drive through many of them. Being a New Yorker, I was impressed at first by the fact that at least here the buildings were not so high and there was a chance for a little sun and air to permeate the filth and squalor. But I soon learned just how bad these alleys were. What crime was bred there, what disease spread from there and what seeds of delinquency were sown in those alley slums.

The question has never been decided whether a human being acquires more characteristics through heredity or through environment. Nevertheless I am quite sure that human beings who live in the Washington slums are conditioned to a great extent by their environment.

The greater number of people living in the slums of Washington are Negroes. There is always a housing shortage for them; they are always being crowded into houses which have been condemned and should be torn down. It is hard to believe, but most of Washington's slums have only outdoor sanitation and sometimes the only running water available is a faucet in the yard.

From these overcrowded rooms servants go out to work in comfortable houses. Children are cared for by women whose children go to segregated schools. Poor food and poor housing make these children a prey to many diseases and as they pass through the streets, or as their elders care for them at home and then go into other homes to work, the diseases may spread.

I only hope that the things the Senators saw will stay more lastingly in their minds than the impressions which I have seen congressional groups gather before.

~

A great theater critic Eleanor Roosevelt was not. In a commentary on Arthur Miller's Death of a Salesman, *she brings her personal taste, favoring strictly realistic drama, to bear on a play that works only if we suspend our disbelief and accept the theater's capacity to interweave reality and fantasy, conscious and unconscious thought. Mrs. Roosevelt also resisted the play's scathing indictment of middle-class life and the hopeful but unrealistic dreams of the salesman. She remained a resolute believer in the soundness of the American economy and the worthiness of the American worker.*

Death of a Salesman *won the Pulitzer Prize and the Drama Critics' Circle Award. It had an unusually long Broadway run for a deeply serious play, from February 11, 1949, through the end of 1950.*

NEW YORK, APRIL 28—Monday night I saw the much-advertised play "Death of a Salesman." It is certainly a remarkable production. The imagination shown in the scenery and in the directing is extraordinary and no one could want better acting than Lee J. Cobb brings to the portrayal of Willy Loman, the unsuccessful salesman. The rest of the cast also was excellent.

Yet I remained untouched and somewhat critically aloof. One does not hear voices at one moment and talk sensibly to the son of one's old employer a little later on. Surely, there are dreamers and there are totally untruthful people in the world, people who are untruthful with themselves, with their families and with the world as a whole. They fail everyone, including themselves, but I don't know whether one really needs a whole evening of gloom to impress that truth upon one.

There are many touches of reality in the play and, as a theatrical performance, it is something to see. But I would not choose it either as entertainment or for its moral lesson. That lesson, in more realistic style, you can find in many an American community. I think I like it better when it points to the fact that a man, if finally brought to face the truth, can pick himself up and create a different ending.

Is this supposed to be the typical American salesman? If so, I don't think it is typical. The mother was the only person who might have given some redeeming features to the boys, but even that ray of hope was not very clearly indicated. If you go to see this play, be sure you don't happen to be in a gloomy mood. If you are you will come out even gloomier than when you went in.

~

A childhood like Eleanor Roosevelt's would have embittered most people for life. She tells us she "lived an entirely lonely life" at her grandmother's house in Tivoli, New York. Diphtheria had killed Anna Roosevelt (Eleanor's mother) when the girl was just eight; her alcoholic though much adored father had been moved to Virginia, without her, before she was ten, and he did not survive for long. Nonetheless, Mrs. Roosevelt rescues good memories from that lonely time.

NEW YORK, MAY 24—The Hyde Park Historical Association placed its first historical marker in Hyde Park Sunday afternoon. The inscription was written by Claude Bowers and placed on what was once the house belonging to Colonel and Mrs. Archibald Rogers. It is now the home of the Roosevelt School.

Since in the annals of my husband's childhood it is written that he used to have lessons in this house with the Rogers children, the Historical Association wished to place their first marker here.

I had not been in the house since it had been turned into a school. I remembered it very well in the old days when we were all children and it was often the center for young people's parties. Dances during the Christmas holidays; coasting and skating, with tea or supper at this hospitable home; and, when we were even smaller, dancing classes all through the autumn weeks, which drew children all the way from Hudson on the north and Fishkill in the south, were only some of the activities we enjoyed. Those were not the days of automobiles. We took a train down from Tivoli, where I lived with my grandmother, had our lessons and our supper and then were driven to the station and took a train home, arriving at what for us was a very late hour after another drive of five miles by horse and cart.

I was usually shy and frightened because I lived an entirely lonely life, with few children of my own age nearby. I had no ear for music and therefore danced extremely badly! My father sang well, loved music and had a real sense of rhythm. My mother played the piano and danced well. Something was certainly left out of me—at least at that early age—and what little appreciation of music I since have acquired has been acquired with toil and effort and was certainly not a gift of the gods!

Senator Estes Kefauver flew up from Washington to speak at this small meeting, which brought together the members of the Historical Association, the children of the school and their parents. Afterward I took the Senator over to see our old house and the library, but it was a hurried visit and he had to be on his way back to Washington.

~

The fierce competition of political interest groups was something Eleanor Roosevelt wrestled with throughout her public life. She took it as a matter of course that expressing her opinion was her civic duty but that criticism would flow in from some quarter, no matter how reasonable her argument. On the issue of public aid to education, the 1940s and 1950s were the era of finding our way. What the country takes for granted fifty years later in relying on massive amounts of federal aid to public education was then largely a new concept. Mrs. Roosevelt's predilection for viewing the United States as a Judeo-Christian nation is clear, but she offers ecumenism as well. Her work in the United Nations was broadening.

HYDE PARK, JULY 15—I am still getting letters from a few people who seem to think that in opposing aid from the taxpayers' money to any but public schools, I must have a particular bias against the Catholic Church. This must be because their parochial schools are more numerous than the schools of any other denomination.

I hate to continue an argument that many people think is based on prejudice, but something was written in a letter to me that seems worth mentioning.

A gentleman writes that the Barden bill was a discriminatory bill against the Negroes in the South. I have not read the bill carefully, and I have been rather careful not to say if I am for or against any particular bill or bills. As a matter of fact, I have not gone into the details of any bills.

I believe in federal aid to public education and I think it should be particularly valuable to the states of the South that do not have the income to spend as much per capita on all children, white and Negro, as should be spent. I believe that all children should have an equal opportunity for education in whatever community they live, and this holds good for the whole of the United States.

Another lady writes that I am against the Constitution, since I would deny religious education in the public schools. I did state that I thought religious education was valuable to every child, but it could not be given in the school alone. The home and the church must cooperate.

This is no real reason why every school should not teach every child that one of the important aspects of our life is its spiritual side. It might be possible to devise a prayer that all the denominations could say and it certainly ought to be possible to read certain verses from the Bible every day. It probably would do children no harm to learn to know some of the writings of other great religious leaders who have led other great religious movements.

~

Few writers of Mrs. Roosevelt's generation, or any other, could walk a philosophical tightrope with as much finesse. Here she defends freedom of speech and criticizes Communist ideology and American intolerance for black people.

Paul Robeson, son of a slave, became an all-American football star at Rutgers in 1917–1918. The sports world lionized him, but the profession he chose—the law—had no place for him. Embittered, Robeson's politics shifted far to the left; his interest in Soviet communism eventually drew him to Moscow. Robeson had meanwhile become a widely admired actor and concert singer in America during the 1920s and 1930s, with starring roles in The Emperor Jones, Show Boat, The Hairy Ape, Porgy *(the original play, later to become the opera and film,* Porgy and Bess*), and* Othello— *and in several concert tours in Europe and one in Russia (1936). When the war came, he returned to the United States and often mixed political monologues with his concert programs.*

HYDE PARK, SEPTEMBER 3—A great deal of feeling has been aroused by the riots that took place in Peekskill, New York, at a meeting sponsored by the Civil Liberties Union. I, myself, cannot understand why anyone goes to a meeting at which Paul Robeson is going to speak unless they are in sympathy with what he is going to say, since by this time everyone must be familiar with his thinking. I have been told that what I once experienced, namely, seeing him turn his concert into a medium for Communist propaganda, is his constant practice, so whoever goes to hear him must know what to expect. They might well want to hear him sing, in spite of knowing that he would sing certain songs that they might not like, or at some point, talk in a way with which they might not agree. If so, in this country, it is their privilege to go to hear him and leave. I think if we care for the preservation of our liberties we must allow all people, whether we disagree with them or not, to hold meetings and express their views unmolested as long as they do not advocate the overthrow of our Government by force.

It seems to me that peaceful picketing of such a meeting is also an unwise gesture. I can well understand why veterans want to show their displeasure, but I think there are other ways of doing it. They can hold a meeting and see to it that their speakers are as well reported as those at any other meeting. They can see that the press carries refutation of whatever arguments are given at any meeting with which they disagree, but I do not think they need fear that the average American is an easy prey to the Paul Robeson type of propaganda.

I believe the average American should realize that rioting and lawless-ness—even when we can prove that they were, as some people are trying to prove in this case, incited by some Communists—are still not good pro-paganda for democracy in the world.

We in the United States should, I think, make it very clear that we dis-agree with and disapprove of many views of Paul Robeson, but it is well also for us to remember that Paul Robeson left this country and took his family to the USSR until the coming of the war. He wanted to find some-thing he did not find here. He was a brilliant law student and could not find a job in any good New York firm staffed for the most part by men and women of the white race. In other words, he could not be a lawyer, so he became a singer—a gain for art—but perhaps there was some bitterness in his heart, brought about by the fact that there was no equality of op-portunity for educated men of his race. He did not want his boy to have the same experiences. Others might feel the same way. In the USSR he was recognized as an educated man, as an artist and as an equal. We disap-prove of his speeches, but we must also understand him and above all other things, we must be jealous to preserve the liberties that are inherent in true democracy.

∼

By late 1949 Mao Tse-tung had succeeded in unifying sufficient support from the sprawling Chinese territories and the intricate web of Chinese in-terest groups, including the military, to declare his revolution a fait accom-pli. *The Nationalist Chinese, under Chaing Kai-shek, had battled Mao ide-ologically and militarily during a protracted civil war. Mrs. Roosevelt did not have a formula to move the Chinese closer to democratic revolution. One could only watch and wait.*

EN ROUTE HOME FROM ATLANTA, SEPTEMBER 10—If the Chinese people as a whole are going to be democratic they will have to get together. This is no recent civil war. This is a war that has been going on for a very long time. China is too big a country, it has too many people for any other nation to be able to fully control unless they wish to invade and control by force.

The Communistic theories are those of a dictatorship and it may be that for a time and on a partial basis they may control certain areas of China. But if the people of China do not become convinced Communists, not even the dictatorship sponsored by Communism will really run a stable government for the whole of China.

I have a feeling that China is slowly emerging into a new and strange era. An unsettled situation may be theirs for a long time, but I doubt if we can do more than remain the friend of the Chinese people and be ready, when signs of stability emerge, to help them in any way that it becomes apparent might be useful.

~

As American as apple pie, but more interesting: the tasty treats concocted in a national baking contest Mrs. Roosevelt attended in New York and reported to her "My Day" readers as though she had been a fly on the wall. A high percentage of her readership were housewives who could identify immediately with the contest winners. Never known for a discriminating palate, Eleanor Roosevelt nonetheless recognized a delicious story, served up with good humor and telling detail.

HYDE PARK, DECEMBER 15—I went to a luncheon on Tuesday in New York City at the invitation of Philip W. Pillsbury, president of Pillsbury Mills, which was advertising on a grand scale but at the same time had a very healthy human touch about it. It was the finals of the national recipe and baking contest at the Waldorf-Astoria that brought women from 37 states, the District of Columbia and Alaska to New York on a trip financed by the Pillsbury company. They were a very happy and excited group of people.

There were $1,000 awards in six categories for the best bread maker, cake maker, cookie baker, etc., but it was for the three big awards that every woman sat on the edge of her chair waiting to find out who the lucky one would be. Those who got the six awards in the various classes were happy, indeed. But I think Mr. and Mrs. Pillsbury must have felt quite proud when they gave out the other prizes, because it is given to few people in this world to give such great happiness to other human beings.

It is a pleasant thing in itself to have the journey and the fun of a baking contest in the Waldorf, and every woman did her baking in a General Electric stove, which she will take home with her. As a by-product, Mrs. Ethel Hansen, from Anchorage, Alaska, who has been a missionary there, saw her brother from Hartford, Conn., whom she had not seen in 36 years. That in itself must have been worth the trip, and more, to her. It must be exciting, too, to see some of your favorite radio people in the flesh, instead of just knowing their voices over the air.

The really tense and moving moment came when Mr. Pillsbury and I went down to the little platform in front of the raised dais where we had lunch and the announcement of the prizes was begun. Third-prize money—$4,000—went to Mrs. Richard W. Sprague, of San Marino, Calif. Her winning entry was named "Carrie's Creole Chocolate Cake." She was asked what she would do with the money and answered: "Well, the baby is paid for but there is still the mortgage on the house."

Then came the announcement of the second prize—$10,000. That went to one of the few unmarried contestants, Miss Laura Rott of Naperville, Ill. Her entry was "Mint Surprise Cookies." I was assured by those who sampled them as they came out of the oven that though they might look like ordinary cookies they tasted like your dream of something highly delectable. Miss Rott was speechless. She could hardly stand up and she had no idea what she would do with the money. She never thought of having so much money at one time in her hand.

Finally came the announcement of the $50,000 prize. It went to Mrs. Ralph E. Smafield, of Detroit, Mich. Her entry was "Water Rising Nut Twist," and we were each given a bite. It certainly is delicious. Tears were in her eyes as she was asked what she was going to do with her prize. She did not hesitate: "We will have a home of our own at last." Her husband is an electrical engineer. A home of their own seemed to be a dream which she had long cherished.

This is a healthy contest and a highly American one. It may sell Pillsbury flour but it also reaches far down into the lives of the housewives of America. These were women who ran their homes and cooked at home; they were not professional cooks.

I almost forgot to say that three men got the trip to New York by qualifying and one man won with an entry which he called "Quick Man-Prepared Dinner."

~

Though she speaks here with graceful charm about sitting for a portrait to satisfy her children, there was more than modesty behind Mrs. Roosevelt's resistance to their request. From childhood on, some in her family instilled in her a self-image of the Ugly Duckling. As a married woman in public life she was criticized for the plainness of her clothes, the inappropriateness of her flower-bedecked hats, the shrillness of her voice. Her willingness, finally, to sit for a portrait was a triumph not so much of her children's persuasiveness as of her own self-acceptance.

HYDE PARK, DECEMBER 16—I might as well own up to the fact that to please my son, Elliott, I have broken all my vows and finally am sitting for a portrait done by Douglas Chandor. He did a wonderful portrait of my mother-in-law when she was an old lady. And while I hope that this portrait of me will be kept from public view until after I am dead, I have to acknowledge that he is a remarkable painter and that my grandchildren will find in me much more that is pleasant and agreeable to look at in an ancestor than really exists! One must look on a portrait as something to make future generations feel that they do not have to be too much ashamed of their forebears.

1950

*T*ension at home, conflict abroad. Mrs. Roosevelt's 1950 "My Day" columns were full of bad news and angry opinions. Since 1945 at war's end, America had poured almost $25 billion in aid and loan credits into other countries. But the postwar world was no friendlier for all of it. In January President Truman initiated the Civilian Mobilization Office, a sign of America's deepening fear of Soviet attack. Truman also revealed that the U. S. was working on the hydrogen bomb, the next right step in what was by now irreversibly an arms race. Eleanor Roosevelt had serious reservations about these developments.

In February Senator Joseph McCarthy of Wisconsin stunned the nation by accusing the State Department of harboring Communists. Many people were convinced or were at least scared into believing him. A Soviet consular officer was found guilty in March of espionage against the United States: perfect kindling for McCarthy's growing fire.

The Supreme Court evidenced its own fear of political subversion by upholding the controversial Taft-Hartley Act requiring union leaders to swear they were not Communists. Mrs. Roosevelt consistently labeled McCarthyism's rabid hatred of communism as dangerous and even insane while maintaining her staunch dislike and distrust for Soviet Communist politics. Yet her acceptance of benign forms of socialism confirmed itself when she visited several of the socialist Scandinavian countries in late spring.

When the "Korean conflict" (never officially a declared war) broke out in late June, with North Korean troops invading South Korea using Soviet military equipment, the case against the Soviet Communists was sealed. The UN Security Council (minus the boycotting Soviet representative) immediately authorized armed intervention to save South Korea. Truman sent the Navy to blockade the Korean coast and the Air Force and Army to lead the way in the UN's land battle. General Douglas MacArthur was appointed commander of all UN forces. Former Secretary of State George Marshall became Secretary of Defense during the crisis.

Late in July the Senate Foreign Relations Committee reported that Senator McCarthy's February speech had had no basis in fact, but the damage was done, and years would pass before the McCarthy witch-hunt for alleged Communists ended. In September Congress passed, over Truman's veto, the Internal Security Act, requiring all Communists to register with the government and authorizing their detention in case of a national emergency.

Mrs. Roosevelt had placed such high hopes in the UN as a means to establish world peace that to see another war break out, so soon after World War II, was profoundly disillusioning. She used her "My Day" columns to educate her readers about the rather complicated history of Russian-Chinese-Japanese-American involvement in Korean affairs.

Throughout much of 1950, on an almost daily basis, Mrs. Roosevelt confronted the UN Soviet delegates, with whom she found it increasingly difficult to work. Except for the Scandinavian trip, a visit to family and friends in California, and a short vacation at the Roosevelts' home on Campobello Island, her UN job kept her busy in New York most of the time.

During the early fall, the UN troops made steady progress in Korea, recapturing Seoul; reaching the 38th Parallel, which divided the two Koreas; and penetrating beyond toward the North Korean capital. Then an unanticipated additional enemy appeared on the battlefront: The Chinese Communists joined the North Koreans and, toward year's end, drove the UN forces into retreat. Soon it became a protracted struggle. General Dwight Eisenhower took a leave of absence from his post as president of Columbia University to assume command of NATO. Truman declared a full national emergency to facilitate his military strategy. General MacArthur urged that the U.S. attack mainland China.

In November, Puerto Rican nationalists staged an unsuccessful assassination attempt on President Truman, who escaped unhurt, though a guard was killed, as was one assailant. It was a time in which almost no one felt entirely safe.

During these years of Eleanor Roosevelt's public life as reported in "My Day," actually from December 1947 onward, there was a parallel private life. Although she would occasionally effervesce in "My Day" about the antics of her grandchildren and from time to time would publicly mourn the loss of a loved one, Mrs. Roosevelt played other cards in her private deck close to her vest. Biographer Joseph Lash observes: "Eleanor was sixty-three when her quenchless desire to love and be loved settled on David Gurewitsch. Her letters to David lack the passionate intensity" of others she wrote earlier in her life, "but they were love letters. She was fifteen years older and a figure now in history, which made even more remarkable her ability to shake free of convention and upbringing to love a younger man."

Gurewitsch had been a longtime friend and was the physician of the former First Lady's friend Trude Lash, the biographer's wife. Her correspondence to Gurewitsch tells an interesting tale of an older woman whose previous marriage and public life made it impossible for her either to find comfort with a disloyal husband or to seek escape through divorce or open displays of anger but who now would come alive again in her heart.

Charming discontinuity: In Mrs. Roosevelt's column about visiting her son John's family in Los Angeles, the first half reads like a letter to a friend about domestic activities anyone of any background or social status might know—kids, schools, clothing, weather. But then it's off for lunch to Romanoffs, the pricey place where Hollywood's elite meet. That day, however, the tables were turned on Eleanor Roosevelt by one Humphrey Bogart—in whose eyes, apparently, Eleanor was the real star.

LOS ANGELES, JANUARY 18—Here in the city of Los Angeles the usual winter rainfall already has exceeded the average mark. My first two days have been beautiful ones, with blue sky and little wind. The grass is green everywhere and the flowers are in bloom. I wish we might have had some of the rain in New York about which they complain here. Then we would not be so short of water.

Here they are accustomed to measuring their water supply, and I was interested to find that in my son's house in Pasadena there is a regular monthly bill for water, and the gas bill comes at the same time. Gas furnaces seem to be a convenient method of heat here and they only turn them on in such sections of the house as they feel have need of greater warmth. In many rooms there is no central heating and often just a small open fire will be all that is needed to take off the winter chill. I can well see, however, that when the good weather goes back on them, they are not equipped to be warm in the way that we are at home in the East.

For the children, though, this climate has many advantages. Little boys wear their overalls the year round, and I went with a friend of mine to take her little daughter, my godchild, to nursery school this morning. The sweater set, which I had sent her for Christmas, was all that was needed; no gaiters or arctics and heavy coats.

Nevertheless, my grandchildren think of snow and ice in the East as something highly enjoyable. I think if they were given a choice as to whether they would come to visit in the summer or winter they would choose winter because their only contact here with snow is up in the mountains on an occasional trip.

My son, John, took Anna, Miss Thompson and me to lunch yesterday at Romanoffs and I had the pleasure of seeing a number of the famous Hollywood people—Walter Wanger; George Jessel; Freeman Gosden and Charles Correll, of "Amos and Andy" fame; and Humphrey Bogart, who flattered me greatly by bringing me a copy of my book, *This I Remember*, to sign. I could not help thinking how many of my youthful acquaintances would have thrilled to see so many people whom they enjoy on the stage and screen and radio actually in the flesh.

~

April 1950: Eleanor Roosevelt was sixty-six. Her vitality and sense of momentum would challenge people half her age who could not cram as much activity into a day and still have resources left in the evening, indeed the late evening, to continue being productive or charming or both.

NEW YORK, APRIL 27—The visit of the President of Chile Gabriel Gonzalez Videla and his charming wife to Hyde Park the other day was an informal and very pleasant occasion. From the time I greeted them, as they walked from the library to my husband's grave, through the visit to the old house, the recording for the Voice of America on the front steps, and finally to the library, the whole party seemed interested and unweary in spite of the whirlwind pace of events arranged for them since they arrived in the United States.

Ambassador Herman Santa Cruz drove with me in my little new car, which I have not yet mastered very well, as I led the official cars through the wood road to my cottage. I was apologizing for the holes left by the winter frost and the spring mud and to console me he remarked: "Many roads in Chile are like this."

I had tacked the flags of our countries on my door and the President at once noticed his own flag. In spite of the fact that we are somewhat crowded in my little cottage when we are a large party and we cannot eat out-of-doors, everybody seemed relaxed and at home. I had a warm feeling about this party, as though it really had created a greater sense of friendliness between the representatives of our two countries.

After my guests had gone to visit their old friend, Mrs. Olin Dows, Miss Thompson and I drove down to New York City, arriving in time for me to attend a meeting of the United Nations Day Committee at 6:30.

After a hasty bite of dinner there was a Wiltwyck School Board meeting at 9 p.m., which, wonder of wonders, ended at 10:30. We are having our usual troubles, reaching the month of April without having raised enough money to cover our summer expenses for Wiltwyck.

A special meeting will be called to consider how this money may be raised. While we have put forward great efforts this past year and have greatly increased the list of subscribers, our budget has gone up but still falls short of increased costs. There is much work to be done for these little boys who still find trouble getting started in life and land in police courts and then in Wiltwyck.

On Tuesday I reached Lake Success [Long Island] in time to do a recording for the YMCA before our morning Human Rights Commission meeting opened.

We started our discussion on implementation of a Covenant of Human Rights, but after a number of preliminary speeches, which took us halfway through the afternoon, we found that the commission was anxious to have a little more time for preparation of this subject. Therefore we postponed further consideration until next Monday, when it was agreed we would take it up and conclude our work on it.

Then we went back to drafting Article 18, as, during my absence on Monday, Article 17 of the Covenant on Freedom of Information had been completed. Later in the afternoon, I looked in for a brief moment at two meetings that were going on—one in the Economic and Social Council and one in a large conference room.

Then I hastened back to New York City and a brief half hour at a brilliant and crowded party given on the Starlight Roof of the Waldorf-Astoria by Laurence Rutman, editor and general manager of United Feature Syndicate. Newspaper people from all over the country were there and I felt a little bewildered as I was engulfed by the crowd and realized that I would have difficulty in locating my host in that sea of faces.

I got home in time to change and eat dinner before going across the street to the Broadway Tabernacle for the annual banquet of the Lemuel Haynes Congregational Church. There I was presented with an award, and an added thrill was hearing Carol Brice sing. She has a beautiful voice.

From there I went to Hunter College, where they were holding a meeting in the interest of the activities carried on at the Inter-Faith Houses which are named after my mother-in-law. There I saw the most interesting and graceful dances presented by a young Indian student from Bombay. There ended a very full "My Day."

~

*Five years after FDR's death, Europe was still commemorating his contribu-
tions to revitalizing the world economy during the Depression and to saving democracy from totalitarianism during the war. Eleanor Roosevelt recognized that the praise lavished on the late President belonged in fact to all
Americans who had shared in these burdens and tasks.*

OSLO, JUNE 9—The crowd yesterday waiting for the King and the royal
party to arrive for the ceremonies of unveiling the monument to Franklin
D. Roosevelt was large and enthusiastic. As I stood listening to our national anthem, I realized anew what a beautiful site has been chosen for
this statue. It stands over the quayside looking down the fjord. The
speeches were fine and warm and I think there was a full realization by all
the people present that this statue symbolizes their gratitude not to one
man alone, but to the people of the United States of America, to President
Truman and Congress. And to the ideals for which they stand—continuing to give cooperation and support to attain peace and justice which
men in the United States military services fought for during the late war,
side by side with their allies.

~

*The late 1940s and the 1950s laid the groundwork for the great civil rights
battles of the 1960s. It took time to build up the momentum that eventually
produced Martin Luther King, Jr., the Freedom Riders, and Supreme Court
decisions outlawing school segregation. Mrs. Roosevelt recognized, while it
was happening, that the momentum would build slowly, and she used her
"My Day" column to praise what she felt were positive contributions to the
struggle.*

HYDE PARK, AUGUST 18—I received a letter the other day from Mr. Joseph
D. Lohman, of Chicago, who is secretary of the National Committee on
Segregation in the nation's capital. The letter carries very heartening news
as regards the fight for civil liberties in this country. He tells me that the
courage of the President and the Secretary of the Interior in running, on a
nonsegregated basis, the swimming pools in the District of Columbia, has
proved successful. This has resulted from the careful planning and training of the police, Park Service personnel, and the organization and cooperation of the community groups. Mr. Lohman points out that St. Louis
without this careful planning had difficulty, but that nevertheless Judge
Rubey Hulen of the United States District Court has handed down an

opinion which ordered the city of St. Louis to refrain from segregating their pools.

It is heartening to find democratic principles being firmly established in the nation's capital and in such big cities as St. Louis. Each time an accomplishment of this kind is brought about, it has a far-reaching effect. It would not be so important if the effect was only in our country, but it will reverberate around the world and be of value to us in every country where the population is largely of another race and color.

~

A lazily rambling late August column: Mrs. Roosevelt, reporting from Campobello Island, touches on half a dozen topics as though she were chatting with friends. We find her here relaxed and playful yet still observant of social problems—the plight of Native Americans—even when they seem to cloud over an otherwise sunny vacation day.

CAMPOBELLO ISLAND, N.B., AUGUST 25—I have not driven a great deal since I arrived on the island. In the years when I spent long summers here we always walked or went by boat so I find it hard to remember to use the car; besides, when one has driven across the island to Herring Cove and up to the head harbor end of the island, one has been about everywhere that one can go by car, whereas by boat there are endless trips to take. One can go up the St. Croix River to Calais, or stop at St. Andrews and see the fashionable world in the big hotel, and buy handwoven rugs and tweeds in the cottage industries shop which has flourished for many years. By now one can probably get some English china and pottery, which was not available during the war and is still not too plentiful in England itself. One can travel in a little boat among endless islands up the coast of Newfoundland, and even out to Grand Manan, and all the way around Campobello Island itself, joining the fishing fleet if one wants to fish.

The seining of a weir here is one of the sights no stranger should miss, for it takes one back to the days of the Bible as one watches the fishermen pulling up the seine and filling their dories with fish. One can stay in American waters and find endless picnic spots up the Denny River which flows down to the west of Eastport, as the St. Croix does on the east.

There is a little Indian village north of Eastport where the Indians still sell some of their baskets and other wares in the town, but on this visit I have not been to Eastport.

I am no happier about the way the Indians have been treated in this part of our country than I am anywhere else in the United States. Had we done a really good job it seems to me that our Indians today would be educated; there would be no need of reservations; they would be fully capable of taking their places as citizens, and the tribes would have had full compensation for the lands they owned. Our inability to work out this small problem satisfactorily and fairly is one of the real blots on our history.

We don't seem to be able to deal with dependent people, and that is why I have always been anxious to see us admit Alaska and Hawaii as states. Once they are an integral part of our country we will have a completely different attitude toward them and their inhabitants. They will be fully represented in Congress and no other state's interests will be more important than theirs.

~

The civil rights struggle began to mix with medical and scientific progress when the Red Cross took a stand against labeling blood according to the race of its donor, a practice it had followed for years. Mrs. Roosevelt used "My Day" to trumpet this news to the nation as a way to make the ethical point about racial equality.

NEW YORK, NOVEMBER 22—That was certainly a very welcome piece of information given out by the Red Cross yesterday.

In the future the blood donor cards will no longer designate whether blood given is white, Negro or Oriental. The Board of Governors announced this decision. Scientists have been urging this for some time, since it is a well-known fact that human blood is all alike, regardless of race.

This discriminatory practice created too much bad feeling during the last war, and it has carried over to the present. All of us should be relieved to know that at last one of our greatest relief organizations will be free of this particular type of discrimination.

~

With discouraging events in Korea, fear of Communist subversion sweeping the U.S., the Pentagon working on ever deadlier weapons, and an ugly civil rights struggle shaping up, the end of 1950 was gloomy. The Roosevelts received sad personal news as well when Anna's ex-husband, John Boettiger, committed suicide in October. Joseph Lash records Mrs. Roosevelt's reaction: "Is there nothing I might have done to help poor John? What dreadful things can happen when people fail each other. I did try to offer him friendship, but what good did it do?" Mrs. Roosevelt had the task of informing her daughter.

The final "My Day" columns of the year have a sense of onrushing darkness and a surprising chill.

HYDE PARK, DECEMBER 20—Some of us feel, as we live through these days, that in a curious, haunting way we know each step of the way. We have lived it before, not only once but perhaps twice if we are old enough to remember the prewar years of World War I as well as World War II. All of us feel that the collective intelligence of mankind should be able to save the world from suicide, and yet nothing seems to indicate that such is the case. We follow the path of the years gone by and we feel a little of the inevitableness of the Greek tragedy.

1951

merica spent much of 1951 focusing its attention on developments in the Korean conflict and Far East. Mrs. Roosevelt was a frequent commentator. War abroad always does damage to the economy at home; U.S. domestic price controls once again became necessary. Congress authorized a price freeze and President Truman instituted it on the first day of the year. The President wrestled with another national railroad strike in 1951, this one lasting twelve days and winning most of the workers' demands.

On March 14 UN troops recaptured Seoul, the capital of South Korea. By this time the United States had 2,900,000 military men and women, twice the number before the Korean war. The courtroom was another dramatic battlefield in 1951. After a controversial trial, Julius and Ethel Rosenberg were convicted of passing nuclear weapons secrets to the Soviets and, in April, were sentenced to death. Pressure on the jury to convict the Rosenbergs probably arose from fear in America about Communist subversion. With McCarthyism rampant, military news from Asia suggested that Chinese communism might be as dangerous to American interests as the Kremlin.

In 1951 Mrs. Roosevelt tried numerous times in "My Day" to disentangle the many threads of opinion about linkage between communism abroad and communism at home. She remained resolutely suspicious of communism of the Chinese variety, under the revolutionary leadership of Mao Tse-tung, and supported U.S. efforts to contain it within Chinese borders. At the same time she became even more disgusted with the paranoid psychology of McCarthyism that, by now, had wrecked many people's careers and reputations while turning up precious few truly subversive Communists.

General Douglas MacArthur, commander of UN forces in Korea, found himself on a collision course not only with the enemy but also with his own commander-in-chief. The general argued publicly that in Korea "there is no substitute for victory," while the President prepared to negotiate a truce with no clear winner. By mid-April the President had had enough from MacArthur, whom he recalled and then replaced with General Matthew Ridgeway. MacArthur remained popular at home among those who shared his worry about the Chinese, and Congress itself provided him the extraordinary forum of a joint session to state his case for expanding the war into China proper. Mrs. Roosevelt gave President Truman full support in the MacArthur affair though she admired the general. She recognized the necessary preeminence of the President and advocated an immediate truce.

In June the Supreme Court handed down two decisions backing the government's right to keep track of Communists. The military continued to expand: Draft age was lowered to eighteen and a half and the required service lengthened to two years. By July truce talks had begun, at Kaesang, in Korea, the UN negotiating with the Chinese Communists. Meanwhile a weather and financial disaster struck the Mississippi River basin in July when a massive flood in several states caused a billion dollars' worth of damage.

Years after World War II had ended in fact, a formal peace treaty with Japan remained unsigned; this was remedied in September 1951 when forty-nine nations signed a treaty with the Japanese. The United States claimed the right to maintain permanent military bases in Japan. Mrs. Roosevelt went to Europe again in the fall for the UN, this time to Paris. (The UN headquarters was still under construction in New York.) She made side trips to Geneva and to Brussels to attend a spirituality conference that deeply influenced her ideas about peace.

The critical importance of cooperative political and military security was reflected in the passage by Congress in October of the Mutual Security Act, which funneled $7 billion in aid to selected countries whose politics the United States felt it could trust or influence.

Technological advances for Americans in 1951 included initiation of the first transcontinental dial telephone service, and the first electricity to be created by a nuclear-powered steam generator sparked through test wires in a government laboratory in the mountains of Idaho.

Although thousands of American lives were lost or damaged by the fighting in Korea and millions of dollars were spent, the United States never formally declared war on Korea. For the first time the United States was fight-

ing as one power among many (though certainly the largest) under the United Nations banner. Few Americans had ever heard much about Korea, let alone visited. There were few cultural and economic ties.

George Kennan of the State Department introduced a foreign policy idea that lasted a generation: containment. *While we could not overcome communism, its roots already being too deep, we could keep it from spreading. The Korean conflict represented an ideological battlefield where Chinese and Soviet communism struggled against Western capitalist democracy; it was the perfect laboratory experiment for Kennan's containment theory.*

Mrs. Roosevelt wrote several "My Day" columns explaining how we became embroiled in an undeclared war in Korea.

HYDE PARK, FEBRUARY 2—I have come to the conclusion that the nation as a whole has a very short memory. A number of people lately have asked me how we happened to be in Korea and why did the President start the war there? These seem to me almost impossible questions.

Anyone remembering back to the last war should know that the Japanese occupied Korea, and when we conquered Japan, we took the country over from them. They should also remember that Russia came into the war as our ally against Japan some months earlier than had been expected. It was originally understood at Yalta that the Soviets could not fight on two fronts, but would come in just as soon as the war in Europe ended. Instead of that they came in ahead of schedule, perhaps because they felt they must guard their Asiatic interests.

In any case, when we took over Korea, Russia quite naturally claimed a part of the responsibility and an arbitrary line was set up—the 38th Parallel. North of that was Soviet responsibility, south of that was ours.

The United Nations was asked by us to supervise a free election in South Korea. Syngman Rhee, while out of the country during the Japanese occupation, had been constantly agitating for Korean freedom. Since this was the first election participated in by the Korean people, it is perhaps understandable that they voted for this man whom they considered the leader for Korean independence. I am told that under him some steps toward a free and democratic government have been taken.

On the other hand, the Soviets refused to allow any interference and set about militarizing the North Koreans. When they were ready, they invaded South Korea. The South Koreans resisted. Immediately our President asked the United Nations to take action. It did so promptly, and the call went out for volunteers to enforce the UN stand against aggression.

This is the history of how we happen to be in Korea and how this whole situation came about. And this is why, having branded the North Koreans as aggressors, we also had to brand the Chinese Communists as aggressors. Whether you are a big or a small nation, aggression must be called by the same name.

If the Russians had not been the ones responsible for the North Koreans' preparation, one might hope that the Chinese had suffered anxiety in seeing us so near their Manchurian border. But I am quite sure the Soviets know that we are a peace-loving people and the Chinese Communists know it, too. Had they listened to what we said—and believed us—they would know that we had no intention of invading China, that we are only anxious to see Korea a peaceful country with a government the people themselves have chosen.

That is our aim today and the aim of the UN. I hope it can be carried out.

~

Mrs. Roosevelt had an abiding admiration for FDR's liberal political philosophy and his ability to help people overcome their anxiety. Responding to the scourge of McCarthyism with its exaggerated allegations of Communist subversion, Eleanor Roosevelt frequently reminded her readers that American democracy was quite capable of defending itself—if only people would rise above their fears. To deliver the message, she borrowed rhetoric from her husband.

NEW YORK, FEBRUARY 16—The Lord meant us to pray when we are frightened and when we feel the need of help. None of us in ourselves can feel that we have the wisdom and courage to meet the happenings in our ordinary daily lives, much less to meet those in the troubled world of today. But there are many verses in the Bible that would remind us what strength there is in faith. And instead of encouraging fear, I would encourage our representatives to have faith in our great destiny which is now shaping up.

The leadership of the world is no easy undertaking and it will not be adequately met by fear. It must be met by strength and objectiveness. We ended World War II with great military strength backed by an enormous productive capacity. We made a very rapid transition to civilian production and stood the strain on our economy in an extraordinary way. We were too quick in throwing away controls; we were too quick in giving up our military strength. Therefore, now we are having to accept more sacrifice than we might otherwise have had to make.

To feel, however, that the people of the United States cannot understand the need, cannot accept the responsibility of leadership, cannot meet the sacrifices and also the goals of production and even the regimentation, if necessary, is to show little faith either in God or in ourselves.

I would not look for a Communist under every bed. I would believe that the vast majority of our people believe in their republican form of government and their democratic way of life. I will accept the fact that we have to improve and constantly try to give benefits to more people within our own nation, but I will not believe that the terror and poverty of Communism and their faith in materialism instead of in God can win in the struggle in which we are now engaged.

~

Eleanor Roosevelt was neither athletic (save for horseback riding) nor interested in big-league sports. But when a betting scandal in college basketball surfaced, Mrs. Roosevelt was quick to defend the importance of athletics in education. Her argument favoring the decommercialization of college sports fell on deaf ears.

HYDE PARK, FEBRUARY 22—None of us can help but be shocked to find that boys have been bribed to throw basketball games. But I feel that the men who did the bribing deserve the severer punishment because they were willing to make money out of young people to whom they were offering a very serious temptation.

Many boys who are working their way through a university have to work very hard. Many of them not only feel the pressure of meeting their own expenses, but sometimes things are happening at home which make it truly difficult not to have money to help out.

I can see the temptation that it might be to many a young person, though I must say some of these boys seem to be old enough to know better. I am rather glad that college games will now, in great part, be taken out of Madison Square Garden.

When you are in college, sports are a vital part of a man or woman's activity. They build health and they give young people good, strong bodies and the ability to use them skillfully.

In addition, we have always thought of sports as an aid to character-building. The old saying that many battles were won for Great Britain on the playing fields of Eton did not come about because of physical development alone, but because of the spirit of fair play, the teamwork, the ability to stick even in the face of defeat developed there. All these things are valuable assets to education. They go by the board, however, the minute there is cheating in a game just as an honor system is of no value if boys cheat in examinations.

Perhaps we have allowed our college sports to become too commercialized. Big gambling was possible on the results of these games and so the gambler tempted the players. Intramural sports are good, but I think it will be a pity if, because of the weakness of a few boys, we wipe out all intercollegiate sports.

I have never liked the practice of the alumni subsidizing good players and thus attracting athletes to college regardless of their mental attributes. But I do realize that the GI Bill of Rights has enabled many young people to go to college who might otherwise not have had the opportunity for an education. Therefore, I am very anxious that some way be devised by which boys who show ability in school shall have an opportunity to attend college regardless of their financial status.

We cannot afford to waste brains in this country. They are becoming more important to us every day. And surely financial position should not bar young people from the education which can give them positions of leadership in our nation in the future.

~

General Douglas MacArthur overstepped his bounds (according to President Truman) by issuing statements about U.S. foreign policy in the Far East. Within days the General's position—that we should expand the war in Korea to include military action directly against the Communists in mainland China—polarized the American political scene. Eleanor Roosevelt maintained that the military should fight and the Congress and the President should set foreign policy. Others lionized MacArthur, a World War II hero. Some believed MacArthur had his eyes on a Cabinet position in an anticipated Republican administration or even on a bid for the presidency.

Mrs. Roosevelt refocused the discussion on policy rather than personality issues: What should America be thinking about the intentions of the Communist Chinese?

NEW YORK, APRIL 9—I have a very great admiration for General MacArthur as a soldier and, from all I hear, he has been a good administrator in Japan who has made some wise and far-reaching reforms. I feel that this country owes him a debt of gratitude for the part he played in World War II, and I hope when he comes home he will be received with the honors due one of the great American generals of that war.

I cannot feel, however, that a commanding general in the field, particularly when he commands for a group of nations, should take it upon himself to announce the policy that in his opinion should be followed in the area of the world where he commands troops. I cannot speak for any other citizen of the United States, and I know there are Representatives in the House and in the Senate who are in complete sympathy with the things that have been said lately by General MacArthur—but, for myself, I am unhappy about them.

As a citizen, I have two great concerns at the present time; first, that the United States policy and the United States troops should continue to support the United Nations in an effort to show the world clearly that aggression by any nation is going to be withstood by the UN as a whole. Second, my concern is that we, as a nation, should do all we can to bring about a peaceful world. We will not help in that direction if any overt act, or anything said by responsible officials, is taken by Communist China as an excuse for charging that we are aiding and abetting aggression against the Communist Chinese government or against USSR-controlled territory in Asia.

Why should we, at this juncture, ally ourselves with any portion of the Chinese people? Whatever difficulties now exist in China must be settled by the Chinese people themselves. It may be they can settle their difficulties without further internal strife. Certainly that is a solution much to be desired. But that we should in any way support a government that could not remain in control of the Chinese people because it was unable to bring about a unified government or the reforms that would give the people hope of a better life in the future seems to me a mistake.

Again we seem to be lining up on the side of reaction simply because we cannot approve of Communism, which is on the opposite side. I think we would be justified in refusing to recognize the Communist Chinese government for some time. In any case, I would think we could not recognize them until they did represent all the Chinese people and had proved their ability to accept the requirements that go with becoming a member of the United Nations. If the Chinese people as a whole live under a Communist regime, I think that regime will either have to satisfy some of their needs or it will cease to be acceptable to the people. Chinese people are a patient people and heaven knows they have lived with civil war a long time. But, having made up their minds to get some reforms, they will be critical, I think, of any sham reforms and will be quick to resent anything which gives them reforms only in name and not in fact. To accept the suggestions made for our foreign policy by General MacArthur would seem to me to put us in a very equivocal and undesirable position.

～

Should the United States pass an Equal Rights Amendment to the Constitution to guarantee fair treatment of women? For a long time Eleanor Roosevelt opposed the idea of a constitutional amendment because in her opinion the biggest offenders were the states themselves, with discriminatory laws. By mid-1951, she had seen enough foot-dragging by the states and had learned enough in the UN Commission on the Status of Women to recognize that a constitutional amendment would probably be necessary.

To educate her grandchildren on women's rights, Mrs. Roosevelt playfully read to them from Rudyard Kipling.

BOSTON, JUNE 16—Kipling has gone out of fashion more or less, whereas when I was young it would have been almost impossible to find a child who did not know "The Jungle Book." It is a rare thing nowadays to find a child who does. But on the afternoons when I am home some of my grandchildren gather around at five o'clock in the afternoon and I read aloud. The other day we read "How Fear Come" from "The Jungle Book."

Some of my contemporaries will remember from that story of a few of the rules of the jungle, as taught by old Baloo, the brown bear. These particular rules apply to the wolves, but as I read I could not help thinking how well they applied to us all. For instance:

> *"As the creeper that girdles the tree-truck the law runneth*
> *forward and back,*
> *"For the strength of the Pack is the Wolf and the strength of the*
> *Wolf is the Pack."*

Isn't that a pretty good picture of why we should have a United Nations and why each nation in the UN should look to its own contribution? The success of the organization depends on what each member is and can contribute.

I could not help looking at my small fry with a smile as I read:

> *"Wash deeply from nose tip to tail tip; drink deeply, but never*
> *too deep."*

And then again:

> *"When Pack meets Pack in the jungle, and neither will go from*
> *the trail,*
> *"Lie down till the leaders have spoken—it may be fair words will*
> *prevail."*

So, even in the law of the jungle the value of conversation before action was recognized.

And here again is one of the human rights expressed as the law of the jungle:

> *"The lair of the Wolf is his refuge, and where he has made his*
> *home,*

"Not even the Head Wolf may enter, not even the Council may come."

So the right of privacy and the ownership of property was one of the laws of the jungle! Kipling even made it clear that in the jungle you could not be completely selfish. Here it is:

"If Ye plunder his Kill from a weaker, devour not all in thy pride;
"Pack-right is the right of the meanest; so leave him the head and the hide."

In other words, if you can get it, you can take the major part. But don't take everything or you may regret it later. And now for the last verse:

"Now these are the Laws of the jungle, and many and mighty are they;
"But the head and the hoof of the Law and the haunch and the bump is—Obey!"

~

Mrs. Roosevelt was in a playful mood again when her subject was, of all things, men's fashions. She had been mocked many times by fashion critics who said her own clothes left everything to be desired. Presumably, Eleanor Roosevelt would never venture into the fashion field as a social commentator. But not so. Clearly, it was time for men to shape up.

NEW YORK, JULY 13—After watching the red fezzes and costumes of the Shriners now in convention here, I have come to the conclusion that somewhere in the male make-up there is a desire to make their costumes a little more interesting and to allow them to express themselves better through their clothes.

I never have understood why every member of the male sex had to dress in the same way. I always liked to look at pictures from the era when our gentlemen wore breeches of beautiful materials and colors, long silk stockings and beautiful shoes with a variety of buckles. Coats and waistcoats rivaled any lady's finery and, if they so wished, men wore powdered wigs tied with gorgeous ribbons.

How they came to be so restrained later on I don't know, unless the difficulty of obtaining this finery in the early days of this country was too great. Perhaps the Quakers and some of the other religious sects had a quieting effect.

I'd like to see our gentlemen follow the rules of nature that govern our animal friends. Almost always the male animal is the showoff while the female remains demure and is less startlingly clad. Perhaps someday we will have the courage to strike a good medium and let the men have a little self-expression in their clothes.

~

There was no more articulate defender of the New Deal than Eleanor Roosevelt. Some historians argue that by the time the U.S. entered World War II, the American experiment with a mixed socialist and capitalist economy was over, but debate continues. Mrs. Roosevelt argued that the New Deal may have seemed radical at the time but in fact served conservative purposes. It calmed fears of an imminent workers' revolution and it put people back to work under circumstances similar to those before the 1929 stock market crash and the Depression, although supported now by a bigger role for government.

NEW YORK, OCTOBER 5—Occasionally I get a letter from someone who feels that in this country we have lost the old virtues of standing on our own feet, of realizing that we have to work for what we get, of being honest in our relations with one another.

This feeling often is attributed to the fact that under the stress of economic disaster people began to look to their government for aid because they themselves were unable to meet the desperate situations in which they found themselves.

Most of the people who write me seem to have forgotten that the businessmen who had striven to find answers to the economic problems up to 1932 had not succeeded in keeping down a wave of foreclosures on farms in the middle part of this country. Thus, many of our farmers were made completely desperate. Factories were closing everywhere, railroads were hardly receiving freight enough to run a full train at any time during the 24 hours, and the economic wheels of our country were practically at a standstill. So much so that many a man who always had operated honestly and expected to ask nobody's help found himself offering his business to his government.

The "dangerous and socialist" schemes that came into being at this time were designed primarily to try to prevent such conditions from ever recurring. The people whose farms were saved, the people who did not lose their homes, the people who found work on government projects until the factories could begin to open again—all these people were not made dependent. They were simply kept from revolution against our government.

When you stand in line in the street for a cup of coffee, you rarely feel that your government is a successful one. I would like those who feel that the people of the United States have been rendered soft and dishonest by the things the government has done for them to remember that there were a good many parts of this country in 1933 where a revolution could have been engineered by almost any enterprising person. And that condition was brought about by the conservative, orthodox business methods that prevailed under the experienced men of business under President Herbert Hoover and his very able Cabinet.

These very people who complain to me that under the almost 16 years in which this country was under the administration of the Democratic Party and who believe that this fact is responsible for all the shortcomings that they now see in various parts of the country are putting the cart before the horse. The Republicans, perhaps because of circumstances beyond their control, but still while they were in office, brought this country to a condition where only drastic measures could keep us from complete disaster. These measures were applied in cooperation with the people of the country, who worked hard to make them succeed.

I cannot believe that the people of this country, by and large, are less honest today or have less independence and moral fiber than they had in the days gone by. We hear today of every shortcoming in public office, in business, or among our youth. Perhaps in the old days these things would not have been so easily discovered or so quickly exposed, but I am glad that we expose them and that they inspire us to work harder as citizens to make an even better record in the future. We have shown that we are no weaklings; we have tried to devise ways of preventing a recurrence of conditions that existed up to 1932.

～

What of the spiritual Eleanor Roosevelt? She was loyal to the Episcopal church in Hyde Park, where generations of Roosevelts had worshipped. She believed deeply in the power of prayer, and during the Depression and the war, Mrs. Roosevelt encouraged her readers to pray for their leaders and for those in great need.

In 1951 she was invited to a spirituality conference in Brussels where European religious leaders, intellectuals, and artists explored how an individual's spiritual development could affect, for better or worse, his or her social action. It is a short step from this question to Mrs. Roosevelt's own longtime belief—that peace in the world begins with peace in the individual's heart. Though steadfastly Christian, she also recognized that other religions may lead in the same positive direction.

PARIS, NOVEMBER 22—I think I should say that the membership of the group [the spiritual conference in Brussels] was highly intellectual. It was composed of university professors, teachers, ministers of many faiths, philosophers and representatives of such religious groups as Bahai.

I think Europe is a more fertile ground than the United States for this type of intellectual and spiritual research. The organizers of this group, I think, feel that the intellectual approach is not a good one; that it must be a purely spiritual approach on the part of the individual. But there were certainly a great many people at these meetings who could not divest themselves of their intellectual capacities.

The one thing that I would fear is that people who become enthusiasts are apt to see in everything that happens to them a corroboration of the things which they wish to believe. To be sure, therefore, that you are not imagining something because you wish it to be true is very difficult.

For instance, if I desire guidance in a difficult decision, and I have done everything possible to prepare myself to receive guidance, might it not be possible that subconsciously I would accept what was my own desire rather than any direct communication from God? Take another instance: If someone were not completely honest, or even if they fooled themselves because they had a desire to do something or not to do it, they could hide behind a feeling of guidance which really was only an expression of their own desire.

Again it seems to me that there is the chance that we were given our intelligence and our gifts as a part of God's plan, and it might well be that each and every one of us should develop our faculties to the best of our ability, that we should seek information from others. In fact, we should explore all avenues that would help us to meet our own problems.

This is not saying that we would feel able to decide without God's help. But the deep religious feeling of many people will not, of necessity, mean that on each action that they take they feel direct guidance from God. Rather, it may mean that what they have learned and the effort they have made to live, if they are Christians, according to Christ's teachings, will have so molded their characters that unconsciously they will do the Lord's will. These people may need contact with their churches and they may not have exactly the type of guidance that the organizers of this movement feel is essential.

I think I believe that the Lord looks upon His children with compassion and allows them to approach Him in many ways. I am glad to have had the opportunity of association with the group at Brussels—it was a rare privilege—and it is a wonderful thing in these times to feel that people are devoting themselves to the growth of spiritual strength and capacity. But I do not think that anyone can feel that there is only one way, since what may meet someone's needs may not of necessity meet another's needs. And one must even beware of too much certainty that the answers to life's problems can only be found in one way and that all must agree to search for light in the same way and cannot find it in any other way.

1952

*N*ot many years so truly represent the end of an era as does 1952. There were changes in Eleanor Roosevelt's life this year which made it seem to her a clear turning point as well. When in January Dwight David Eisenhower announced that he would accept a draft to run for President on the Republican ticket, it was the beginning of the end of a twenty-year period of continuous Democratic dominance of the White House. The country was ready for a change, generally in a more conservative direction. "Ike," as Eisenhower was called, would fill the bill. Mrs. Roosevelt, as a lifelong liberal, naturally supported the Democratic candidate, Adlai Stevenson; however, even she had such deep respect for General Eisenhower that she made no dire pronouncements about the fate of the country should he become the next President.

But Harry Truman had twelve months of chief executive work still to go. In January he reached an accord with the once-again prime minister of Great Britain, Winston Churchill, in which the United States promised never to initiate an atomic bomb attack on Europe without British consent. Late in the month, the Korean truce talks stalled.

Always on the go, Mrs. Roosevelt began 1952 in Paris, where the UN convened. In the early spring she traveled eastward on her first round-the-world journey, making stops in India, Nepal, and other countries over a three-week period. By late April she was back in New York to take up her UN work once again.

McCarthyism headed into its heyday. Eleanor Roosevelt's reactions to what she saw as the scourge of McCarthyism grew stronger and more hostile as she condemned the Red-baiting and character assassination techniques of Senator McCarthy and his congressional colleagues on the House Un-American Activities Committee. The Supreme Court ruled in March that people termed subversive could be barred from teaching in the public schools; by October New York City had begun a purge in which eight teachers, alleged Communists, were dismissed. Also in March Senator William Benton of Connecticut tried to discredit Senator Joseph McCarthy's earlier attacks on the credibility and patriotism of the Foreign Relations Committee and the Pentagon by claiming that McCarthy had used Hitlerite scare tactics. McCarthy countered with a suit (for slander, libel, and conspiracy) against Benton. Benton hit back with a move to have McCarthy expelled from the Senate. Who won? Neither Benton nor the nation: In November a pro-McCarthy challenger defeated Benton, while McCarthy was reelected. Anti-Communist foreign-policy hard-liners were pleased when George Kennan, architect of the containment policy, became ambassador to the Soviet Union.

Mrs. Roosevelt made one more important trip in 1952, at the request of outgoing President Truman. Chile was to inaugurate a new president of its own, and the esteemed former First Lady carried Truman's and the nation's good wishes to Santiago as unofficial U.S. ambassador.

With a popular general about to assume the presidency, the year ended on a military note. In November the United States successfully tested the first hydrogen bomb, blowing up a tiny atoll in the Marshall Islands. John Foster Dulles, whose foreign-policy ideas fueled the arms race for years to come, was selected as the next secretary of state. In an attempt to break the stalemated Korean peace talks, President-elect Eisenhower, long familiar with Army life on the front lines, went to Korea but did not bring home the hoped-for peace.

Even the literary world seemed hooked on the military theme in 1952: The Pulitzer Prize went to Herman Wouk's *The Caine Mutiny*, a gripping novel about the paranoid lunacy of a naval commander drunk on his own power, obsessed with a rigid battle plan. In "My Day" Eleanor Roosevelt reminded Americans that McCarthyism represented just such a madness in its insistent search, often in entirely wrong places, for alleged subversives who usually turned out to be innocent.

Early in 1952 Mrs. Roosevelt returned to Paris, continuing her UN work, and from there wrote an idealistic column about converting the American economy (and others) to full-time peacetime production. World War II had forced a complete military mobilization of all U.S. resources, effectively putting the country back to full employment. But was entering the war the only way out of the Depression?

PARIS, JANUARY 4—Occasionally over here somebody says to me: "What will happen if peace comes? We are all geared from the economic stand-point for a war economy. It would mean economic collapse."

Many of us who have a habit of looking backward as well as forward re-member people who came home after traveling in Germany before World War II. They would tell with great admiration of the fact that there was no unemployment in Germany, that everyone was working, that conditions, on the whole, were very good. But these conditions were brought about almost entirely by Hitler's preparation for war.

Now, many people in Europe feel a certain analogy between prewar Germany and the United States of today and wonder if, rather than face an economic collapse, certain people in our nation would not rather have war.

Of course, this is utterly ridiculous and unnecessary. Those of us who know the needs of the underdeveloped areas of the world today are con-scious of the fact that there is a need for production that will go on for many, many years. When it is possible, the production for defense can be quickly changed to production for peacetime usages.

This cannot happen, however, unless there is a blueprint and unless a decision is taken now as to the steps that will be followed when we reach the point where we feel we can face the Soviet Union on an even basis.

That day we should be ready to enter into worldwide development, which probably could be started now but probably cannot get into full swing until less money has to be devoted to defense preparation.

We should know how and what we will produce, where we will place it, what we will get in return for it and how we are going to develop a per-manent peacetime economy, moving according to priority from one sec-tion of the world to another until we have a well-balanced international economy.

This requires thinking and planning on a world scale. I am sure that it should be done within the United Nations or, in any case, in close cooper-ation with the UN. A well-thought-out plan needs us to increase the heights of freedom and higher standards of living, but only if we have the imagination and the brains of the people who have built great enterprises in their own sections of the world, proving their ability to achieve greater benefits for the whole world.

Only the unimaginative could ever ask the question: "Do we have to have an economic collapse if our defense preparation comes to an end?"

We should face a peaceful world not only without fear but with great joy at the realization that the creative powers of many people can be let loose for good instead of being directed toward developing the type of goods that are essential for defense but which bring no return on the economic level. When these goods for defense are used in war they are destroyed and a chain of destruction is started, instead of a chain of constructive development such as peacetime activity can produce.

⁓

Mrs. Roosevelt knew about high levels of citizen participation in voting and campaigning in remote, undeveloped, illiterate India, which she would soon visit. Americans, to Eleanor Roosevelt's consternation, were more casual about civic responsibilities. This column is a not too subtle reminder to her fellow Americans: If you value democracy, exercise your right to vote.

PARIS, FEBRUARY 6—I was particularly interested in a story here reporting the voting of certain wild tribes in India. I had been wondering, as perhaps so many people in the United States might have, why it should take so long to go through this process in India. This story cleared this up, describing how many of the Indian tribes from deep in the jungle had marched miles to reach the polling booths and how others had left the worship of their Babylonian gods in order to travel long distances to worship the god of "vote."

We cannot get out more than 51 percent of our vote at home, if I recall the statistics correctly, and yet whole tribes in India can trek through jungle and over desert with drums and flutes, leading processions to cast their ballots. Think what this must mean for the campaigners!

We think it is quite a task to cover a state by car and make speeches to our constituents. How would we feel about making our way through tiger-infested jungles to make stump speeches and later to vote!

Perhaps someday it will be the Indian people who will be teaching the rest of us how to use our precious secret ballot, which we are inclined to take so much for granted and even to neglect.

⁓

En route around the world, stopping in more than a dozen nations and often acting as an unofficial UN-U.S. ambassador, Eleanor Roosevelt turned travel writer. For three weeks "My Day" reported exotic sights, sounds, and smells. In far-off lands it was often working-class people whose dignity impressed Mrs. Roosevelt most. She took pleasure, too, in spreading American culture, albeit with a twist.

New Delhi, March 1—Many of the people of this area are refugees; many of them are just poor people; but some of them are leading a life they would not change. For instance, we saw one of the hill tribesmen who had spent the winter down in this warmer area and was on his homeward trek. He had probably lived on the sand in one of those odd little round huts they build with bent bamboo ribs and which open out like a folding basket to hold up the outside. The front is open and the family cooking goes on the outside. The inhabitants need only mats to lie on at night and their animals are herded around.

For transportation everything is loaded on donkeys, and the other travelers we saw who were on their way back to the hills were trudging single file over the roads that led there.

The faces of the people are extraordinary and their carriage is regal in its dignity for both the men and women, the women carrying large burdens on their heads.

We returned in time for a reception given at the Ladies Club in Lahore. Then I spoke to a group of students at Lahore University and later attended a large women's dinner at which some of the younger women did folk dances for me. And in a very few minutes I taught them the Virginia reel, dancing it to their own Pakistani music.

~

A devoted Hyde Park family worker died after fifty-five uninterrupted years of service on the estate. Mrs. Roosevelt went home to pay her respects, and she eulogizes him in "My Day." Such a loyal employee had become "family."

There was a funeral of another sort this spring at Hyde Park: Often written about in "My Day," the Roosevelt family dog, Fala, died of old age. Mrs. Roosevelt buried him near FDR in the Rose Garden. Her son Elliott said later, "She had not wept at Father's burial, but the tears came this day. I had never seen her openly give way to grief before. . . . In lamenting the end of the scottie, Mother wept for his master."

New York, April 18—Instead of going to the Human Rights Commission meeting on Wednesday morning, where the work up to now has been moving slowly, I took the train to Hyde Park to attend the funeral of Mr. William Plog, who had worked for my mother-in-law and then for my husband as superintendent of the Hyde Park place. Mr. Plog stayed on when we turned the place over to the government and continued to do the flowers in the house, just as he had always done them for my mother-in-law, and to superintend the gardens, particularly the rose gardens which he had always loved.

It is rare that someone works in one job for nearly 55 years. Mr. Plog was 30 years old when he came and 84 when he died. He was a faithful and loyal employee. He had seen my husband grow up from a young boy and he was always fond of him. I was glad that I could be at the funeral and that my cousin, Mrs. Theodore Douglas Robinson, was at home and able also to go to the funeral.

Fifty-five years is a long time to be associated with anybody as closely as one is with those who live on the same place. Mr. Plog will be missed very much because he was active almost right to the end. At 84 it probably is fortunate, though, when one has to die, to do so without suffering or too long an illness. The men who worked with him were devoted to him, for he was a good and kind person. It will seem very strange to me to go over to the old place and not see his familiar face and hear his warm and friendly greeting.

〜

America Firsters—isolationists between the two World Wars—believed that no matter what our European cultural ties, we had no responsibility to defend Europe against totalitarianism. To Mrs. Roosevelt this was a morally reprehensible position. Equally unacceptable was to impugn the patriotism of the American war hero General Eisenhower. Insinuations of Communist sympathies were rife amidst McCarthyism's paranoia; they made Eleanor Roosevelt wince in embarrassment for her country.

NEW YORK, APRIL 19—I wonder if many of my readers noticed that an organization that seems to stem somewhat from the old America Firster group was formed the other day to prove that General Dwight D. Eisenhower is closely associated with Communists. This type of thing is becoming so ludicrous that each time it happens we should point it out and say to ourselves: "How stupid can we be? Is hysterical fear turning us all into morons?"

〜

The UN Commission on Human Rights brought Eleanor Roosevelt face-to-face with Third World delegates whose countries were starving for cash to invest in their feeble, primitive economies. Though she may sound here simplistic about the pressure for guaranteed capital support, Mrs. Roosevelt articulated well the fact that for Third World investment to work effectively, it must be advantageous to both giver and receiver. Here, also, we glimpse the inner workings of the UN commission Eleanor Roosevelt chaired with what most observers considered remarkable aplomb.

New York, April 24—The sins of the past are rising up to make life difficult for us today in many ways! In the Human Rights Commission last Monday one of the most evident examples came to light. The delegate from Chile presented an article to be attached to an article already passed in general terms on the right of self-determination. This article stated that the right of people to self-determination included the economic right to control all of their natural resources and not to be deprived of their use or their means of existence by the action of any outside power.

The article was loosely drawn and could be interpreted in many ways. Therefore, as it was for inclusion in a legal document, the United States was opposed to it. I recognized at once, however, the reason why this article received such immediate consideration from all the underdeveloped countries sitting around the table. All those who have to borrow capital were in favor of it.

The reason came out in private conversations. One after the other told me how contracts had been made and natural resources granted for development, and then either they were left undeveloped or developed for a short time and closed down to meet some world situation and keep the price of some article at the desired level.

People would be thrown out of work under these circumstances; royalties would not be paid to the government, which would result in higher taxes for the people.

I pointed out that all these abuses could be remedied by better contracts; that the difficulty they had labored under was unfair and unsafe contracts, but that an article phrased in the way they were proposing would result in no capital being available for development. No nation is going to risk its taxpayers' money outside its own country if there is no regard for contractual agreements, and no group of private individuals is going to feel that they can risk their money or their clients' money without proper safeguards.

One recognizes the evils that underdeveloped nations were trying to correct, but one also fears that they are cutting off their sources of future supply for development.

For those of us who take a serious view of the obligations imposed by a covenant drawn in treaty form, such articles as this create great obstacles. It may be possible to make reservations, but what amounts practically to confiscation of property of foreigners without compensation being legalized by a treaty is going to be extremely difficult for a great many nations to accept.

~

Mary McLeod Bethune was a black Southern educator who founded a col-
lege for black women in 1904, served as the college's president for twenty
years, and became an important member of FDR's New Deal team, direct-
ing the Division of Negro Affairs in the National Youth Administration
from 1936 to 1944. The mere idea of alleging that Mary Bethune was a
Communist sympathizer convinced Mrs. Roosevelt that Senator McCarthy,
if not the whole country, was going mad.

NEW YORK, MAY 3—A few days ago I read a newspaper account here that
shocked me. A group of people, evidently without much knowledge, had
so frightened a school organization in Englewood, N.J., that the school re-
scinded an invitation to speak which it had extended to Mrs. Mary
McLeod Bethune.

It seemed to me so preposterous that I waited day by day to see if they
had reconsidered, apologized and invited her again to come. But I have
seen nothing further, and I cannot let this incident go by without protesting such treatment of an elderly woman who is a leader among the American colored citizens and loved and admired by all American citizens who
know her.

Mrs. Bethune is probably a little older than I am. She really worked for
her education, and when she had obtained it, literally on a shoestring, she
founded a college in Florida to help Negro people. Hundreds of people
have helped her because one could not meet her and not recognize her
sincerity, her deep and simple Christianity. She has built up this university.

She has headed and worked for the Negro Council of Women, and made
it into a strong organization. She has the gift of getting people to cooperate with her. She is the kindest, gentlest person I have ever met.

She lent her talents to the federal service in the National Youth Administration during my husband's administration, and there are countless
other positions and responsibilities that she has taken and filled with
honor both for her country, for organizations and for individuals. She is
the last person that I can imagine any thinking person would believe to be
a Communist.

This is again that pernicious thing that we are allowing to bedevil us:
guilt by association.

She is accused, I believe, of having gone to Communist-front organizations to speak, even of having belonged to some of these subversive groups.

If she did belong to any, I am sure with her keen mind she soon discovered something wrong and was not a member for long. If she went to

them to speak, she undoubtedly did them good. Mary McLeod Bethune would meet the devil and confront him with Christ and I would feel quite sure that she and Christ would triumph.

If it were not so sad to have respected and beloved American citizens insulted and slighted, it would be funny. But those of us who have loved and known Mrs. Bethune for many years must speak up in her defense. If we do not, then this country of ours is in danger of curtailing the liberties for which our forefathers fought.

I still believe that people should be considered innocent until they are proved guilty under the law. I still think that a life of work and service should carry some weight against the idle accusations of a group of extremists.

I know the danger of Communists in this country, and I know the subversives can do us harm. But it does us much more harm to tear down the fabric of justice and fairness and trust in our fellow human beings who have a life record to disprove an idle accusation.

Let us hope that this possibility, having been drawn to our attention in this little magazine, will never actually come to pass in America. There are moments when I listen to Senator McCarthy and hear about an un-American activities committee when I wonder where our freedoms are going and hope that the academic tradition, which is perhaps one of the strongest in this country, will save us from the kind of complete conformity which kills originality and truth.

~

We may take for granted cultural institutions like Lincoln Center in New York City or the Kennedy Center in Washington, D.C., but they required grand efforts to create. Mrs. Roosevelt was in on the ground floor in the campaign for a national cultural center in Washington.

NEW YORK, JUNE 6—There is a bill before Congress to build in Washington, as a national war memorial, a great cultural center, to include a theater and an opera house, as well as the Smithsonian Gallery of Art, which had been authorized by a 1938 act, but for which public funds were never appropriated.

Our national capital could become a very great cultural center and its influence could be felt in every other great city of the United States if we did something of this kind. We have in Washington representatives from all the countries of the world.

We could have there a center that would encourage modern art in all its branches. We might develop a place where young artists could feel they would receive a sympathetic and understanding opportunity. To do something of this kind would prove to the older nations of the world, which are now turning to us for economic and military leadership, that we have come of age and also have much to offer in the way of leadership in the cultural field.

~

Truman declared he would not run for President in 1952. The field for Democratic nominees was open for the first time since 1932 when FDR drove Republican Herbert Hoover from office. As chairman of the UN Commission on Human Rights, Mrs. Roosevelt remained uncharacteristically disengaged from the hurly-burly of American domestic politics.

Within her family, political enthusiasms were sharply divided. Son Franklin Jr. campaigned for Governor Averill Harriman of New York; son James supported Senator Estes Kefauver of Tennessee; Eleanor liked Governor Adlai Stevenson of Illinois. At least these were Democrats. Son Elliott, privately, and son John, publicly, favored Eisenhower, the Republican. So, Mrs. Roosevelt welcomed an excuse to keep hands off.

Yet "My Day" may have damned Stevenson with faint praise. She respected his intelligence and platform but believed he lacked sufficient charisma to govern. Labeled an egghead by opponents and even by the liberal press, Stevenson stood aloof from the people. Eleanor Roosevelt's model President was FDR—also a well-educated man—but with a joie de vivre that charmed and reassured. Eisenhower overwhelmed Stevenson in November, and the Democrats were gone from the White House after a long, uninterrupted reign.

HYDE PARK, SEPTEMBER 13—As the two presidential candidates tour the country I really wonder whether we can count on people as a whole listening to or reading in full their speeches. If they do, they cannot fail to be impressed, I think, by the fact that there are more real issues being discussed in Stevenson's speeches than in General Eisenhower's.

This is probably because Governor Stevenson is more personally familiar with the domestic questions in the country, having been governor of Illinois and being in active politics for some time and with a family background that would have led him to the study of day-by-day political situations.

They might feel, however, as I do, that occasionally the Governor is a little academic. Please remember, Mr. Governor, we are usually sitting down after a long day's work to listen to you in our living rooms. We want to feel that you are visiting us, that you have something which you want us to know about in order that we may help you. We don't want to be talked down to; we just want you to tell us very simply what your problems are and what you face in the great task you are asking us to help you meet by voting for you in November.

~

"My Day" columns were used many times to expose particularly virulent racism that Mrs. Roosevelt believed must be addressed legally and morally. Here she asks Caucasian readers to imagine how they would feel if while traveling abroad they were denied medical help because of their race. Anyone who took the point to heart would immediately see the absurdity, Mrs. Roosevelt hoped, of denying medical assistance to black people in America—simply because they were black.

NEW YORK, OCTOBER 17—I have just received from the Southern Conference Educational Fund, Inc., a most interesting pamphlet entitled "The Untouchables." It deals with the question of segregation in hospitals and the difficult situations that arise when hospitals do not accept all sick people but put limitations on their service.

The Southern Conference Educational Fund is a Southwide, nonprofit organization with headquarters in New Orleans. The little prospectus sent out with the pamphlet states that "it is dedicated to the fight against racial segregation and discrimination in all fields of social endeavor."

Through pamphlets and publications, conferences and opinion polls, the SCEF seeks to achieve a more equitable sharing of our democratic heritage. Its funds come from voluntary contributions from some 3,000 individuals throughout the country. "The Untouchables" is one of its pamphlets. Ben Shahn has contributed the illustrations and layout as a gesture of his concern with the great social problems the pamphlet discusses. The text was written by a native Southerner and a former New Orleans newspaperman, Alfred Maund.

No one could look through this pamphlet without being deeply troubled that such things as it describes should happen anywhere in the United States. Some of the instances it mentions go back many years, but also detailed are some occurrences of recent years that seem fairly shocking.

For instance, on "August 27, 1950, three victims of an auto accident were denied beds in Breckinridge County Hospital, Hardinsburg, Kentucky, because the establishment had no facilities for colored people." They were left lying on the floor of the emergency room for three hours, their wounds were untended, and the only medication given them was morphine. One of the men died on the floor, and, ironically, his family later received a bill for "services rendered." The others were removed to Louisville General Hospital, where they eventually recovered. One sustained partial permanent paralysis as a result of a broken back.

Also, in February, an 18-year-old boy suffering from sugar diabetes died after being refused admission to the Akron, Ohio, City Hospital.

These two stories would make sorry reading for any American finding himself in the Near East or Asia. Suppose we white people were taken ill in those areas of the world and this type of segregation were practiced against us. Yet, that would be the normal and natural thing to do, according to some standards, because we would be in the minority, since two-thirds of the world's people are colored.

The picture is changing, however, in the South. As of last February, the Kentucky state senate passed by unanimous vote a bill forbidding all licensed medical institutions to deny care to any person on the basis of color or creed. In at least six cities similar citizen's movements combating Jim Crow medical care are under way.

It is such organizations as the Southern Conference Educational Fund that will really bring about the changes all of us hope for—not only in the South but throughout our country. Then we can say with truth and conviction that we move forward to ever better conditions for all of our people.

1953–1962

First Lady of the World

1953

$\mathcal{T}$he transfer of power in 1953 from one administration to another in the White House was a sea change of ideology. After decades of Democratic hegemony, at last the Republicans moved back into 1600 Pennsylvania Avenue. Though Eleanor Roosevelt hoped to stay on as a UN delegate under the new Eisenhower administration, she quickly saw that such was not to be. The year began with her resignation from the post that had established her professional diplomatic credentials around the world. Almost immediately she began to work for the American Association for the United Nations, becoming busier than ever during the year that in October saw her sixty-ninth birthday.

In his final State of the Union address, President Truman warned of the increasing dangers of atomic war, while worry grew in many quarters of American life about Communist attack or influence. The day after Dwight Eisenhower was inaugurated in late January, a federal jury in New York convicted thirteen Communists on charges of conspiracy to overthrow the U.S. government. The political atmosphere was ripe for McCarthyism.

In February, Senator Joseph McCarthy, a Republican of Wisconsin, alleged that Eisenhower's foreign policy was sabotaged by the Voice of America radio network. McCarthy made outlandish, unsubstantiated claims, often about individuals, insinuating that Communist subversion was rampant. In November, responding to the pervasive Red Scare, President Eisenhower decried McCarthy's tactics and defended Americans' right to confront their accusers face-to-face, something McCarthy never seemed willing to do. The next day the Senator declared sweepingly that the entire Truman administration had been "crawling with Communists."

McCarthy's influence and that of the House Un-American Activities Committee were spreading, despite the apparent illogic of their allegations. In June Julius and Ethel Rosenberg were put to death for espionage related to communism, the first American civilians to be executed for treason. The General Electric Company and other major businesses declared that as a matter of policy all Communist employees would be fired. Mrs. Roosevelt joined President Eisenhower and many other more sensible Americans in questioning McCarthy's and HUAC's good sense and intentions.

The Republicans did not favor wage and price controls as had the Democrats. Beginning in February, the bureaucracy and executive orders controlling everything from the price of eggs to automobile tires, as well as workingmen's wages, were dismantled. Laissez-faire Republicanism took hold in Washington again after an absence of many years. Eleanor Roosevelt, long a supporter of moderate price and wage controls, was skeptical about the changes but saw no chance of stemming the Republican tide or the pent-up demand for a freer market among workers and consumers.

The country suffered three tornado disasters in 1953 (during May and June, in Texas, Ohio, and Massachusetts), killing 349 people. In March the United States protested the Soviet's firing on an American bomber in international airspace. At the end of July a U.S. B–50 bomber was shot down off Vladivostok, Siberia, by Soviet forces, adding fuel to anti-Communist fires.

While Mrs. Roosevelt enjoyed a prolonged Far Eastern trip (late May to early August), a Korean armistice was finally signed at Panmunjon. In the fall, over much protest from the liberal establishment, including Eleanor Roosevelt, the administration struck a deal with Spanish dictator Francisco Franco, promising to provide military and economic aid in exchange for the right to build air and naval bases in Spain—a strategy to augment U.S. influence in the Mediterranean and North Africa.

One of Mrs. Roosevelt's great heroes in public service, former Secretary of State George C. Marshall, architect of the Marshall Plan for postwar European recovery, won the 1953 Nobel Peace Prize.

Briefly, after Eisenhower was elected but before Truman left office, Mrs. Roosevelt believed she could continue her role as UN delegate. Democratic political friends told her bluntly that her time was up. No invitation to stay on had come from Eisenhower. There were rumors that FBI Director J. Edgar Hoover wanted her out. The change in Eleanor Roosevelt's life by no means meant she slowed down. Enlivening her appearance (new hair styles, brighter clothes), she launched into volunteer work for the UN and renewed her discreet romance of the heart with Dr. David Gurewitsch.

HYDE PARK, JANUARY 5—On New Year's Day many of my close neighbors came to call on me at home in the afternoon, and I was asked quite frequently whether I would now be staying here more of the time. Suddenly I realized that I would probably be here less.

As my readers doubtless know, all Democrats who have been presidential appointees either to the U.S. delegations to the UN General Assembly or to any of the UN councils or commissions are expected, with the change of administration, to send in their resignations. It is, of course, only fair that a new president should have an opportunity to appoint people of his own choice to represent him in these positions. For this reason I have sent to the State Department, for presentation at the proper time, my resignation as a delegate to the present General Assembly, which has only adjourned and will reconvene in February.

Having resigned both from the General Assembly delegation and the Human Rights Commission, and not having lost any of my interest in the United Nations, I tried to think of the most useful thing I could do. It seems to me that the most essential thing is to strengthen the American Association for the United Nations in this country. This, of course, can only be done by finding ways to enlarge our existing chapters, to increase the number of chapters throughout the nation, and to make all of them centers from which information flows to every other organization in the community. In that way, knowledge of all UN activities will not only be available, but practically thrust upon the attention of every American citizen. Therefore I am going to start work on Monday morning as a volunteer under Mr. Clark Eichelberger, and I hope that I can be of use to him and to the United Nations.

~

Eleanor Roosevelt had a fine sense of humor about family lineage. Keeping track of the Roosevelts, whose American forebears went back to the early Dutch settlement of the Hudson Valley, required, as she said, deep concentration. The Roosevelt grandchildren referred to here are from Mrs. Roosevelt's fifth son, John: Haven Clark Roosevelt, born in 1940; Anne Sturgis Roosevelt (Nina), born in 1942.

NEW YORK, JANUARY 13—Because of the miserable weather over the weekend we all decided not to go to the country, so I took my two grandchildren, Haven and Nina, to Roosevelt Memorial House at 28 East 20th

Street. Mrs. Joseph Lash brought her son Jonathan to meet us and we went through the house, beginning with the nursery on the second floor.

I had had the great privilege many years ago of going through that house, which was the birthplace of my uncle, Theodore Roosevelt. At that time I was with my aunt, Mrs. Douglas Robinson. So, on last Saturday I tried to remember all the stories she used to tell us.

There is the story of his saying his prayers, as a little boy, to his mother's half-sister. This half-sister later became Mrs. James K. Gracie, a great-aunt whom we all adored as children. She must have really suffered in those early days when she and her mother were sheltered in their Northern son-in-law's house when all of their interests were wrapped up in the South. The story of the prayer was that little Theodore prayed for the success of the Northern army and his aunt was beside herself in tears. His mother heard him from the corridor and came in to reprove him for being so thoughtless and unkind. His answer silenced her, for he said: "But, mother, I thought I could tell the truth to God."

Down on the second floor the middle room has the old horsehair furniture of that day and I could remember Auntie Corinne telling us how much as children the horsehair scratched their legs and how they squirmed and were reproved by their father. She even remembered the Bible verses she had first read aloud as a child in that room.

We went through the museum side of the house also, and the children were interested to see some things similar to what I have and which they had seen at home. For instance, there are some samples of the pink-and-white china that belonged to my grandmother Roosevelt, who was their great-great-grandmother.

It is a little confusing to them, however, to follow the family lineage that leads back to Theodore Roosevelt, Sr. on my father's side and on my husband's side to Isaac Roosevelt. There is one less generation on his side and that is also confusing, and to work out that their grandfather, Franklin D. Roosevelt, and I were fifth cousins once removed is a real problem in higher mathematics.

～

Having visited India and seen firsthand what had been accomplished under the guidance and inspiration of Mohandas Gandhi, before and after his assassination in 1948, Mrs. Roosevelt was deeply moved. Her own Christian spirituality was in fact ecumenical. She saw wisdom in other traditions and tried to bring it into her own. Perhaps it was Mrs. Roosevelt's conviction that even the most intractable of political problems begins to dissolve when people open their hearts to one another that most attracted her to Gandhi's philosophy.

WASHINGTON, JANUARY 27—"I prophesy that if we disobey the law of the final supremacy of spirit over matter, of liberty and love over brute force, in a few years' time we shall have Bolshevism in this land which was once so holy."

What Gandhi said about India is something for every one of us to ponder. Most of us are constantly concerned about material things and yet the people whom we like best to have with us and who make the best impression on those with whom they come in contact are the people who rarely give much thought to material things. Their minds dwell on the deeper questions of life.

Mahatma Gandhi often urged that we "turn the searchlight inward." By this, of course, he meant that we must understand our own weaknesses, our own faults, before we can conquer them. All these teachings of Gandhi are applicable to our modern way of life just as they were in the kind of life he was urging on his people. His inspirational leadership finally won freedom for his people—and it was achieved without war.

I do not know that Gandhi's plans for living could be applied to modern life, but there is no doubt in my mind that the more we simplify our material needs the more we are free to think of other things. Perhaps what we all need to do is to sit down and think through how this could be accomplished without the loss of gracious living.

I used to think that, of necessity, comfort and beauty cost a great deal of money. I have learned that that is not true. But I still think we encumber our lives with too much, and that perhaps that is the part of Gandhi's teaching that should remain with us today.

No one who has been in India and seen some of the things that he established and felt the impact that his presence has left on material things—such as the feeling one gets when one enters the very simple room he occupied so frequently at the boys' school for Untouchables—can doubt the power of the spirit. Gandhi used to sell his autographs in order to keep this school going.

Some of the things the boys are trained to do, such as spinning and weaving, seemed to me less necessary now that India is free and they do not have to prove that they can live independently of any goods brought from outside. But the spirit is as valid as it ever was.

I think that here in our country it would be well for us to give more time to studying how we must preserve our freedoms and our liberties and, above all, how we must preserve our belief in one another.

~

Nobody likes to see a house they have built torn down. Eleanor Roosevelt had to swallow a bitter pill when the Republican administration, heavily

*influenced (some said intimidated) by Senators Joseph McCarthy and John
Bricker (of Ohio), refused to subscribe to the UN Declaration of Human
Rights. The administration argued that U.S. foreign policy might be hampered by restrictions about dealing with countries not in agreement with
the legally binding promises on human rights.*

*Mrs. Roosevelt considered the UN Declaration of Human Rights one of its
(and one of her own) most important accomplishments. She gave seven
years to the project as chairman of the Human Rights Committee. Even if
she had not been the U.S. delegate, her moral principles and foreign policy
savvy would have led her to the same embittered critique of the Eisen-
hower-Dulles-Republican position.*

NEW YORK, APRIL 9—I was not really surprised when I read in the newspapers yesterday about Secretary of State Dulles' testimony on the subject
of executive agreements and treaties. I had heard rumors that this abandonment of the human rights covenants was to be the position of the
State Department and the administration, but it was hard to believe that
it would be done in quite the way it has been done.

It is quite evident, as the Secretary of State said, that executive agreements are necessary for the safeguarding of the country in certain situations and to prevent them or insist that they be accomplished only in cooperation with the Senate would be endangering the working of our
foreign relations.

To say, however, that it is improper to have a treaty that is going to
change the social customs of a country and its legal practices as regards
the protection of its individual citizens and their civil liberties seems to
me an utterly strange position to take. I wonder if all of the Republicans
will agree with this stand on the human rights covenants.

I am very happy to say that the present administration did not carry on
the bipartisan policy followed by the Democratic administrations in the
immediate past by which many Republicans were given opportunities for
service, and gained experience. Had the present administration carried
on this bipartisan policy, I might have been asked to finish out my last
year on the Human Rights Commission. Had I been asked I probably
would have felt obligated to accept and now I would be in the unpleasant
position of having to resign in the face of the administration's attitude toward these covenants.

Mrs. Oswald Lord, now representing the United States on the Human
Rights Commission, must find herself in a curious position. She has
joined representatives of 17 other nations in Geneva, where they are
scheduled to draft two covenants that her government has announced it
will not present to the Senate.

It would seem more logical to withdraw from the Human Rights Commission if this is to be the U.S. attitude. Even the Soviet Union, though many of us are fairly sure it will not ratify, have not announced through their government that they will not ratify. The Russian representatives are not in quite as awkward a position as those from the United States.

True, this attitude will not take away from us in this country our social, political or civil rights, but there are many areas in the world where our leadership, even if it had been confined to civil and political rights, might have helped vast numbers of people to gain these rights.

In spite of all that has been said, we would have been in no danger of losing any of our rights, and there were many ways—either through reservations, through working for a federal-state clause, or in improving the wording of the present articles—in which we could have made it possible to ratify the covenant on civil and political rights. But now we are not even going to try.

We have sold out to the Brickers and McCarthys. It is a sorry day for the honor and good faith of the present administration in relation to our interest in the human rights and freedoms of people throughout the world.

~

Mrs. Roosevelt had chilly feelings about Clare Booth Luce, who deserted FDR to support Wendell Wilkie in the former Vice President's renegade run for the presidential nomination in 1940. Mrs. Luce did not always have kind words for Eleanor Roosevelt. Nonetheless, Mrs. Roosevelt cited Mrs. Luce as a sometimes admirable model: as a playwright (best known for the 1936 satire The Women) *and as congresswoman (Connecticut, 1943–1947). She was married to American publishing giant Henry Luce (founder of* Time, Fortune, Life). *Mrs. Roosevelt, at sixty-eight, had another weighty issue on her mind: staying trim after fifty, always a bipartisan problem.*

NEW YORK, APRIL 13—On Thursday afternoon of last week I went to a tea given by the N.Y. Newspaper Women's Club in honor of Mrs. Clare Booth Luce, our new Ambassador to Italy. It was her 50th birthday and, she told us, someone had said to her: "Well, the worst part of the century is behind you."

Mrs. Luce does not look 50. She is a very lovely-looking woman who has kept her slim, slight figure, and she has much charm. They say the Italians were uncertain about accepting a woman as ambassador, for it was a somewhat new departure in their area of the world. But in Mrs. Luce they will find not only a beautiful woman, but an able ambassador, with brains which any man might be proud of. I feel Mrs. Luce will represent us well.

Her powers of observation and analysis, sharpened by her training both as a writer and as a member of Congress, should make her very valuable.

~

On April 12, the eighth anniversary of FDR's death, Mrs. Roosevelt lost a co-worker and companion who had served for decades: Her secretary, Malvina "Tommy" Thompson, died. There had been for years now a team of secretaries carrying out Mrs. Roosevelt's work. Some handled correspondence; others did research, tracking down facts and figures to give reliable authority to Mrs. Roosevelt's arguments in "My Day," magazine articles, and hundreds of speeches. But Malvina Thompson was her personal secretary, a cross between confidante and administrative director. They worked together virtually every day, and on most domestic and international trips, Miss Thompson went along.

Eleanor Roosevelt left New York for Hyde Park at 4:45 a.m. to be on time for ceremonies at FDR's grave. Afterwards, she went directly to the hospital, and Tommy died just as she arrived. Miss Thompson had indeed been a Roosevelt family member. Anna wrote to her mother: "I know there is no use dwelling on how much you (& we . . .) will miss her but still, not having her around is going to be hellishly hard to take."

NEW YORK, APRIL 14—Miss Malvina Thompson, who had been my secretary for 29 years and who is known to most of my friends and to all my family as "Tommy," died on Sunday afternoon in New York Hospital after 12 days of very serious illness. We all hope that she suffered very little pain.

I am quite sure that no one ever lived a more selfless life. She gave of herself willingly and lovingly. She had a tremendous sense of responsibility about her work and a great sense of dignity. But because to her what she did was so important, whether the task was little or big or whether it was menial or intellectual made no difference whatsoever. She did every job to the best of her ability, and her greatest satisfaction lay in helping me to do whatever work I was doing as well as she thought it should be done. Her standards were high for me, as well as for herself, and she could be a real critic.

She had met a great many of the great in her life, but she always valued them as people and not because of their names or their position. A young friend of hers and mine said to me after her death that one would always have memories of good times with her, for she had humor, was a shrewd judge of people and could be caustic, though never really unkind.

One does not weep for those who die, particularly when they have lived a full life. And I doubt in any case whether the gauge of love and sorrow is in the tears that are shed in the first days of mourning.

People who remain with you in your daily life, even though they are no longer physically present, who are frequently in your mind, often mentioned, part of your laughter, part of your joy—they are the people you really miss. They are the people from whom you are never quite separated. You do not need to walk heavily all your life to really miss people.

The children who have so constantly come into Tommy's living room, who have used her typewriter—and sometimes abused it—who have been scolded, who have been cared for, who have been loved, they will talk of her as naturally and as often as they do the things in which she played so big a part. Their elders might make their memories into sadness. Children will keep them bright with laughter.

I am sure that no day will pass when in her own family, among her brothers and sister, her nieces and nephews, someone will not remember kindly her loving deeds of remembrance. I know that in my large family, with its many ramifications, there will never be a day when Tommy will not live.

~

Mrs. Roosevelt was busy before taking one of the longest trips of her life. The nearly continuous "My Day" column that began in 1936, interrupted for a few days after FDR died, would now be shut off for two months. The trip would take her around the globe, starting westward to the Far East—Japan. Accompanied by Maureen Corr, her chief secretary, and by Minnewa, her son Elliott's wife, the voyage was underwritten by the U.S. Committee on Intellectual Exchange. She would meet David Gurewitsch in Athens; together they would visit Yugoslavia.

Mrs. Roosevelt asked Secretary of State John Foster Dulles if he preferred sending a Republican woman to Japan. His lofty response indicated indifference: Mrs. Roosevelt would not be representing the United States anyway. Dulles ignored her offer to come to Washington to be briefed.

Social invitations Mrs. Roosevelt declined because of her travel plans demonstrate the high esteem world leaders such as Ambassador Abba Eban of Israel, Queen Elizabeth II of England, and the Norwegian royal family held for her.

NEW YORK, MAY 13—I have found much to my regret in the past day or two that I have to have time to do a few personal things before leaving next week for Japan and Europe.

As a result, I had to forgo the pleasure of attending on Monday night the dinner given by the United Jewish Appeal for Ambassador Eban. It was a real disappointment to me personally, but I was somewhat relieved because I felt it would cause less consternation than if I had had to give up something where I was the only speaker and the whole meeting depended on my being there.

As always happens when one is going away, unexpected things come up and one has to try to finish odds and ends hurriedly as the date for departure draws closer.

I am prepared to work very hard in Japan but on leaving there I hope to travel in more leisurely fashion, not spending much time anywhere except in Yugoslavia, where I will be for about two weeks. And I hope there will be no speeches or official engagements, so that I can really enjoy sights and sounds of new places and get a little impression of the places and peoples.

I was very much touched the other day to be invited to the coronation by Queen Elizabeth, and I was very sorry that, because of my commitments in Japan, it wasn't possible for me to accept.

In the same way I would have liked very much to be at the wedding of Princess Ragnhilds. I felt it was very kind of Prince Olaf and Princess Martha to invite me and because of old associations I would have liked to have been there. I am glad, however, to hear the young people will be coming to New York, as the young husband's family has business connections here, and I look forward to someday soon when I shall see them.

~

As much as Eleanor Roosevelt loved globe-trotting, few pleasures could compete with family gatherings and community activities at Hyde Park. The Roosevelts were competitive, playful participants, entering animals in contests at the county fair, marching in the town parade.

Mrs. Roosevelt's wry observations of human behavior—how vanity precedes a fall, how we tend to hear just what we want to hear—were inspired by the personalities and antics of her own children and grandchildren.

HYDE PARK, SEPTEMBER 3—We went this morning to the opening of the Dutchess County Fair. My first interest was of course to visit Franklin Jr.'s Hereford cattle and his sheep. They had changed the hour for judging the cattle so they will not be judged until tonight and I do not know at what hour the sheep will be judged. Going so early we missed some of the exhibits.

I always enjoy the flower shop, particularly the flower arrangements, and I was looking forward to seeing them today and comparing what I saw with what I had learned about flower arrangements while I was in Japan. I brought home two books on the subject and watched many classes, even those in factories where girls were being taught to arrange flowers. In our hotel a lady who was taking courses arranged the flowers in the lobby each day and I watched with keen interest to see how she created such a variety of beautiful designs and used comparatively few flowers. Since the flower show was being judged and we could not go in, neither could we see the arts and crafts show nor the grange exhibits, as the judges were busy.

I did get into the 4-H Club building, however, and looked with interest on what the boys and girls were doing in dressmaking, in food preparation, in craft work of different kinds and even in flower arrangements. I saw some of their animal exhibits, too, and spent a little while watching some of the horse show entries. While we were there they were showing medium-sized ponies and large-size ponies. Miss Deborah Dows with her beautiful white stallion won first prize with her really beautiful little horse.

Our children went through all the booths of different kinds for entertainment and tried their hands at many things. Only two of the small boys were lost when it was time to go home. We had their names called over the loudspeaker, but when they finally appeared they blandly said they hadn't heard a thing, which shows how easy it is not to hear when you do not want to.

We all went to lunch at the Vanderbilt Inn on the way home and I felt that when we walked in we must have looked like an invading army: 11 children and eight grownups. That really is quite a crowd!

Sad to say, I will not be able to go again since I go to New York early tomorrow morning and my niece with her four children and a friend, Mrs. Wagner, will be leaving here for Michigan. I shall be anxious to hear what happens to Franklin Jr.'s pet bull because he thinks he should win over anything in his class. But every owner has that feeling about his particular pet animal and I learned long ago not to count my chickens before they were hatched. This is a very valuable lesson which I hope Franklin Jr. has also learned.

1954

*T*he threat of communism at home and abroad fanned a smoldering debate all year long in 1954. Many "My Day" columns wrestled with particular cases of alleged Communist influence in foreign or domestic affairs. Although Mrs. Roosevelt's positions were usually consistent, she joined in the country's frustration over the excessive expenditure of energy on a single but amorphous issue—because she saw so much else the society should be doing to improve itself and to help the less fortunate elsewhere.

In Eisenhower's State of the Union message in early January, Congress heard a call for cuts in military spending. Five days later Secretary of State Dulles announced America's commitment to a policy of "massive retaliation" against any nuclear attack and promptly suffered a barrage of criticism. On January 21 the United States launched its first nuclear submarine, the *Nautilus*. Within the next six weeks Eisenhower reported twice to the nation that the military had successfully tested the new hydrogen bomb on two atolls in the Pacific. While America built its nuclear arsenal, it also participated in unsuccessful Big Four talks on the reunification of Germany. Mrs. Roosevelt was as eager as anyone for Europe to be stabilized, for oppressed people to be free, for the spreading influence of Soviet-bloc communism to be checked. But she remained skeptical about a re-empowered Germany.

Foreign policy and military activity in 1954 seemed to draw the United States repeatedly to Asia. In mid-March the French reported that U.S. military aid in fact covered most of the cost of the French-Indochina war in which France, a former colonial power in Southeast Asia, tried to stave off Communist control in Vietnam. The United States opposed a negotiated settlement, fearing that communism would spread even faster. Dulles urged air support for the French battle at Dien Bien Phu, but Congress was leery without cooperation from Britain. On April 7 Eisenhower gave a speech, using the phrase "falling row of dominoes" to describe what he feared the Southeast Asian countries would become if the United States did not take a military stand there against communism. For years to come, the "domino theory" prevailed in U.S. foreign policy thinking as a corollary to the containment theory. Eleanor Roosevelt had little argument with this position, though she believed humanitarian aid could work better in the long run than arms.

In early May, Dien Bien Phu fell to the Vietnamese Communists. France began to back out, American commitments to the French unraveled, and the Communists took over North Vietnam. By August a situation with similar potential confronted the State Department. Having lifted its protective blockade of Taiwan earlier in the year, the U. S. found itself and its ally, the Taiwanese non-Communist government-in-exile of China, threatened by invasion from Communist mainland China. Eisenhower did some saber-rattling, reminding Chou En-lai, the Chinese Communist foreign minister, that the U.S. Seventh Fleet could easily interpose itself, but by mid-September the United States had decided not to get involved in a direct military way. Nonetheless, seeds were now sown for U.S. commitments in Southeast Asia (defense treaties were also signed in 1954), and as a prognosticator, Eleanor Roosevelt could see there would be trouble for years to come as long as America continued in its role as chief defender of democratic rights worldwide.

Among the more successful battles being won on the home front, however, were two that Mrs. Roosevelt was particularly pleased about. The Salk polio vaccine was out of the lab and into the doctor's office, at least in Dr. Jonas Salk's own office in Pittsburgh, where real testing on children began and appeared to be working. And in a landmark case, *Brown v. Board of Education.* the Supreme Court pushed the country a giant step forward in achieving justice in civil rights. In *Brown* the Court defined segregated schools that are "separate but equal" to be "inherently unequal." It demanded desegregation "with all deliberate speed." Liberals cheered; outraged Southern conservatives showed their resistance to change by refusing to implement the Court's orders. Mrs. Roosevelt praised the Court and pressed for reasonable discussion and obedience to the law, yet she knew the struggle would take years.

Another grand drama and debate also absorbed the nation—primarily on television—throughout much of 1954. Republican Senator Joseph McCarthy of Wisconsin opened hearings in April into his allegations that the Army was in some quarters infiltrated by Communists. His tactics in the hearing room and in press conferences were so outlandish, irresponsible insinuations which threatened to ruin many careers, that his Senate colleagues realized at last something must be done to put him in check. By June McCarthy had expanded his charges, claiming that the CIA too was infiltrated by Reds. In August a Senate committee began to investigate charges of misconduct by McCarthy himself.

McCarthy and his allies were still having some success, however. They had passed the Communist Control Act, which Eisenhower signed in late August. By mid-October—just after Eleanor Roosevelt's seventieth birthday—the Civil Service Commission, using this new law, had dismissed more than 2,600 employees suspected of having Communist sympathies. Nonetheless, by the end of September, the evidence against McCarthy had become overwhelming. The Senate committee unanimously recommended censure; on December 2 he was condemned by the full Senate, and within weeks his power was gone.

In 1954 Americans initiated two bold engineering projects. The St. Lawrence Seaway Project was launched with massive commitments of capital from both Canada and the United States. Groundbreaking took place for the first atomic power plant, at Pittsburgh. Two Americans of note were awarded Nobel Prizes in 1954: Dr. Linus Pauling was recognized for his work in biochemistry (on the role of vitamins in health), and the coveted prize capped Ernest Hemingway's career as a writer. The name of America's most popular fiction writer at mid-century barely receives a brief mention, if that, in the whole run of "My Day" columns. Hemingway's male chauvinism, belligerent personality, heavy drinking, and conviction that politics never really solves any problems were all anathema to Eleanor Roosevelt.

Foreign policy analysts may count dollars, guns, tons of grain, and other quantifiable things when assessing the outcome of a potential move. Others focus on attitudes, beliefs, even feelings. Mrs. Roosevelt was never oblivious to the value of the first approach. As FDR's adviser and as UN delegate, she was renowned for being well-informed about objective facts. To evaluate a contest of wills (between two countries), Mrs. Roosevelt looked at the overriding feelings expressed by the governments and their people.

Concerning the testy relationship between India and Pakistan, Mrs. Roosevelt wanted to see communism contained within the Soviet Union, China, and the Warsaw Pact nations in Eastern Europe. In this respect, Eleanor Roosevelt was in step with mainstream U.S. (Eisenhower administration) thinking. But she reiterates an old Eleanor Roosevelt idea: that humanitarian aid may do more to win the battle against communism than will all the arms America could ever supply.

NEW YORK, JANUARY 7—Day by day we see the question of military aid to Pakistan or a military agreement with Pakistan discussed in our newspapers and each time it seems to me it is being made more clear to us that, whether reasonably or not, still the Indians are completely opposed to this arrangement. They feel that Pakistan is safe from the Soviet Union, having both Afghanistan and India on its borders, and that in accepting military aid from the United States, Pakistan will bring the cold war to the Indian world.

We seem to be jeopardizing the friendship of 370 million people in order to establish a military agreement with 70 million people. It is certainly not fear of Pakistan that makes India appear to object to this, for even with the United States military aid Pakistan would not be a threat to India because of India's predominance in her area of the world as to resources and population.

It is perhaps natural that Pakistan should seek to strengthen her position. From the United States point of view there is undoubtedly no feeling that we want to control either India or Pakistan and because the idea of political control is very far from our thoughts we are sometimes surprised that the rest of the world does not take it for granted that our intentions are good—that all we are trying to do is to make the world safer for democracy.

In the old sense of military bases and military alliance this arrangement with Pakistan seems to be entirely different. We are simply willing to strengthen Pakistan against the Communist world. It is true that India has tried all along to remain completely neutral in the cold war and this strengthening of Pakistan by a Western democracy might well seem from the point of view of the Indians a dangerous step. There is no question that we want to be friendly with both India and Pakistan and there is no question that we trust both countries as far as their desire for freedom and democracy goes.

It may well be that we would strengthen Pakistan more by economic aid than by military aid and perhaps give India less cause for suspicion. This whole question it seems to me requires careful study and thought. It is important for the people of the United States to demonstrate in every possible way their friendship for both countries and their feelings that it is important not to do anything that endangers that friendship. It may well be that a change in the type of aid that we propose may be the solution to this problem. All of us may feel that India is unreasonable but there are times when all nations are unreasonable. Some people have even felt that that could be said sometimes of the United States.

LEFT: Though dwarfed here by the modernist architecture in the chamber of the United Nation's General Assembly in New York, Eleanor Roosevelt's prominence at the UN was incontestable. The occasion was "United Nations Day," October 24, 1952. Mrs. Roosevelt would soon move into (nearly) full time volunteer work for the United Nations Association, a world-wide organization dedicated to educating people everywhere about the importance of the UN. *(United Nations)*

RIGHT: Andrei Gromyko had been the Soviet Union's ambassador to the United States in the 1940s and later played a key role at the United Nations, where he and Mrs. Roosevelt often found themselves at odds ideologically. When Mrs. Roosevelt left her post at the UN in January 1953 in the clean sweep of Republican patronage following Eisenhower's election, the tributes to her were many. None meant more than the respect she was accorded by Gromyko, one of her ablest foes. *(FDR Library)*

RIGHT: B. C. Gardner, chancellor of McGill University, Montreal, applauds as Mrs. Roosevelt accepts an honorary doctorate of laws in November 1953. Such honors were particularly gratifying to her—she eventually had dozens of them—because she had never attended college. *(FDR Library)*

ABOVE: Especially after World War II, when the harsh truth of the Holocaust became widely known and the establishment of Israel as a state was under way, Eleanor Roosevelt was an indefatigable worker for the Jewish cause. Chosen woman of the year more than once by Jewish groups, she was always ready to join in fundraising efforts for the budding new country in an ancient land that she had visited and found fascinating, even inspiring. This photograph was taken in Akron, Ohio, in early 1954. *(FDR Library)*

LEFT: Two great communicators met in New York in February 1955 when the American Foundation for Overseas Blind gave a testimonial dinner for Helen Keller. Eleanor Roosevelt was a guest. Miss Keller admired Mrs. Roosevelt's dedication to social causes and to promoting respect for the handicapped. Eleanor Roosevelt applauded Keller's exuberant and courageous determination to live a full life despite her blindness. *(American Foundation for the Blind, Helen Keller Archives)*

ABOVE: Ten years after the end of World War II, Europe was still plagued by serious problems with refugees and displaced persons. Among the most heartrending situations were those of the orphans of war and its aftermath. In 1955, at Campous, near Montpelier in southern France, Mrs. Roosevelt visited with Moroccan Jewish refugee orphans. She had a magic touch with children everywhere. *(FDR Library)*

Eleanor Roosevelt was married to the man who served longer than any other in the White House and supported the man who failed in three consecutive attempts to become President. Many in the country's liberal wing looked to Governor Adlai Stevenson of Illinois as their conscience and intellectual standard-bearer. Mrs. Roosevelt sometimes urged greater warmth upon him but always found his ideas persuasive. Here she rallies with the governor at the Democratic National Convention in Chicago in 1956, where he won the party's nomination for the second time. *(FDR Library)*

By reporting from behind the Iron Curtain in 1957, particularly in her interviews with Soviet Premier Nikita Khrushchev (whom she visited at Yalta in September), Mrs. Roosevelt broke new ground for American journalism. The United Feature Syndicate editors extended her "My Day" columns to accommodate the serious and detailed text she filed from deepest Russia. The interviews revealed a Khrushchev at once more human and more rigidly ideological than had been seen or heard before. Khrushchev later visited Mrs. Roosevelt at Hyde Park in September 1959. *(FDR Library)*

ABOVE: It took Eleanor Roosevelt several months to warm to Senator John Kennedy, particularly after the failure of the draft-Stevenson movement she had helped to spearhead at the 1960 Democratic National Convention. Kennedy was candid about his gratitude for Mrs. Roosevelt's support, and she saw in him the promise of greatness. *(USIA I FDR Library)*

ABOVE: Seventy-two-year-old Eleanor Roosevelt carries her own suitcase to a plane at New York's LaGuardia field in 1960. Fiercely independent and determined, Mrs. Roosevelt traveled thousands of miles every year until the last few months of her life. *(Lawrence Jordan, Jr.)*

In June 1960, part of Dore Schary's *Sunrise at Campobello* was filmed in the Roosevelt family residence at Hyde Park. Between takes Mrs. Roosevelt chatted with the film's stars, Greer Garson (who played the young Eleanor Roosevelt) and Ralph Bellamy (who played FDR). Mrs. Roosevelt counted playwright Dore Schary among her friends and did provide some insight and information to encourage his work, but she and her children found it strange to see their lives transformed into those of literary and historical characters. *(FDR Library)*

Eleanor Roosevelt's heart, soul, and mind went into her Val-Kill Cottage at Hyde Park, New York. Built in 1926 as the shop for Val-Kill Industries, a furniture-making business Mrs. Roosevelt ran with two friends to help local young farmers expand their incomes, the house was remodeled in 1936 when the factory closed. It served well as an 18-room "country retreat" for entertaining countless guests and family. Following FDR's death, Val-Kill became Eleanor Roosevelt's permanent home. *(George I. Browne)*

Val-Kill Cottage was cozy, even humble when compared to FDR's austerely grand ancestral home on the Hudson River at Hyde Park, New York, a mile or so away. The living room in the converted furniture factory was crammed with Mrs. Roosevelt's books, overstuffed chairs in cotton slipcovers, and photographs of family and distinguished friends and visitors. Val-Kill is now a National Historic Site, administered by the National Park Service. *(FDR Library)*

At Eleanor Roosevelt's funeral in Hyde Park in November 1962, three American presidents joined other friends and family to bid her farewell. From left: President John F. Kennedy; former President Harry Truman; former President Dwight Eisenhower; Adlai Stevenson. *(John F. Kennedy Library)*

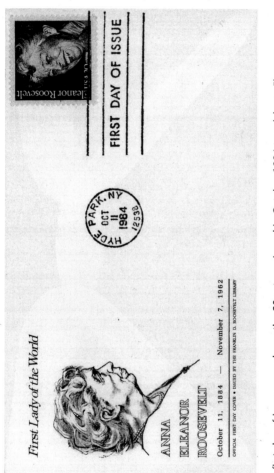

A first-day-of-issue cover shows the 20¢ stamp issued in October 1984 to celebrate Eleanor Roosevelt's hundredth birthday. The postmark was, of course, Hyde Park, New York, Mrs. Roosevelt's legal and emotional home. *(FDR Library)*

McCarthyism caused liberal-minded career service people in government to leave their jobs lest they end up being unfairly accused (by McCarthy, his Senate cronies, or by the House Un-American Activities Committee) of having Communist sympathies. The result: a brain drain from the federal government. The Red scare drove people away even from applying for government jobs for fear that their reputation might be ruined by unfounded insinuations. Eleanor Roosevelt lamented McCarthyism repeatedly. She refers to Henry Ford II, grandson of the automobile industrialist, who became president of Ford Motor Company in 1945. Ford had spoken on world peace when accepting the Poor Richard Club Medal, January 16, 1954.

NEW YORK, JANUARY 23—I think Mr. Ford's statement the other day that he found many of the foreign representatives in the United Nations mystified about our attitude on communism in this country and feeling that we were a great big frightened giant looking for a mouse with a club, was most interesting. It never does give confidence to people to find that someone they feel they should rely on for calm and clear judgment is frightened.

This mad rush on the part of Senator McCarthy to accuse people in government of communism has forced us into searching for Communists under every bed when as a matter of fact the Senator discovered comparatively few in positions of importance. I think the performance has been harmful to the trust that citizens as a whole have in the conduct of their government and in their government servants.

Mr. Dulles may well believe that in the Foreign Service the witch-hunt in the Department of State has had no effect. On the whole our people are so loyal and courageous that as long as they stay in the service they will try to send in reports which do represent their thinking. However, I know of a number of young people in the service who were just beginning to be of value who had resigned because they did not feel it was worth staying in under present conditions. That is a loss to the Foreign Service in the future and the mere fact that in the recent past fewer young people have been applying to enter is an indication of how they feel.

～

Mrs. Roosevelt heard from Japanese women protesting the contamination of Japanese fishing grounds by American hydrogen-bomb tests in the Pacific. Her ambivalence about the value of the tests is clear. While she wanted the U.S. to retain military superiority (remembering its weak position before World War II), Mrs. Roosevelt feared the very weapon designed to ac-

complish that end would be impossible to control. Numerous "My Day" columns, speeches, and magazine articles by Eleanor Roosevelt contributed to the nuclear arms race debate (though in the minority report). The Eisenhower administration decided that the best defense against nuclear attack was to arm America to the teeth with nuclear weapons sufficient to deter any hostile initiatives by the Soviets.

NEW YORK, APRIL 16—Increasingly people are talking to me about the new H-bomb and its dangers. Even on "Meet the Press" I was asked if the knowledge that one could carry a devastating bomb in a suitcase didn't frighten me, and so I have decided to tell you what I feel about this whole situation.

It seems to me that the discovery of this latest bomb has actually outlawed the use of atomic bombs. The power of destruction is so great that unless we face the fact that no one in the world can possibly use it and therefore it must be outlawed as a weapon, we risk putting an end to all civilization. However, this realization makes it necessary to think of other things much more critically.

The day that we agree the world over that no one can use an atom bomb, we must either agree immediately on total disarmament, except for a united force in the United Nations, or we must make sure that we have better weapons than anyone else. We must have the best of the less destructive weapons, such as tanks, guns, etc. We are not equal as to population with the Communist world.

Therefore, the free world must stand together to defend itself. It will not do to rely on a weapon that we cannot use for protection. It is entirely obvious that were we, because we had no other strength, to use the H-bomb, let us say against an enemy that seemed to threaten us or that seemed to threaten the security of an area of the world that we felt should not fall to Soviet domination, instead of having the sympathy of the world we would, by that one action, have created fear and hatred of us.

No one can use this new destructive weapon without destroying innumerable innocent people. It would not be only our enemies that would condemn us, it would be our own conscience.

The conscience of America is a very real thing and if, because of any temptation whatsoever, we use this terrific weapon first, there are few of us in this country who could live with our own conscience.

Before we drift into war in one way or another, I feel that every possible agency, primarily the United Nations and its negotiation machinery, should be called into play. Sometimes I think we rely too much on negotiation only among the great powers. True, there is no force set up in the

United Nations and you cannot rely on the enforcement of peace through an already set-up compulsory force provided by every member nation in the United Nations.

Just because of this, however, the mobilization of world opinion and methods of negotiation should be developed and used by every nation in order to strengthen the United Nations. Then if we are forced into war, it will be because there has been no way to prevent it through negotiation and the mobilization of world opinion. In which case we should have the voluntary support of many nations, which is far better than the decision of one nation alone, or even of a few nations.

I dislike fear and I confess to being on the whole rather free from it. But not to look at the dangers of the present and make up our minds that we do not want to drift, but that we want to use all the machinery there is to prevent war, seems to me foolhardy.

I think the women of this country, if they face the fact of the present situation, will agree with me that this is a time for action—not for war, but for mobilization of every bit of peace machinery. It is also a time for facing the fact that you cannot use a weapon, even though it is the weapon that gives you greater strength than other nations, if it is so destructive that it practically wipes out large areas of land and great numbers of innocent people.

~

To say that Eleanor Roosevelt was filled with admiration for David Gure-witsch (her personal physician and intimate friend) is an understatement. The doctor could deliver both physical and psychological help to a patient (especially to children) in ways that were direct and tangible—compared to the more abstract efforts a writer, diplomat, and intellectual like Mrs. Roosevelt could make to improve society.

Accompanying Mrs. Roosevelt on this midwestern trip was Bernard Baruch, the financier who advised Presidents Woodrow Wilson and Franklin Roosevelt and who, like Eleanor Roosevelt, served as a United Nations delegate.

ATHENS, OHIO, APRIL 28—Just in a week, spring is with us. Last Saturday I drove to Westchester County and all of the blossoms were out. Dr. Gure-witsch and I went with Mr. Baruch on a visit to Blythedale Hospital. Dr. Gurewitsch is the medical director there and he was anxious to show Mr. Baruch the experimental work being done for handicapped children.

There are children in plaster casts lying on their stomachs. There are others lying on their backs and many who look perfectly normal but who have some disease which requires bed rest and treatment. There are others with deformities of one kind or another, but for all of them treatment is being administered. The experimental part is the effort to find out how to treat the whole child so that one handicap will not mean that the child acquires several handicaps during the years required for a cure or for amelioration of the condition that he may suffer from.

I saw, in walking around, great improvements in the training of the staff since I had been there a few years ago, and much had been done to develop the specific things needed by certain children. They were dedicating last Saturday a dental clinic with a movable chair so that a child who was in a bed could be wheeled in and treated without leaving his bed. They had also enlarged and improved the examining room so that one felt the doctors had a much better opportunity to make really satisfactory examinations of their patients. Altogether, I thought the board of directors and the administration director were doing a fine piece of work in cooperation with the medical director.

Dr. Gurewitsch has with all his patients, but especially with children, a very remarkable intuitive way of knowing what they need. They are taking advantage now of psychiatry for the children but I think every doctor practices psychiatry, even though a specialist is essential to help fully meet the needs of the patients.

~

The Supreme Court decision in Brown v. Board of Education *declared separate public schools for nonwhite children inherently unequal and therefore unconstitutional. Mrs. Roosevelt appears to assume the Court's decision will end school segregation. "My Day" columns over the ensuing years indicate that after some reflection Mrs. Roosevelt saw the 1954 ruling as critically important but not by itself adequate to effect the social change she hoped for. Coming was a complicated test of wills among the federal government and school administrators, state and local officials, ordinary citizens, and the National Guard—before black children could safely attend classes in previously all-white schools.*

NEW YORK, MAY 20—While I was on the "Tex and Jinx [television] Show" I was given the news of the unanimous Supreme Court decision that wiped out segregation in the schools. I am delighted this was a unanimous decision because I think it will be difficult for the states with segregated school systems to hold out against such a ruling.

If it were not for the fact that segregation in itself means inequality, the old rule of giving equal facilities might have gone on satisfying our sense of Justice for a long time. It is very difficult, however, to ensure real equality under a segregated system, and the mere fact that you cannot move freely anywhere in your country and be as acceptable everywhere as your neighbor creates an inequality.

Southerners always bring up the question of marriage between the races, and I realize that that is the question of real concern to people. But it seems to me a very personal question which must be settled by family environment and by the development of the cultural and social patterns within a country. One can no longer lay down rules as to what individuals will do in any area of their lives in a world that is changing as fast as ours is changing today.

~

Visiting son Elliott and daughter-in-law Minnewa at their ranch in Meeker, Colorado, Mrs. Roosevelt encountered a new challenge, the word game sweeping the country, Scrabble. *Evidently being one of the most articulate women in America did the former First Lady little good in the competition with her grandchildren.*

NEW YORK, JULY 24—On my return to the ranch I was introduced to Scrabble, which practically has become an obsession with some of us. Those who play it know how competitive one can become in finding combinations of words. In spite of the fact that I found it extremely irritating because I was so slow at making these combinations, I think I shall get a game and start the children at home on it. I am so bad at games, though, that I always find I can start and teach the children and then they rapidly become so much more proficient that I am again relegated to my knitting.

~

Throughout 1954 Eleanor Roosevelt maintained a hectic schedule of speeches and meetings with the chapters of the American Association for the United Nations. While in Los Angeles, she observed air conditions vexing to anyone with high standards about the quality of urban life. Smog was not yet a common word, but the seriousness of the problem was gaining recognition. Mrs. Roosevelt's optimism made her foresee an early solution, one of her few wrong guesses. In New York or any other city with good subways or buses, Eleanor Roosevelt had no qualms about riding as a straphanger. The absence of public transport in Los Angeles seemed conspicuous indeed.

LOS ANGELES, NOVEMBER 6—On arrival in Los Angeles I went directly to Long Beach, where a very charming hostess allowed me to bathe and change and have a little rest before their buffet dinner. This was an informal and delightful party in a house situated on a hill, with a beautiful view of the many lights far below. In the daytime it must be really gorgeous. These California houses seem almost to take in the outdoors—you feel that you live outside and the world of nature is very close. Flowers are everywhere. Trees and vines apparently grow with great rapidity.

Smog, however, is what seems to be on everybody's mind. They told me all sorts of things that would have to be done. I had not realized quite how bad smog can be. People say their throats are raw, their eyes are runny and it is really a great discomfort.

Governor Knight recently called some specialists together who said it was not really dangerous to health. But others believe it may have lasting bad effects, so no one is very happy about the situation. In spite of the beauty of nature and the fact that today the sun is shining and everything looks lovely to me, my hosts last night were troubled by the whole smog situation.

Los Angeles is a city with rather poor public transportation, so there are an enormous number of cars. And while there are machines that can be placed in oil-refining plants which might do away with smog, nothing small enough has yet been invented to use in motor cars. I suppose, with the need, inventors will go to work and the problem will be solved. But at present it is a very unpleasant situation, I gather, for those who live in this whole area.

~

Norman Thomas, America's most famous socialist, appears in numerous "My Day" columns. Mrs. Roosevelt, always the teacher, tried many times to distinguish between capitalism, socialism, and communism. Social critics on the right in America believed any ideas originating in the socialist camp were in fact Communist ideas in disguise. Mrs. Roosevelt looked at socialism through a different lens. Had she been a European intellectual, she might have been a socialist herself. In modified form, several ideas originating with the American socialists worked their way into the New Deal and into subsequent legislation sponsored by Democratic liberals.

Mrs. Roosevelt toasts Norman Thomas, who joined the Socialist Party (1918), helped found the American Civil Liberties Union (1920), and ran for President as the perennial socialist candidate (1928–1948). The record of his ideas later enacted into law is impressive: unemployment insurance, minimum wage, five-day workweek, abolition of child labor. A prolific author, Thomas spent his last years campaigning for nuclear disarmament. He died in 1968.

NEW YORK, NOVEMBER 23—On Saturday last Norman Thomas was 70 years old. He has led American socialism in this country for a half century. He still seems full of vigor and enthusiasm. He is no more afraid of new ideas today than he was 50 years ago.

It seems to me that men who have had a purpose, and have really worked for it, come to their older years still with a vitality and an interest in life which is lacking in those who have been less dedicated. Though he has not been elected to public office, Mr. Thomas has seen many of the ideas that he tried to persuade people to accept finally become acceptable in the most conservative circles. So I think he must have the satisfaction of feeling that he has done something to make the world a better place for the majority of people to live in.

1955

*I*f the airline companies Mrs. Roosevelt used in this one year alone had offered frequent-flier mileage credits, her 1955 travels would have put a considerable dent in their revenues. She circled the globe and crisscrossed the nation in a flurry of activity, driven by her abiding political and moral passions but at times, like the United States itself, somewhat uncertain of her focus or of the impact her work might have.

In January, Eisenhower's Foreign Operations Administration made the fateful decision to send military aid to Southeast Asia (Cambodia, Laos, South Vietnam). Few people, Eleanor Roosevelt included, foresaw the protracted struggle there in which the U.S. would eventually become embroiled. Sam Rayburn was reelected Speaker of the House of Representatives when the 84th Congress convened; he would wield the gavel for another six years. Among the Senate's early 1955 actions was an 84–0 vote to continue its investigation of Communist activities by government employees: The spirit of McCarthyism lived on. If such behavior was old hat for the Senate, President Eisenhower tried something new by giving the first televised presidential news conference.

Typical of Mrs. Roosevelt's hectic schedule was a winter trip to the Southwest for AAUN lectures and meetings. In a span of a few days she covered Little Rock, Memphis, New Orleans, Houston, Dallas, Corpus Christi, Denver, and Odessa, Texas. When she hit the ground again in New York, she was still running. She was a young seventy. Another ten-day trip (to the Midwest) followed in February. By March she was en route to France and visits in Italy and Israel.

Although now ten years past, the geopolitical aftermath of World War II was still current business. In April 1955 the Senate agreed to negotiations on the future of West Germany, and the Big Four powers consented to the establishment of sovereignty for the Federal Republic of Germany. Eleanor Roosevelt kept a close watch on Germany's political behavior. Austria's status, too, was clarified in 1955 by a Big Four treaty: Its borders returned to their pre-1938 positions; economic union with Germany was prohibited; occupying forces were withdrawn.

There were relatively few giant steps forward in 1955 for the social causes liberals such as Mrs. Roosevelt supported, but among those, two are worth noting. In May the ruling elders of the Presbyterian church decided to admit women to the ministry through ordination. Late in the year, the Interstate Commerce Commission banned segregation on trains and buses crossing state lines.

Reflecting the continuing tensions between the United States and the Soviet and Chinese Communists, Congress extended Selective Service for another two years. In June the Soviets shot down an American military plane over the Bering Strait, which did little to calm American nerves upset about the prospect of nuclear war. Not long after a July summit meeting in Geneva that did little to advance the cause of peace, President Eisenhower suffered a heart attack.

Late summer saw Eleanor Roosevelt heading west to Asia for an extended trip, including visits in Tokyo, Hong Kong, Manila, Djakarta, the island of Bali, and Bangkok. Much of the trip was devoted to work for the international federation of United Nations associations.

Toward year's end Mrs. Roosevelt celebrated one traditional occasion and a new development. About Thanksgiving at Hyde Park she wrote: "We were only seventeen for Thanksgiving dinner Thursday evening here. . . . But we had six children, which always makes a celebration at home more worthwhile." And the labor movement gave her something new to applaud: Under the leadership of George Meany and Walter Reuther, their two nationwide organizations (American Federation of Labor and Congress of Industrial Organizations, respectively) joined forces to create the AFL-CIO, which meant more strength from greater numbers, a positive fact for working men and women.

Eleanor Roosevelt respected artists who told the truth about human experience and who found ways beyond their art to contribute to society. The hugely successful photography exhibit The Family of Man *was the brainchild of photographer Edward Steichen. Born in Luxembourg in 1879, Steichen eventually joined Alfred Stieglitz in the vanguard of American photographers. Around the turn of the century they organized shows revolutionizing the public's concept of photography as art. Steichen served in World War I, pioneering aerial photography; in World War II he led the naval combat photo unit. Garbo and Chaplin were among his portrait subjects between the wars.*

The Family of Man exhibition showed the human race to itself in all its splendor and shame, joy and agony. Photographs, from every corner of the globe, represented many races, creeds, political systems, and cultures.

SARASOTA, FLA., JANUARY 27—On Monday evening I attended a preview of the photographic exhibit called "The Family of Man" at the Museum of Modern Art in New York. This collection of 500 photographs by 280 photographers from 68 countries was conceived and prepared by Mr. Edward Steichen, director of the museum's department of photography.

Mr. and Mrs. Carl Sandburg were there to commemorate the occasion and it was a joy to see them. In fact, there were many people I was glad to see, such as Mr. and Mrs. Eugene Meyer, who had come on from Washington, and Dorothy Norman, and Nelson Rockefeller, who paid tribute to Mr. Steichen in a stirring short speech.

Thousands and thousands of photographs were examined before Mr. Steichen made his choices, which makes "The Family of Man" a memorable exhibit.

Some of the young people who worked under Mr. Steichen, like my young friend, Doris O'Donnell, told me that his favorites are the collection showing birth and motherhood. There is one among these particular pictures of a baby's arms that I thought simply entrancing.

The captions were not as yet on all the pictures when we viewed the exhibit, and that was because at the last minute they did not entirely please Mr. Steichen.

I could not, however, have enjoyed anything more than I did the first impact of the collection. Joy is depicted by such a beautiful collection of photographs—fun, enjoyment, and, finally, the pleasures of food, drink, of daily living, of the dawn of love. Eventually, one comes to the sorrow of death, the horror of fear and despair and the cruelty of man to man.

How strange it is that there can be such perfect love and such cruelty side by side!

I liked the photograph of the United Nations General Assembly with the words of the Charter, which are used as a caption for the entire exhibition. In a way they symbolize the hope of man. If enough of us can cling to those aims, some of the cruelty will disappear and more of the maturity of love and understanding may emerge.

It seemed to me that perhaps one area was somewhat neglected, and that was the area of the work of man. That is a most important part in the lives of men and women, in some lives the most important part, particularly when the work is creative work. It is often such a large part of man's existence that it would seem to be essential to mark it more clearly in a collection such as the museum's.

Perhaps I am wrong, however. There was such a crowd at the preview that even with Mr. Rene d'Harnoncourt's kind guidance I had difficulty in not starting at the wrong end of the exhibition and going backward. I may well have missed some of the photographs.

There is one special photograph of Mr. Steichen's own mother, showing her bringing out food from the house, which one should not miss. I know I shall return to be sure I have not missed any part of this remarkable exhibition.

~

Undue fear of Communist subversion in the United States and the spread of Communist influence abroad were major concerns of the fifties. Mrs. Roosevelt's prescription for a cure was more education. In "My Day" she frequently delivered an almost set speech on the differences between Communist ideology and Communist practice.

Mrs. Roosevelt struggled with the containment theory of foreign policy. She stood firmly with those who resisted the spread of communism into lands where people had no choice of government; she also campaigned for what a later generation called détente, *disengagement by major powers to avoid war. Should the U.S. or the UN defend Formosa (Taiwan) against attacks from the Communist mainland? Mrs. Roosevelt's analysis leaned in both directions.*

The subject of communism versus democracy was so fascinating to Eleanor Roosevelt it could serve equally well as dinner party conversation. "My Day" of February 12 outlines Marxist doctrine considered ideally and compares it to Marxism in its not-so-ideal practice. Why respectable intellectuals were attracted to communism was a question Mrs. Roosevelt was not afraid to ask. The column refers to Mr. and Mrs. Julius Rosenberg (but not the recently convicted spies). The wife is Anna Rosenberg, a close adviser of Mary Lasker, the art connoisseur and supporter of medical research and public health, causes Mrs. Roosevelt supported as well. Anna was also a staunch supporter of Democratic presidential hopeful Adlai Stevenson.

NEW YORK, FEBRUARY 8—It is true that the island of Formosa was acknowledged as a part of China, but that was before the mainland was overrun by the Communist forces in China. Once that had happened, naturally the area to which non-Communist forces had retreated became an area which must be defended by the non-Communist world against aggression.

Both the Soviet Union and Communist China should recognize the fact that no one intends to interfere with them within the borders that they now control. On the other hand, the rest of the non-Communist world does not intend to have Russia and Red China swallow up little by little other areas of the world, nor do they intend to have them, through infiltration, gradually induce more areas of the world to develop discontent at home and eventual revolution.

We are making a very concerted attempt to try to bring about a peaceful world within which people may live together in spite of differences of economy and political beliefs, but we cannot sit by quietly and see new areas swallowed up by constant Communist aggression.

To take Formosa would be the beginning of the use of force by the Communist Chinese. It is true that Communist China has not as yet taken over satellites in the manner of the Soviet Union, but it might easily become a practice of the Chinese Communist government, as it has become a habit on the part of the government of the Soviet Union.

There is certainly no desire on the part of the U.S. to bring about active war, but if we are to have a world with some kind of security there must be some understanding of the fact that communism cannot spread beyond its present boundaries and territorial ambitions.

NEW YORK, FEBRUARY 12—Last Wednesday evening I went to a most interesting dinner party at the home of Mr. and Mrs. Julius Rosenberg. There I had the pleasure of talking with Senator William Benton at the dinner as well as with my hostess and many other delightful people.

After dinner the group gathered together for general conversation, an enlightening procedure that is rather rare at a dinner party nowadays. At an appropriate time I asked a question which had been asked of me during the day:

"How do you explain why communism has any appeal at all to intellectuals or to the intelligent people of countries that are not suffering from great economic distress?"

The consensus, as I judged it, was that many people did not think of communism in the terms of what actually exists today in the Soviet Union. They thought of it primarily as a Marxist doctrine, more or less of an economic Utopia with ideals that are similar to those phrased for me some time ago by Marshal Tito.

I had asked Marshal Tito to give me his definition of communism. His answer was that no country had real communism as yet—least of all Russia, where there existed state capitalism and an imperialistic form of government. He disclaimed true communism in his own country, saying that they were trying in Yugoslavia to establish a socialist state, which was only the first step toward true communism.

True communism had not yet been achieved anywhere, he said, since it required that all people should cease to be greedy and be willing to see each individual receive according to his need from communal production.

I pointed out to Marshal Tito that this existed in an Israeli kibbutz, and he insisted this could not exist anywhere since people were not unselfish enough as yet to live together in this way!

I think the feeling in our group at the dinner party was that it was this idealistic concept which appealed to intellectuals, the idea of reaching a state where no one suffered and where there was a standard of achievement that was not financial, so that everyone could share in a decent and happy existence.

But, since this ideal does not resemble what actually happens in those countries where there is so-called Communist rule today, it did not entirely explain the acceptance by certain types of people in different parts of the world.

It was finally suggested that to these people the faults that exist today probably seem the necessary steps, in themselves wrong and perhaps reprehensible, but steps that must be gone through before the desired goal could be reached.

One of the members of the group pointed out that we were not taking into consideration the differences in the characters of people throughout the world, and the fact that communism might never have an appeal to people in certain countries because bread might mean more to them than ideas. In other countries, however, the appeal of martyrdom for an ideal might be much more compelling than any financial success.

~

Of all the Israeli leaders Mrs. Roosevelt met, none impressed her more than the young country's elder statesman David Ben-Gurion, whose home she visited in Tel Aviv. She welcomed opportunities to see kibbutzim in action, for in the U.S., government-sponsored residential and work cooperatives were rare. Eleanor admired the high-spirited young workers who chose to help build the still-new state of Israel by forsaking personal needs for the benefit of the group.

NEW YORK, APRIL 1—In Tel Aviv last week we arrived just in time to keep an appointment with Mr. Ben-Gurion. We were met at the door by his wife, who greeted us warmly, and it was a great pleasure to see the Minister of Defense himself in such good physical health and such happy spirits.

Mr. Ben-Gurion typifies, as does Mr. Baratz of Degania, the pioneer in Israel, a man who felt he must live on the soil and make things grow and be as self-sufficient as possible. It was characteristic when he said to me, "The happiest years of my life were the first years I spent in Israel in a kibbutz and the last ones I've spent in the Negev."

He lives in a new settlement not far from the Egyptian border and he says, "God made the rocks but forgot to put soil on them. Therefore, it is up to us to do it."

In his mind's eye he sees the picture of his home surrounded with flowers and fruit trees and a garden and green grass everywhere. As I left he said, "One must see the picture and then one can make it come true."

~

There were few women in America Eleanor Roosevelt admired more than Mary McLeod Bethune, whose death she laments here. Even if Bethune had been white and had accomplished the same things—rising from poverty to obtain a fine education; founding a college (Bethune-Cookman College, Daytona, Florida, and its normal-school predecessors); serving as Director, Division of Negro Affairs, in FDR's New Deal—she would have been remarkable. Dr. Bethune demonstrated to white and black worlds that with supportive parents and ceaseless hard work, even a poor black girl could achieve renown.

NEW YORK, MAY 20—I was distressed to read in the newspapers Thursday morning of the death of a really great American woman, Mary McLeod Bethune.

Dr. Bethune started life under conditions which must have made her education seem almost impossible, but both she and her parents had a great desire for her to gain knowledge and they seized on every opportunity. And the opportunities came, as they so often do, when people are ready to use them.

The newspapers were full of stories of how she led her remarkable life. Beginning with a dollar and a half she built a Negro college in Florida. She fought for the rights of her people but never with resentment or bitterness, and she taught both her own people and her white fellow Americans many a valuable lesson.

I always liked the story of how once a patronizing Pullman car conductor, asking her for her ticket, said: "Auntie, give me your ticket." She let him repeat it twice. Then, looking up sweetly, she said: "Which of my sister's sons are you?" This was a way of turning the tables on a gentleman, which was far more effective than any amount of anger would have been.

She had a deep religious faith and religion was not academic with her. It was both a weapon and a shield. She has told me very simply how time after time she has prayed for things, never for herself, but she always believed that if they were good things the Lord would hear her prayer. And there must have been many, many times when people were moved to answer her needs just because of this faith. She helped herself and the Lord helped her.

I knew Dr. Bethune best, of course, in the years when she worked for the National Youth Administration and she did good and courageous work for the young people of her race in a difficult period. But I have kept in touch with her all through the years and I will miss her very much, for I valued her wisdom and her goodness.

I would like to be at her funeral but I doubt if that will be possible. I have many commitments that would mean disappointment to various causes, which I think Dr. Bethune would be the first to feel should come before one's personal desires. Nevertheless, I will cherish the spirit she lived by and try to promote the causes that she believed in, in loving memory of a very wonderful life.

~

In a section of a column devoted to other subjects, Mrs. Roosevelt returns to a favorite political and philanthropic theme, the plight of political refugees. A figure not yet well-known appears here, a name destined to dominate the American political landscape: Senator John F. Kennedy. Theirs was an unsteady friendship until well into the presidential race of 1960.

HYDE PARK, JUNE 28—Senator John F. Kennedy has written a letter to Senator William Langer, chairman of the Senate subcommittee on refugees and escapees, that should be read by all of us. Senator Kennedy suggests amendments to the Refugee Relief Act of 1953 in order to allow more help to be given to escapees and refugees from behind the Iron Curtain, so that they may be resettled in other countries. Secondly, he wants the expiration date extended and unused quotas made available to other groups, such as Greeks, Italians, Poles, French, etc., and he hopes the limit will be raised far over the present 209,000 people.

I like the quotation at the end of Senator Kennedy's letter in which he says the Refugee Relief Act should not be what John Boyle O'Reilly once termed:

"Organized charity, scrimped and iced
In the name of a cautious, statistical Christ."

Let us hope that we can approach this question in our Congress, in our homes, and in our communities with generosity, for in the end we will benefit.

～

Summer pleasures were frequent "My Day" subjects. The Fourth of July was a holiday the Roosevelt family never ignored. They enjoyed festivities in the village, Hyde Park, and the day offered a welcome excuse for family to gather at Mrs. Roosevelt's Val-Kill cottage. Despite urgings from adults to sit still briefly for a reading of words written long ago by the Founding Fathers, other activities were clearly more important to the youngsters. Eleanor Roosevelt had a forgiving heart whenever children were involved.

HYDE PARK, JULY 7—We celebrated the Fourth here in very quiet fashion, staying at home most of the day but having a goodly number of people to play tennis during the morning and for lunch.

I asked my son John to read the Declaration of Independence and the Constitution to all of the young people, for we had 10 youngsters between the ages of two and 16 over the past week-end. The youngsters, however, were much more interested in sparklers after dark and spending all possible time in the pool. The Declaration of Independence and the Constitution and the Bill of Rights remind them of school!

It was a good thing that the long week-end came during such a hot spell, for many people were able to get to the country and find some relief. Our swimming pool has been in almost constant use. I don't think anything gives the children more comfort than being able to plunge into the pool and stay there for an hour at a time. They have a wonderful game they call "Red Rover," and that seems to take all their interest and energy for long periods of time.

～

Many writers tried to distill from FDR's long and complex story the essence of his genius for leadership, of his contribution to American history. Few succeeded as well as political historian and literary critic Isaiah Berlin, whose forte, Mrs. Roosevelt thought, lay in seeing patterns in both historical facts and the human feelings behind them.

Berlin emigrated in the 1930s from his native Latvia to England, where he became a lifelong Oxonian as both student and professor. Among his better-known works is The Hedgehog and the Fox, *about Tolstoy's view of history (1953).*

NEW YORK, AUGUST 1—In the Atlantic for this month there is an article entitled "Roosevelt Through European Eyes" by Isaiah Berlin. It is most interesting to me that someone who never met or saw my husband, but only heard his voice over the radio, could write this article. He was writing, however, of how Franklin D. Roosevelt appeared to Europeans, and most of them could not see or meet him and probably did not often hear him on the radio.

Mr. Berlin says certain things that to me are very interesting as coming from an outsider, so to speak. He writes, for instance, "It is not too much to say that he altered the fundamental concept of government and its obligations to the governed. In this respect Lloyd George was no more than a forerunner. The welfare state, so much denounced, has obviously come to stay: the direct moral responsibility for minimum standards of living and social services which it took for granted, are today accepted almost without a murmur by the most conservative politicians in the Western democracies. . . . But Mr. Roosevelt's greatest service to mankind (after ensuring victory against the enemies of freedom) consists in the fact that he showed that it is possible to be politically effective and yet benevolent and civilized: that the fierce left and right wing propaganda of the thirties, according to which the conquest and retention of political power is not compatible with human qualities, but necessarily demands from those who pursue it seriously the sacrifice of their lives upon the altar of some ruthless ideology, or the systematic practice of despotism—this propaganda, which filled the art and talk of the day, was simply untrue."

To have changed permanently a concept of government and made it more humanitarian, to have won a further victory over the enemies of freedom and to have proved that you may hold power and still be a really human being—that isn't a bad summing up as the results of an active political career. I am grateful to Mr. Berlin for his insight and understanding.

～

Although Japan had been as much an enemy of the Allies in World War II as had Germany and had even attacked the United States directly at Pearl Harbor, Mrs. Roosevelt moved more quickly toward rapprochement with the Japanese than she ever did with the Germans—whom she held responsible for starting both world wars. Little sense of resentment appears in "My Day" columns from this journey to the Far East.

Eleanor Roosevelt, the travel writer, was certainly never a great stylist, but, charmed by the foreignness of Japan, she could nonetheless evoke in her columns a scene—here, the rigorous discipline of the Japanese tea ceremony; in another "My Day," the enigmatic calm of the Buddha. She had a knack for seeing below surface details to cultural values beneath. Her close friend, Dr. David Gurewitsch, accompanied her.

TOKYO, AUGUST 20—Mr. and Mrs. Matsumoto and Dr. Takagi joined us at noon and took us to a delightful Japanese restaurant for lunch. The first dish placed on the table was so lovely in color and so artistically arranged that Dr. Gurewitsch insisted on having it carried out into the sunlight so that he could take a picture of it in color. The charming courtesy of everyone in Japan impressed you wherever you go but especially when you go to the kind of restaurant we went to today. After our very delicious lunch the lady who owns it showed us the tea ceremony. Only the very best Japanese tea is used and they do not ship it to the U.S.A. Dr. Gurewitsch was instructed in the guest's role of the ceremony by Mrs. Matsumoto, who showed him how to turn his bowl and hold it correctly, but he liked the tea—which proved that he is more adaptable than I am, for I have never quite been able to get used to the taste.

I remember that when I was here two years ago I was envious of my daughter-in-law, Minnewa, because she had shoes that she did not have to untie every time we went into a shrine or into a house. So this time I brought a pair to wear that I can just slip on and off without bothering to tie them.

1956

$\mathcal{T}$he new year began with a burst of energy from Eleanor Roosevelt. In its first month alone she visited these cities on two trips for the American Association for the United Nations and to keep other business and social appointments: Bellingham, Seattle, and Longview in Washington State; Los Angeles; San Antonio, Houston, Lubbock, and Dallas in Texas; Philadelphia; Albuquerque, New Mexico; Phoenix, Arizona; and, of course, New York City and Hyde Park.

Tensions were rising in the civil rights debate. Early in February the University of Alabama broke the color line by enrolling its first black student, Autherine Lucy. Liberals hailed the step. Overnight, riots ensued on the campus and within days, to restore order, the school suspended Lucy, a major setback for desegregation. A week later a federal court in New Orleans declared all state laws supporting segregation invalid. By March 1 the National Association for the Advancement of Colored People had sued the University of Alabama to force readmission of Lucy, but, to get clear of the problem, the school countered by expelling her altogether. In May the Methodists joined the Presbyterians, who, the preceding year, had voted as a church to call for an end to segregation. Eleanor Roosevelt had been for some time a director of the NAACP, and in midsummer she agonized over whether to vote to obey a court order segregationists had obtained to force the organization to surrender its membership lists.

Springtime brought news of different kinds. Royalty-watchers everywhere were given a rare treat when an uncommon commoner, the Academy Award–winning actress Grace Kelly, married Prince Rainier III of Monaco. Dr. Jonas Salk, a hero in Mrs. Roosevelt's and many other people's minds, announced in June that the polio vaccine he had developed with colleagues stood a good chance of eliminating the disease in the U.S. within three years.

International tensions in the Middle East boiled over into armed conflict in July. The United States had offered $56 million to Egypt to support the Aswan Dam project on the upper Nile, but shortly withdrew the offer on learning of Egypt's close political ties to the Soviets and of Soviet arms sales to Egypt. Even larger World Bank loans were offered for the project and then withdrawn under U.S. pressure. Egyptian President Gamal Abdel Nasser retaliated by nationalizing the Suez Canal (which had been an open waterway, under British control, since 1875) and by withdrawing guarantees of safe passage for Israeli ships. By autumn Israel and Egypt were in military battle over land rights in the Sinai Desert, which Israel had occupied. British and French troops fought on the Israeli side until the United States successfully arranged a cease fire—to be enforced by United Nations troops. Mrs. Roosevelt saw the entire string of events (particularly the lack of coordination among the Western powers) as a monstrous foreign policy debacle for the Eisenhower administration.

It was an election year. Ike and Vice President Nixon were renominated by the Republicans after the Democrats renominated Adlai Stevenson for president, this time with Senator Estes Kefauver for Vice President. Mrs. Roosevelt squeezed in a month-long European trip just after the conventions, visiting Holland, Denmark, and France. Back home by mid-September to join the campaign, she fought hard for Stevenson and other Democratic candidates. She took the unusual step of closing up part of her Hyde Park house because she simply didn't have time to go there. In mid-October, after noticing that, like Moby-Dick, Mrs. Roosevelt seemed to have the knack of being everywhere at once, the *Boston Globe* sent a reporter to follow her: The editors could not believe anyone of seventy-two could keep up the pace of her travels and appointment schedule. The reporter was soon exhausted and went home.

The incumbents held fast in the White House, garnering almost seven times as many electoral votes as the losers. But the liberals held sway and even gained seats in both houses of Congress. Mrs. Roosevelt and other political observers foresaw a difficult four years ahead resulting from this ideological stalemate between the White House and the Capitol.

Election week in America, no matter how it turns out, demonstrates at least one thing: that political choice is relatively free in the U.S., at least for those who can muster the necessary funds to run for office. But in the Eastern-bloc countries of Poland and Hungary, early in the same week when Americans were choosing new representatives, the story was dif-

ferent. The Soviets used massive military force to crush popular uprisings against Communist control by the Kremlin, uprisings which many
people, including Eleanor Roosevelt, thought stood a good chance to
blow apart the ten-year-old Warsaw Pact alliance of Soviet satellites.
They were wrong. It would be another thirty-four years before real political freedom would begin to return to Eastern Europe.

*Eleanor Roosevelt foresaw that the desegregation process would be a pro-
tracted struggle to change ingrained customs. Here she comments on the
early boycotts, in Alabama, of buses with "whites only" sections and on efforts to integrate the University of Alabama. Mrs. Roosevelt consistently recommended the same course of action as would soon be recognized also as
Dr. Martin Luther King, Jr.'s strategy—nonviolent resistance.*

NEW YORK, MARCH 12—I think everyone must be impressed by the dignity and calmness with which the boycott of the bus companies in Montgomery, Alabama, has been carried on by the Negroes. Gandhi's theory of
nonviolence seems to have been learned very well.

I would also like to speak in praise of those white people in the South
who have long fought for the rights of all their fellow citizens. They are
probably being made to suffer more than any of us in the North can imagine at the present time. I am interested to find that there is even a group of
University of Alabama students who want to know how they can restore
sanity to their fellow students. They do not regard with fear the admission
to the undergraduate body of one young woman, and they deplore the
methods used to keep her out.

I feel Miss Autherine Lucy has behaved with a great deal of dignity. She
has apparently not enjoyed the publicity which the NAACP has thrust
upon her; but she has acted with quiet dignity both in Washington and in
New York, and her attitude gives one confidence that if she can be given a
chance in the university she will act with wisdom and discretion.

Personally, I would like to see not one student but ten admitted. Also, if
there are others at the present time that the university is considering, it
would be well to bring their consideration to a rapid close and accept
these students, as well as to rescind their foolish refusal to permit this
rather gentle and mild young woman from returning to the university.

The Supreme Court recognized that there must be local adjustment in
certain states in desegregation of the schools. They placed good faith in
moving forward in the hands of the courts, and we must wait to see how
this progresses. But there is nothing which prevents the Administration in
Washington from moving at once in the area of protection for all citizens

who desire to vote. In many states, this means paying a poll tax. That in itself may make voting difficult in some cases and really requires two campaigns: (1) to get people to pay their tax, and (2) actually to get them to the polls.

No matter how many promises the NAACP wishes to extract from candidates at the present time, nothing can be achieved of real value for the coming ten months except by the Republican party and the Republican administration, since they are now in power. The question now being addressed to Democratic candidates might much better be addressed to the President of the United States. He can act, and where he cannot act he can ask Congress to give him the power to do so, or to give it to his Department of Justice. I think it is fair to ask any candidate what his position is. But I think it is a waste of time, if you want something done in the next few months, not to concentrate your continuing efforts on the only people who can actually do anything—the President and his administration.

~

Mrs. Roosevelt, like many American women, loved to shop for something fresh to wear. She had as well a single-minded passion for leadership in politics and society, where few women had dared to work. The former First Lady was completely comfortable with the blend in her personality of the ordinary and the unique.

NEW YORK, MARCH 20—One almost expects blizzards early in March, but this one was a little late.

And since Friday was a difficult day to get around on the streets of New York, I decided to go out and buy myself a spring hat! I bought two of them, in fact, in Sally Victor's and I hope that by April, when I finally receive them, the weather will not resemble that of last weekend.

Saturday morning I gave a short speech on "The Changing Role of Women in the Modern World." This subject seems to be one that is growing in interest. It perhaps has particular value at the present time, since women are playing a larger and larger part in developing areas in many countries. So this is a good subject for study by women all over the world.

~

Clear evidence that the child within Eleanor was still very much alive in her seventy-first year appears in a column about her reaction to a freak snowstorm that brought New York City to a standstill.

NEW YORK, MARCH 22—On Sunday afternoon I went out to speak in the evening in Englewood, N.J. A car came for me and we simply crawled the whole way. But the car was heavy and the driver was excellent, managing to keep control so that we did not go too fast down the hills.

I arrived on time to find that, in spite of the snowstorm, a full attendance was present for the dinner. The only thing that worried me was how, in returning, I could climb the hills I had come down. Another route was suggested to my driver and he took it successfully, bringing us back safely at about 11:30 p.m.

With my usual passion for fresh air at night—which, I am told, is quite out of fashion now—I could not resist opening a window before retiring and at 6:00 a.m. I awoke to find that the snowstorm was in my bedroom!

I got up and found a dustpan and pail, filling the pail with snow over and over again until my poor maid woke up and put the finishing touches on my efforts to remove the outdoors from my bedroom. Everything within reach of the snow was soaked, and from then on I kept my window closed!

I was supposed to go to Philadelphia for the whole day on Monday, for both lunch and dinner speeches. So I decided that if I could do nothing else, I could walk to 59th Street, get a subway and then shuttle across to Pennsylvania Station.

But the Pennsylvania Railroad would give me no assurance that the trains would be on time going over or coming back. At the same time, it occurred to me that in this weather there would be no audience in Philadelphia, so I called those in charge there and they promptly agreed, asking me to give them a "snow" check for later on.

I had a free day! Such a wonderful thing!

First, I took my little Scotty, who loves the snow, for a walk. Then I did all the dictating that has been accumulating for months, some reading, wrote letters, talked on the telephone with my snowbound son, Franklin Jr., on his farm. I also talked with my son Johnny, who had managed to get out of Hyde Park and catch a train down, but the rest of his family was snowbound in Hyde Park.

I called my office and asked if they really needed me and, if so, I could have walked there, if necessary. But I was allowed to stay home.

Then I was told that a grandson was marooned, unable to fly or catch a train to join his family in Florida, and I was asked if he could stay with me. Of course, I was delighted to have him.

All of this was pleasant, but I wish the snow were gone.

The superintendent of our building has just told me there is no oil for the furnace and we will have no heat except from our two fireplaces! I mildly protest that the oil should be allowed to get so low, but we are fortunate to have fireplaces and wood!

∼

The civil rights struggle of the 1950s and 1960s spawned great leaders and embarrassing scoundrels. Much of the real work in winning recognition for equal rights for black people was done by strong-willed, courageous men and women who otherwise made no claim to fame. One such heroine was Rosa Parks, the black woman who started the successful Montgomery, Alabama, boycott to force the city bus company to allow blacks to sit anywhere whites could sit.

NEW YORK, MAY 14—A few days ago I met Mrs. Rosa Parks, who started the nonviolent protest in Montgomery, Alabama, against segregation on buses. She is a very quiet, gentle person and it is difficult to imagine how she ever could take such a positive and independent stand.

I suppose we must realize that these things do not happen all of a sudden. They grow out of feelings that have been developing over many years. Human beings reach a point when they say: "This is as far as I can go," and from then on it may be passive resistance, but it will be resistance.

That is what seems to have happened in Montgomery, and perhaps it will happen all over our country wherever we have citizens who do not enjoy complete equality. It may be that this attitude will save us from war and bloodshed and teach those of us who have to learn that there is a point beyond which human beings will not continue to bear injustice.

∼

Was using the atomic bomb against the Japanese to end World War II morally justifiable? Few doubted its military effectiveness, bringing the war to a rapid conclusion after years of killing. But the nuclear bombs dropped on Hiroshima and Nagasaki did considerably more damage than even the physicists and generals had predicted. The cities were essentially leveled, their populations decimated, their landscapes contaminated with radioactivity.

Here Mrs. Roosevelt responds to those who questioned the legitimacy of using the A-bomb. She tries to resolve the dilemma by reexamining what she believed to be a fact: President Truman hardly had any choice. And she reminds her readers of the United States' obligation to help rebuild the targeted Japanese cities.

HYDE PARK, MAY 31—I was surprised to see an article from The Pilot, an official publication of the Catholic Archdiocese of Boston, reprinted in large quantities and sent out by the American Friends Service Committee of Cambridge, Mass., entitled "I Confess."

The article was reprinted with the permission of the editor of The Pilot, America's oldest Catholic weekly newspaper, and, therefore, editorial boards of both the newspaper and the Friends Service committee seem to have approved it.

It was written some time ago marking the anniversary, August 6, of the day ten years before when we dropped the first atomic bomb on the city of Hiroshima, Japan.

The purpose of the article is to say that the American people and their leaders who were responsible for dropping the bomb on Hiroshima, and on Nagasaki the following day, should have confessed their "guilt" long ago.

It goes on to say that the people of Asia feel that much of the aid we have given them since that time came from a feeling of guilt, but that until we confessed this guilt, nothing would be of any avail.

I would like to review the circumstances which led up to this first use of the atomic bomb.

Our military people were almost ready for the last stage of the war, which was the actual attack on Japan. They had counted the costs such an attack would have involved—at least a million lives of American soldiers in addition to complete destruction of as much of Japan as would have been defended. This would have meant cities, towns, villages, men, women and children, for modern war is no longer a war between soldiers; it is a war between peoples.

Because of the plea of one of our American art lovers, we never had bombed two of the historically beautiful cities in Japan, Kyoto and Nara. These, of course, would have had to be destroyed.

All of these facts were presented to the President. In addition, he was told that one bomb would not be sufficient. Two, in quick succession, were our only hope of bringing about complete and rapid surrender. The reason for this was that we had people who had seen the defenses in Japan and they reported that these were so strong it was not believed possible for any army to penetrate to the interior.

So the only possible chance was to deal the Japanese such tremendous blows that they would realize that if they wanted to save themselves from complete destruction, they must surrender at once.

I think everyone in this country should have a horror of the conditions which brought about the need for using the atomic bomb. They should have grief and pity for the people affected and do all in their power to help the innocent who suffer.

But if you had to make this decision, I do not think any decision could have been made other than the one that was made. Leaflets were dropped over Hiroshima before the attack, warning the people to leave the city, and the same thing was done at Nagasaki. But it is human nature to stay where you are and not believe the worst until it happens.

I would not confess guilt for the American people or their leaders, only pity and a deep desire to aid those who suffered through no fault of their own and certainly through no fault of the American people and their leaders.

~

A day's work for Mrs. Roosevelt often ranged fluidly over personal and family matters, local political issues, and larger international concerns, and sometimes (usually in her writing or speeches) reached far back or far forward in time as she tried to articulate where we have come from and where we are heading. She had a global vision, matured by years of personal interaction with people from all walks of life, all corners of the globe. This column reports a not unusual Eleanor Roosevelt day of work and play.

HYDE PARK, JUNE 19—The meeting of the African groups at New York's International House on Friday morning seemed to be very successful and those participating told me they all enjoyed hearing Chester Bowles the day before. Their motto is "Unity in the Family of Man," and I was particularly impressed by the type of questions asked me.

We Americans have much to learn about other peoples of the world, and I think we know less about those on the African continent than anywhere else. It is impressive and encouraging to find so many of their students over here and able to compete on a high intellectual level with our own, in spite of differences in their educational backgrounds, particularly when they come from the areas of South Africa.

The young woman who came for me was from South Africa and had been in this country for two years. No one could have asked for a more charming, gracious and poised person, and her introduction of me as the speaker of the morning was beautifully done.

As I left International House, I drove straight to Hyde Park where everything is now lush and green, perhaps even more beautiful for the slowness of spring. We have jumped quickly into summer. I picked rhubarb and asparagus Saturday morning in the garden, and many flowers are beginning to be available for the house.

At tea time, Abdul Sbihi from Morocco came with his daughter, who is studying in this country and will return to her homeland next autumn. Several other persons were with them and all spent a little time with me before going over to the Memorial Library to lay a wreath on my husband's grave.

Dr. Nyozekan Hasegawa, an 80-year-old Japanese professor, in this country on the cultural exchange program sponsored by Columbia University, came with his interpreter for dinner and to spend the night.

The children were fascinated by the Japanese kimono he wore and the way he wore his hair, which made him look somewhat like our own Walt Whitman. He told us he once was called the Japanese version of Tagore, the Indian poet.

We found him an altogether delightful person and only wished he could have stayed longer, but on Monday morning he left for New York after I had taken him over to the Library.

Dr. Yasaka Takagi persuaded Dr. Hasegawa to come for the visit, and the latter has the same gentle philosophy and charming approach to life which endears Dr. Takagi himself to everyone.

The interpreter who came with him from Japan was taken ill Sunday. He is 30 years younger than Dr. Hasegawa, and the professor twinkled when he mentioned this difference in age.

Dr. Hasegawa has a delightful sense of humor and was particularly pleased to see my youngest granddaughter, Joan, at breakfast. But she would not approach him very closely, being, I think, awed by his hair and his clothes!

He told us that when he was young he hated to go to the barber, so he found a way that he could cut his own hair and he never has been to the barber since!

~

In a quintessentially hard-nosed campaign-season column, Eleanor Roosevelt took on the top three players in the Republican administration: President Eisenhower, Vice President Nixon, and Secretary of State Dulles. She claims they had so badly botched U.S. foreign policy in recent years that even America's best allies, Britain and France, had vetoed U.S. proposals in the UN Security Council. Stevenson would set things right, if elected President, and America would be secure once again.

At this time, Egypt was courting the Soviets for financial assistance with the Aswan Dam; Israel, allied with Britain and France, aggressively defended its occupation of the Sinai Peninsula; and Egypt's President Nasser nationalized the Suez Canal, rendering international shipping insecure.

On November 5—just before the U.S. election—the U.S. brokered a Sinai cease-fire. UN peacekeepers moved in. Eisenhower swamped Stevenson at the polls, and Mrs. Roosevelt had to eat humble pie.

SAN FRANCISCO, NOVEMBER 2—Like most other persons in the country, I felt that the last few days have been painful, indeed. Every day the news from the Near East has been full of anxiety—anxiety for which we had not been prepared by the administration nor by the President himself, who only a week ago told us that the news from the Near East was good.

Most of us then had some misgivings but hoped that perhaps there might be some truth in what the President was saying. Our common sense told us, however, the situation could not be as rosy as we were led to believe.

The greatest shock came when a resolution presented by the United States in the United Nations Security Council was vetoed by the two most important allies of the United States—Great Britain and France. How could such a thing be?

It could not be possible that our Secretary of State had let our relationships so deteriorate with our closest allies and our most important friends that we were not aware they would veto our resolution!

It could not be possible that we would present such a resolution, knowing that we would find ourselves lined up with the Soviet Union and the dictator of Egypt, against Great Britain and France and the only democratic country in the Near East—Israel! What a false and confusing situation!

If we felt our allies' position was wrong, had we lost all our influence that they would not listen to us? Something must be seriously wrong.

Then on Wednesday morning I opened a metropolitan paper to see on the front page that our Secretary of State accused our allies, Great Britain and France, of having entered into an agreement and instigated Israel's latest action in Egypt.

Again my heart sank. Did we not know whether or not our allies had entered into any such agreement with Israel? What had happened to our relations with these two important countries in the world?

Then I read that Vice President Richard M. Nixon said in a speech that now, of course, the people of this country would decide that they must keep a tried-and-true general as our leader and as our President because it would be unwise to change at this crucial time to untried and poor leadership.

I could not believe my eyes! How could we have had worse leadership than that which brought us to this present situation? Do we want to continue with the kind of leadership that has led to a war in which, if we are not with our old allies, we have to side with the Kremlin and the dictator of Egypt? What a decision to have to make!

Where has our influence, which ought to help shape such decisions in the world, failed so that we find ourselves today in such a position?

I listened to the President on television and noticed that he never mentioned a most important point, namely that the Kremlin has succeeded in dividing the West and we are, indeed, weakened. Does he not realize the seriousness of the situation he and John Foster Dulles have created?

I feel sure that every woman in this country will feel it her obligation to beg her friends and neighbors—men and women, young and old—to change this leadership as quickly as possible.

I think if we elect Adlai Stevenson and Estes Kefauver next Tuesday and give them the support in the Senate and the House which they need, we will not find ourselves unexpectedly in situations of this kind. We will have a leadership which, I hope, will give us a knowledge of what conditions really exist in the world and, therefore, will ensure greater security for us and for the world as a whole.

~

If Eleanor Roosevelt had had more administrative ability (something she confessed she lacked), she might have made a colorful Secretary of State. As journalist, former UN delegate, and First Lady, she saw foreign policy issues broadly enough to critique President Eisenhower's performance. Mideast tensions worsened as British and French troops helped Israel in the Sinai against Egypt. Mrs. Roosevelt believed Republican leaders unnecessarily placated Arab interests to protect the flow of oil to America. And she sensed a dangerous long-term pattern of kowtowing to the Soviets. The memory of two world wars taught her that appeasement does not work.

HYDE PARK, NOVEMBER 26—In our own country we are faced with a difficult decision in the Egyptian crisis. Egypt is demanding that all troops from Great Britain, France and Israel be removed from Egyptian territory at once, and that the UN police force be in no way considered as a "military presence." But the British, French and Israelis, before they withdraw their military forces, want some assurance that Egypt and the other Arab states will negotiate a permanent peace. They feel that otherwise they are apt to find themselves in the same position which existed when they were goaded to the point of making this attack.

It is reported, however, that President Eisenhower feels the best way to proceed "for the solution of the basic problems of the area" is to get all military personnel out of this area as soon as possible. If one could also move all Arab military power from the area, this might be a satisfactory solution. But, I must say, one does not have a great sense of confidence that the Arab states will be moved by any kind of reasonable attitude. If the UN force was considered a real military force and of sufficient size to constitute a power that would enforce all United Nations decisions, this would seem to me a very wise solution. But if it is merely to be a token police force, with no ability to enforce the will of the majority in the United Nations, then I can see a real dilemma for the United States. We will be asking our best allies to withdraw with the possibility that we are reducing them to a hopeless situation, with arms coming into the Arab states from the Soviet Union and nothing being done to protect the interests of the world in the Suez Canal and to assure the safety of Israel, all of which is essential to the survival of democracy in the Near East.

~

A hint of things to come: the first mention in "My Day" of the civil rights leadership of Dr. Martin Luther King, Jr. Eleanor Roosevelt recognized in the wisdom of his thoughts and the eloquence of his expression that, like Mahatma Gandhi, King's best contribution to the struggle would be in the symbolic power of his nonviolent resistance to discrimination.

HYDE PARK, DECEMBER 24—Throughout the country our eyes are turned on Montgomery, Alabama, as the Supreme Court's order ending segregation on buses goes into effect. The Negroes celebrated this order at mass meetings on Thursday night and they have already gone back to using the buses on a nonsegregated basis. Their spiritual leader, Rev. Martin Luther King, Jr., cautioned them not to allow any violence. "This is a time when we must observe calm dignity and wise restraint," he said. "Emotions must not run wild."

Only one or two minor incidents occurred the first day of nonsegregation on buses. The Negroes in Montgomery had been given careful schooling in a nonviolent approach to any difficulties that might arise. Special emphasis had been laid on "remaining peaceful even if others strike first." It is to be hoped that everything will continue to move quietly, for this experiment of nonsegregation is already in force in the airlines in the South, and in the North there is no place where one may not sit next to an individual of any nationality or color in public conveyances. Once it is accepted, I am sure it will seem as natural for the people of the South as it does for the people of the North.

1957

*P*resident Eisenhower and his foreign policy advisers, including Secretary of State John Foster Dulles, believed in early 1957, when they articulated what became known as the Eisenhower Doctrine—a guarantee of U.S. arms sales to any Mideast country requesting them—that providing arms would help stabilize an area of the world threatened from without by Soviet communism and from within by ages-old ethnic and political conflicts. The White House unwittingly fueled the possibilities for armed conflicts there, conflicts that rarely resolved anything for the better or for long. By early March Congress had approved the Eisenhower Doctrine, and there was no turning back. Mrs. Roosevelt wanted to see Israel kept strong enough to defend its borders, but she was among the first to call for a serious reconsideration of arms sales as an instrument of foreign policy. Her voice went mostly unheard.

In the meantime, Ike was inaugurated for his second term as President, riding a high tide of popularity. Eleanor Roosevelt continued to scurry back and forth across the United States, in fair weather and foul, mostly for AAUN meetings and lectures, occasionally stopping to see friends and family en route. In January she went to Florida and the Midwest; in February to Washington State and to California, Arizona, and Texas; in March to Minnesota and Iowa—for several days of grueling work and travel in each state. Also in March, Mrs. Roosevelt and an entourage of friends (including David Gurewitsch) and secretaries took an excursion to Morocco and other parts of North Africa. Though she had been practically everywhere else in the world, the lure of exotic places like Casablanca was still strong for her.

At the end of April the United States dedicated its first working nuclear reactor for domestic electricity production, located at Fort Belvoir,

Virginia. The event was hailed as the harbinger of an era of safe, cheap power.

Senator Joseph McCarthy died in early May, just about the time Mrs. Roosevelt was filing the first of her "My Day" columns from London at the start of a two-week trip to the United Kingdom and the Continent (primarily Vienna). Also early that month, the young, ambitious senator from Massachusetts, John F. Kennedy, captured the year's Pulitzer Prize for biography with his book *Profiles in Courage.*

President Eisenhower remained concerned about the potential spread of communism in Southeast Asia. In May he met with South Vietnam's President, Ngo Dinh Diem, to firm up commitments between the two countries in the struggle against the Soviets and the Chinese, a step similar to that of the French there years before. A historical note was also sounded at midyear: The *Mayflower II,* a replica of the boat that brought the Pilgrims to Plymouth Rock in southeast Massachusetts in 1620, arrived at the same spot after a fifty-four-day commemorative voyage across the Atlantic.

Blowing off the Gulf of Mexico uncommonly early in the hurricane season, a terrible storm took 531 lives along the Texas-Louisiana coast at the end of June. By late summer another type of storm was brewing in the South. The Civil Rights Act of 1957 was signed by the President in late August. The Act included strong provisions to protect voting rights. Strong opposition ensued: South Carolina Senator Strom Thurmond set a filibuster record (twenty-four hours, twenty-seven minutes) in his attempt to thwart the bill's passage. Days later, defying federal Supreme Court rulings calling for school desegregation, Governor Orville Faubus of Arkansas called out his state's National Guard to prevent black students from entering the all-white Little Rock high school.

Much of the nation was outraged, though the action drew praise also from fellow segregationists—who immediately lionized Faubus. President Eisenhower and the governor conferred a few days later. A federal injunction forced the governor to withdraw the National Guard. Black students entered the school, and riots broke out, lasting several days. Finally the President sent in regular Army soldiers to make peace and to protect the nine black students who had tried to integrate the school. Federal authorities and the black students prevailed, but damage had been done to America's international image and to the segregationists' political position. The events radicalized many otherwise patient black people, making them now willing to fight for their rights.

Eleanor Roosevelt engaged in a drama of her own. She made her first visit to the Soviet Union (Moscow and the interior), returning after a month's stay with valuable reportage on Russian life. Her interviews with Khrushchev required additional space in her "My Day" columns. Overnight, in addition to being a leading expert on United Nations affairs, Mrs. Roosevelt now became, at seventy-two, a much-sought-after expert on Soviet affairs. Invitations to lecture on the USSR all but swamped her already overly packed schedule.

When the Russians launched the first unmanned satellite, Sputnik, on October 4, the U.S. space program got an unflattering surprise. Indirectly, the American educational system (especially the sciences) was shocked, too. Though Eleanor Roosevelt never became a supporter of the space program, thinking that all those dollars could better be spent solving earthly problems, she quickly joined the critics who said Sputnik's success was a litmus test for the success of the Soviet educational system—and by implication for the sluggishness of its American counterpart.

The familiar ring of the call for campaign finance reform: Mrs. Roosevelt was thoroughly egalitarian insofar as the two major parties were concerned, but she makes no mention of "third parties" that might also deserve a slice of the pie. Third party challenges to FDR and the unhappy history of the American Communist Party may have kept her from believing that a multiparty system would be good for American democracy.

SEATTLE, FEBRUARY 13—The cartoon on this newspaper's editorial page dealt with a subject which is of interest to the whole country. It showed a GOP elephant and a Democratic donkey, the latter warming his hands at a little wood fire and looking very ragged, having spent only $10 million on the election campaign. The GOP elephant, having spent $20 million on the campaign, looks resplendent in good clothes and a diamond pin. He says, "Money well spent, I say."

I wonder if others throughout the country feel strongly enough about this situation to do something about campaign expenses. I have long felt that the same amount should be spent by both parties, that both should be given free radio and television time, and that an equal amount of newspaper advertising and railroad travel should be allowed in the different categories and paid for by the public.

~

*Always an intensely loyal Democrat, Eleanor Roosevelt was also a fine re-
porter of behind-the-scenes political machinations. Here she is a sharp
critic of Southerners contemplating secession from a too-liberal Democratic Party ready to support civil rights.*

SAN FRANCISCO, FEBRUARY 18—My first greetings in the hotel here were
from delegates from Hawaii who had come for the national meeting of the
Democratic Committee and the Advisory Committee, which met at the
same time. Saturday night the big fundraising dinner was addressed by Adlai
Stevenson, but panels on many subjects continue to be held. My son James
and Senator Lehman [New York] were on the panel on human resources,
where the Senator brought up the question of the attitude of the Democratic
Party on civil rights. The papers have long articles on the subject.

Governor Harriman was here only for 24 hours, but like many others he
agrees with Senator Lehman that the President and the Republican Administration have not faced up to their responsibility as regards integration in this country. They agree also that the Democratic Party, because of
its Southern membership, has not come out strongly and honestly in its
stand, and they are determined that there shall be a clear cut decision as
to where the Democratic Party does stand.

They acknowledge the fact that this may bring a political explosion,
since this is the question which deeply divides the Democratic Party. The
South, solidly Democratic for many years, though it is now beginning to
move into a less solid status and show signs of having a two-party system,
still has held, because of seniority, many of the most important and influential party positions in the Congress. The Congressional leaders in both
the Senate and the House are opposed to anything which will mean a
clear cut stand on civil rights legislation.

There are among the Southerners those who realize that change must
come. But they are also faced with the fact that they must be reelected,
and their role is a difficult one. For the liberals in the North to force on the
whole party a stand which is impossible for the South to accept is going to
be a very serious step, and I hope that wisdom and patience will be used
in the discussions which are to go on in the next few days.

~

*Eleanor Roosevelt goes abroad again. After visiting Madrid to see master-
pieces at the Prado, she and her entourage cross the Straits of Gibraltar to
Morocco. Though traveling privately, Mrs. Roosevelt is received as if she
were a high government official. "My Day" travel columns combine a
friendly letter to family and guidebook reportage.*

Fᴇᴢ, Mᴏʀᴏᴄᴄᴏ, Aᴘʀɪʟ 2—Here we are in the old capital of Morocco and I feel sure that we will find it interesting.

The Hotel Palais Jamal is on the outskirts of town, but as the city lies in a valley and the walls and defenses were built all around it, the view of the city from the top of the hill in approaching it is lovely.

As we were driving along this morning, we came through a village in which the whole population seemed to be trekking to a hill covered with trees. We decided to join the procession and discovered they were going to the weekly fair.

We wandered among the vegetables and fruits, dyes and spices. Then we came upon the meats, and here again I was struck by the cleanliness. There were few flies and everything was washed and fresh-looking. One should not eat uncooked food here, but it is hard to follow the rule when everything looks so sanitary.

We looked at the sheep and cattle, and I spoke to a young man bargaining for them with the Moroccan farmers. This young man, a Swiss, was buying cattle for three farms and he told me he bought sheep at about $6.25 a head, fattened them for a few months, and sold them at the time of the great religious feast for a neat profit.

We lunched in the town of Meknes with the Pasha and had an even more sumptuous meal, if that were possible, than the day before. The food here is rich, prepared with much butter—very good, and very fattening!

We saw the Sultan's imperial palace—enormous but largely in ruins and then drove through the town and saw a beautiful mosaic-covered gate where the letter-writers were plying their trade. Finally, we came here by the most direct road, for we were rather tired of sightseeing.

The Hotel Palais Jamal was built as a private house, but a strange house it must have been, with many stairs and many rooms at different levels. It has a lovely garden and terrace.

My son Elliott is managing his big party of travelers well, and the Sultan has provided us with a delightful traveling companion. The Sultan also notifies his governors along the way to look after us, and they are more than kind.

This country needs more industries and help from various sources. I heard an amusing story about the labor unions. They are struggling to get recognition for collective bargaining, and so far the industrial leaders will not accept them. Consequently, there are strikes.

One strike was called at one of our United States bases where the strikers announced that they understood that in the United States employees are always paid by their employers while on strike. They were surprised and aggrieved when they were told this was not the case.

Perhaps some of our good labor leaders should come over here and help them organize. It would be better than leaving it to the Communists.

~

Filing this "My Day" column from London, where she began her second foreign trip of the year, Mrs. Roosevelt gives her readers a glimpse of the British royal family's private life. A lifelong anglophile, Eleanor Roosevelt never questioned the monarchy's legitimacy.

NEW YORK, MAY 15—I had an appointment to see Queen Elizabeth in London, so George Spencer, who accompanied us from Nottingham on the train, urged the engineer to see to it that we arrived on time, and we did.

It was very kind of the Queen to receive me, since she had not realized that I was leaving Britain so soon and little Prince Charles had had his tonsils and adenoids out the day before.

I arrived at the Palace at 6:30 p.m. to be met by a charming young man who took me into a small sitting room where the Queen's lady-in-waiting came to speak to me. Then we went upstairs to another small sitting room where in a few minutes someone came to say the Queen was ready.

I went into the Queen's study and found her just as calm and composed as if she did not have a very unhappy little boy on her mind. I asked if he had felt well enough yet to demand ice cream and she said he already had had two portions, making me feel that he probably was on the mend.

Forty minutes after I had arrived and after a nice talk, the Queen thoughtfully said she knew she must not keep me longer, as I had a dinner engagement, and we parted.

I have the greatest respect for this young woman who must combine the responsibilities of a Queen with the requirements and emotional stresses of a young mother. I think, too, the British people are fortunate in having the royal family to hold them together. Everywhere you go, you see that the Queen, Prince Philip, the Queen Mother, and Princess Margaret are loved as well as deeply respected.

~

The sheer boldness of Mrs. Roosevelt's request to interview Nikita Khrushchev is noteworthy. Other reporters failed even to gain admission to the country, much less the Kremlin. Her international stature, stemming from years at the UN as a U.S. delegate, put Mrs. Roosevelt in a powerful position, as though she were a self-appointed ambassador-at-large. "My Day" was syndicated widely enough so that foreign leaders, including Khrushchev, knew it was an excellent way to reach the American people.

NEW YORK, OCTOBER 3—I can best begin this series of articles on the Soviet Union by letting Nikita S. Khrushchev, leader of the Communist Party of the USSR, speak for himself. I was asked to submit my questions, but Mr. Khrushchev did not have them before him when I appeared. And he answered my questions as though he was speaking completely spontaneously.

This first article will cover only in part some of the recorded answers, and while I have his answers in Russian, I can give you only the translation as it came from my interpreter, Mrs. Anna Lavrova, who told me she had translated for my husband at Yalta.

I opened by asking her to tell Mr. Khrushchev that I appreciated his taking the time to see me when he was on vacation and I added that I had enjoyed and had been much interested by my trip in his country. Mr. Khrushchev answered, "Politicians never cast aside political obligations."

Here are my questions and his replies:

ROOSEVELT: I came to the USSR for the newspapers I write for and to use what information I could gather for lectures which I will be giving in the coming year, but I have the hope that being here I can gain greater understanding and clear up some of the questions we get at home from some of our people who do not understand certain things they hear about the USSR.

KHRUSHCHEV: I appreciate your coming here and I want to speak of President Franklin Roosevelt. We respect him and remember his activities because he was the first to establish diplomatic relations between the USA and the USSR. President Roosevelt understood perfectly well the necessity of such relations between our two countries.

He was a great man, a capable man who understood the interests of his own country and the interests of the Soviet Union. We had a common cause against Hitler and we appreciate very much that Franklin Roosevelt understood this task, which was a common task of our two countries. I am very happy to greet you in our land and to have a talk here.

ROOSEVELT: Mr. Khrushchev, may I ask the questions which I have submitted? Then if you have any questions to ask me, I will be happy to try to answer them, and may we have some further informal talk, not for direct quotation?

KHRUSHCHEV: Yes, Mrs. Roosevelt, you are welcome.

ROOSEVELT: At home people would say, "How does the Soviet Union expect us to disarm without inspection when she forced us to re-arm after World War II? We reduced our army from 12,000,000 to 1,000,000 men." That would be one of the first questions asked, sir.

KHRUSHCHEV: I believe, Mrs. Roosevelt, we have different points of view on this armament complaint. We do not agree with your conception. We consider that demobilization took place in the U.S. and in the USSR.

You mention that you had 12,000,000 army men but in our country men and women were all mobilized. In our country perished roughly the number of people which you mention made up the army in your country, almost the same number of people. Mrs. Roosevelt, I do not want to offend you, but if you compare the losses of your country and the losses of ours, your losses just equal roughly our losses in one big campaign, one big attack by the Germans.

As you know, Mrs. Roosevelt, what terrible ruins we got and destruction because we lost our mining, our metallurgy. We lost our cities. That is why our country was so eager to establish peace and to establish firm peace. No country wished it so eagerly as our country.

When you consider demobilization, just some circles in your country wanted it. Others thought and believed that the Soviet country would perish as a socialist state, so they just hoped that it will perish, that it will die.

ROOSEVELT: I can't quite understand that. You mean, Mr. Khrushchev, that you think we thought, or rather that some circles believed, that all socialist countries would die.

KHRUSHCHEV: That is exactly. But these hopes failed and you see now that our socialist state was established out of the ruins, has established its economy and has become even more powerful.

ROOSEVELT: I understand, Mr. Khrushchev, but the Soviets kept a much greater proportion of men under arms than we did at that time.

[Dr. David Gurewitsch, who made the trip to Russia with me, was making the recording of the conversation and, at the same time, listening to make sure the translations were correct, since he knew Russian and was allowed to take photographs. So he broke in here to say, "Not just the proportion but the absolute figures were far greater—6,000,000 men under arms in the Soviet."]

KHRUSHCHEV: Dr. Gurewitsch, you may perfectly know the number of your army men, but don't feel so sure of the number of our army men. You don't know it. [Turning to Mrs. Roosevelt] I do not reject that our army was bigger than yours. We approached this question in a quiet way, in a calm way. Then it can be looked at reasonably and easily understood.

Take a map and look at the geographical location or situation of our country. It is a colossal territory. Mrs. Roosevelt, if you take Germany or France, just small countries which keep their army either to defend either their East or their West, that is easy. They may have a small army, but if we keep our army in the East, it is difficult to reach the West, you see, to use this Western army in the East, because our territory is so vast. Or the army which is in the North cannot be used in the South.

So, to be sure of our security in our state, we have to keep a big army, which is not so easy for us. When people speak about borders, they speak about 3,000 kilometers, which is the distance between the continents. But when we move our army from East to West, it means 3,000 kilometers.

ROOSEVELT: I understand all this, of course, but you have nothing to fear from the North. I understand that at Yalta Germany's defeat was accepted and you did not want Germany built up as a military power and you wanted a group of neutral countries between you and Germany. I understood at that time that these countries were to be free countries but to be closely tied to the Soviet Union, since the USSR was actually thinking of its protection.

Today, certainly, Great Britain, France and Germany are not a military menace. I don't say they might not become so, but they are not today. They are purely on a defensive basis, so I think it is possible to discuss very calmly how a country like the Soviet Union can be secure, which I understand perfectly the need of and the desire for, and still it should be possible not to have in the Soviet Union an army that can be an offensive army, because that frightens the rest of the world.

KHRUSHCHEV: What can I tell you in answer, Mrs. Roosevelt? When we increase our arms, it means that we are afraid of each other. Russian troops, before the Revolution, never approached Great Britain and never entered America. Even in old times they never came to the United States of America, but the troops of the USA approached our Far East, Japanese troops were in our Far East in Vladivostock, French troops in our city of Odessa, and that is why we must have an army. Your troops approach our territory, not we yours.

We never went to Mexico or Canada, but your troops went there, so that is why we have to have an army in case of danger. Before the time when troops will be drawn out of Europe and military bases will be liquidated, of course, the disarmament will not succeed.

ROOSEVELT: The actual type of armament today that is important has changed. It is not what it used to be in the old days. We are reducing our army, but what matters today is atomic weapons, and that is why I imagine the emphasis will have to be on how we can come to an agreement.

~

In an excerpt from a subsequent Khrushchev column, we see that Mrs. Roosevelt had lost patience with the slow process of international arms reduction negotiations and had decided to see what she could do herself, and right in the lion's den. The time and space given to nuclear war and disarmament reflect an overriding Cold War concern of the late 1950s.

CINCINNATI, OCTOBER 5—

KHRUSHCHEV: We are for international inspection, but there first has to be confidence and then inspection. Mr. Dulles wants inspection without confidence.

ROOSEVELT: I think the confidence and the inspection have to come together. We have to start and gradually increase our plans.

KHRUSHCHEV: Quite right. Only gradually it can be done.

ROOSEVELT: Would you agree to limited inspection if we could make a beginning?

KHRUSHCHEV: But I quite agree. That is what we proposed. We proposed inspection in ports, on highways, on roads, at airports, and it is to be an international inspection. But in answer to our proposal, Mr. Dulles makes a statement which sounds as though he was making propaganda for the atom bomb, trying to make it palatable. He talks of a clean bomb as if there were such a thing as a clean bomb. War is dirty thing.

But you refused our suggestion. You insist on this flying business and looking at our factories. You know those rockets made the situation more frightful. Now we can destroy countries in a few minutes. How many bombs does it take to destroy West Germany? How many for France? How many for England? Just a few. We have now H-bombs and rockets. We do not even have to send any bombers.

ROOSEVELT: And soon small countries will have atomic bombs.

KHRUSHCHEV: Why not? Research goes on. They learn about it. Let's get together so there shall be no war. We are ready to sign such an agreement
now.

ROOSEVELT: Your people certainly want peace, and I can assure you that
our people want peace, too.

KHRUSHCHEV: Do you think we, the government, want war?

ROOSEVELT: Not the people, but governments, make war. And then they persuade the people that it is in a good cause, the cause of their own defense.
Those arguments can be made by both your government and by ours.

KHRUSHCHEV: That's right. Can we say we had a friendly conversation?

ROOSEVELT: You can say we had a friendly conversation, but we differ.

KHRUSHCHEV: Now, we didn't shoot at each other.

~

*Mrs. Roosevelt turns her attention to a political squabble involving an in-
famous fur coat given to First Lady Mamie Eisenhower. Tempest in a
teapot? Even in the ridiculous, Eleanor Roosevelt uncovers the substantive
issue—the ethics of giving gifts to government officials. And she sends sympathy to the First Lady because she knew the vulnerability of a President's
spouse to merciless public scrutiny.*

ANN ARBOR, MICH., NOVEMBER 9—Congress, it seems to me, is becoming
rather confused about the gifts-in-government question in Washington.

The Constitution bars public officials from accepting gifts from a foreign government, and this has been construed in various ways by the
State Department. But as far as I know there is nothing which deprives a
person who is not actually in employ of the government from accepting
from a foreigner something to show appreciation of kindness or good
service.

There is also nothing except good taste, as far as I know, to dictate what
the wife of a President shall or shall not do. It is this point that is not
touched upon either in the Constitution or in any law I know of. And it is
this which I would like to write about because I think Mrs. Eisenhower has
been made uncomfortable by criticism resulting from her acceptance of a

fur coat from the Fur Trappers of Maine and the Beaver Fur Trappers Association.

The beaver trappers of Maine presented Mrs. Eisenhower with some skins. This was done in the obvious hope that she would have these skins made up and wear them and that a domestic industry thereby would get some sorely needed attention. Not many people know that the trapping of beavers is one of the industries of the State of Maine.

Mrs. Eisenhower herself paid for the making of her coat and it is nobody's business what she paid for having it made up. She was doing an American industry a kindness.

The effort was made, I think, to make her feel that this was wrong in some way, and yet no strings were attached to this gift. She was not asked to award a contract or to change somebody's road or to see that oil was imported here or there. She was simply given a gift which those who gave it hoped would give her pleasure, knowing that if it did and she wore the skins, it would bring them some attention.

Nobody was going to be forced to buy a beaver coat, but they would know where they could buy one. I believe it would have been more unkind and she would have been open to severer criticism if she had refused the gift rather than accepting it.

There is little enough pleasure attached to being the wife of a President, a position that involves a great many responsibilities. Why the press apparently should draw critical attention to a perfectly innocent act of kindness I cannot understand.

Mrs. Eisenhower has conducted herself with dignity and grace in the White House. She has fulfilled the duties expected of her, and this type of criticism seems to me petty and small and not worthy of the American press or the American people.

~

The civil rights struggle in the U.S. did not blind Eleanor Roosevelt to similar if not worse conditions of prejudice in other countries. She was among the early prophets of eventual radical change in South African apartheid. Mrs. Roosevelt supported a universal Declaration of Conscience concerning opposition to such virulent racism.

NEW YORK, DECEMBER 2—People all over the world have been asked to sign a Declaration of Conscience to observe a day of protest against South Africa's apartheid policy. An international committee, composed of more than 150 world leaders from more than 43 nations, has designated Human Rights Day, December 10, as this worldwide day of protest. Particularly in India and in Africa, as well as in many other countries of the world, there will be demonstrations protesting the policy which is felt to be harmful to human relations the world over. Therefore it cannot be the domestic concern of one nation only, but of all nations.

More than 20 American communities have already said they would hold similar meetings. The Very Rev. James A. Pike is the U.S. national chairman and Rev. Martin Luther King, Jr. is the vice president of the committee in this country. The list of those who have signed the Declaration of Conscience is composed of the names of men all over the world who are known to have stood for equal rights for all human beings. It is true that there are peoples who are not as advanced as others, but as a rule this is due to lack of opportunity and can be corrected in one or two generations by education and environment.

When I was asked to sign this Declaration of Conscience, I at first hesitated. I felt that a country which needed to look at its own situation and acknowledge the basic rights of all its own citizens and work for the necessary changes which would bring every citizen in the United States the opportunity for complete development of his powers might better perhaps first sign a Declaration of Conscience covering his own country. I signed, however, because the situation here, bad as it is, is not quite the same as the situation in South Africa. The Negroes of our South have good leaders and though their education has been insufficient and their opportunities for advancement certainly not equal, still they have begun their upward climb. They are able to do much for themselves, and on the whole in this country there is a vast majority of people who are ready and willing to help them achieve equality of opportunity in every area of our complicated civilization.

Bitter as the feeling is at present in the South and in spite of the fact that communications between the races in many Southern states seem to have deteriorated, the Supreme Court decision and the feeling of the majority of the people of the nation will eventually, I am sure, bring about a solution to the present difficult situation. Someone suggested to me the other day that it might be started in the South by dividing boys' schools and girls' schools and putting all boys without discrimination into one school and all girls without discrimination into another, which would remove one of the chief objections of the Southerners. Whether this would help or not, I don't know. But I am confident that the pressure of the majority feeling in this nation will be so overwhelming for equal rights for all our citizens that sooner or later this problem must have a solution which satisfactorily safeguards these rights.

When she went home at last for Christmas at Hyde Park, the pleasures and travails of managing an aging country house (her beloved Val-Kill) absorbed Mrs. Roosevelt's attention. It had been an astonishingly full year for Eleanor Roosevelt. It was time, for a few days, to focus on family and fun.

HYDE PARK, DECEMBER 30—There is an old saying, often quoted by my husband's father, which said "No very stiff frost will come until the springs are filled."

I think our springs in the country must be nearly filled by now. We have had rain and rain and rain. The brook always overflows into my cellar at Hyde Park when it rises above a certain level, and it already has done so.

There are certain places in the roofs of the playhouse and my own cottage which we have tried to mend but which, under certain conditions, leak and cause a near-flood in the back kitchen and in one of my living rooms. But during the last heavy rain only the back kitchen suffered.

This, however, is not a happy situation when cooking for a large number of persons, as my people at Hyde Park have been doing the last few days.

My grandchildren are so delighted to go horseback riding every day during the holidays, so the lack of snow or ice does not upset them at all. But the rain does! So, while we are not praying for snow, we are praying for clear weather!

1958

Not again until the mid-1980s, when President Ronald Reagan was at the height of his popularity, was a person in the eighth decade of life chosen as the most admired American in a Gallup poll. In 1958 that honor went to Eleanor Roosevelt, who would turn seventy-four in October. By 1958 Mrs. Roosevelt had redefined her role as that of gadfly, speaking often for an advanced progressive minority, making all the more remarkable her selection as America's most admired woman.

The Cold War continued to heat up. Reports of military advances and scientific progress carried out in the name of international competition, generally with the Soviets, dominated the news. Protracted discussions of disarmament went nowhere. In January the Air Force implemented unremitting surveillance aloft, keeping strategic bombers always at the ready should the Russians attack. By May the United States and Canada had formed NORAD (North American Air Defense Command)—radar stations across the Canadian tundra to guard against a Soviet attack. Perhaps as an indication of the diminishing presence of Communists in America, *The Daily Worker* cut back to once-a-week publication.

Secretary of State John Foster Dulles, dueling with the Soviets, recognized that outer space could become the next battlefield. In January he proposed an international agreement guaranteeing peaceful use of the heavens. The U.S. space program played catch-up with the Russians'. Explorer 1, America's first satellite, was launched by the Army from Cape Canaveral in Florida. In March the Navy launched Vanguard 1. By July incipient rivalry among the military services in the space program resolved with the creation of NASA (National Aeronautics and Space Administration). Eleanor Roosevelt persisted in her chilly opinion about the space program. She argued that humanitarian needs on earth should be addressed first, a viewpoint not widely shared at the time.

American foreign policy met with hostile resistance in the spring and early summer. Vice President Richard Nixon, on a goodwill tour of Latin American countries, was assaulted by a mob in Venezuela; American-sponsored libraries in Lebanon were attacked after U.S. Marines had landed in that country to help quell an insurrection. Many "My Day" columns in 1958 analyzed America's difficult role in world politics. Mrs. Roosevelt believed the United States had a major role to play as the richest, most powerful country in the world, but her favored tactics contrasted with Eisenhower's preferred strategy, which usually relied on arms sales to foreign governments. During the dog days of August, the U.S. Navy sent its premier atomic submarine, the *Nautilus*, to make the first under-ice crossing of the North Pole, a technical and military triumph.

The Democratic Congress and Republican White House, after much debate, passed the National Defense Education Act to make loans available to students for higher education. The theory was that America needed better-educated young adults to fight the good fight against Communist influence at home and abroad. Mrs. Roosevelt approved of the program but thought there was no need to link the aid-to-education bill directly to international tensions. In the South, the integration struggle continued. In September, Little Rock, Arkansas, sought more time to effect integration, but the Supreme Court denied the request. Governor Faubus closed four public schools in defiance of the Court's orders.

The end of the year saw liberal Republican Nelson Rockefeller, whom Mrs. Roosevelt admired, take a major step in developing his political career when he won the governorship of New York. The Democratic Party in New York was in poor shape, as Mrs. Roosevelt candidly documented in her "My Day" columns, and she worked hard to help rebuild it.

In 1958 James Agee—who with photographer Walker Evans had produced in 1941 one of the most moving books about the Depression and about poverty in general, *Let Us Now Praise Famous Men*—was awarded the Pulitzer Prize for fiction for his *A Death in the Family*. In August, when the Russian novelist Vladimir Nabokov's titillating *Lolita* was published in English in the United States, it barely survived censorship challenges.

Eleanor Roosevelt had long before developed a concern for the financial fate of older people and those with disabilities. She participated in White House debates about the establishment of the Social Security Administration. Few early proponents, however, took inflation into account. By the late

1950s Mrs. Roosevelt, among others, recognized that without periodic benefit adjustments in veterans', widows', and retirees' benefits, living on a fixed income could be difficult indeed. Mrs. Roosevelt's idea here—linking Social Security payments to the Consumer Price Index (inflation barometer)—later gained broad acceptance as "Indexing."

NEW YORK, JANUARY 10—I have a letter from a woman who tells the sad story that I hear more and more often these days.

She is a widow whose husband, a war veteran, died 27 years ago and left her to raise five children. She wrote to draw my attention to the fact that even though widows of veterans get a pension, it is not enough for them to live on. Her pension is $54.18 a month.

This woman lives in southern Texas, but even there her pension is not sufficient to live on. She has worked hard all her life. Her husband was a bodyguard for President Theodore Roosevelt on many of his speaking tours.

She is unable to make ends meet because she no longer can work. Her children, she says, are married and have their own families to raise and she does not think it right to burden them with her support.

I feel that it is not too much to ask that each child give her a small amount, yet I have great sympathy for her feeling that after a life of hard work she should be entitled to a pension covering the necessities of life so she need not depend on her children.

I feel a reassessment of Social Security benefits in the pension field should be made. The cost of living has gone up. Of late, prices always seem to be going up and never coming down. Perhaps there should be a sliding scale for pensions to meet the changes in living costs.

I think, too, that pensioners are a group which probably should be given some of our surplus foods, for no one in this country should be on a diet below the standards of healthy living.

Most of these people are old, and perhaps Congress will not think their votes amount to much. But this group is certainly getting larger in this country and, therefore, even from a political standpoint, this situation should receive consideration from both Republicans and Democrats.

~

The Soviets stunned America by successfully launching the first satellite, "Sputnik," in 1957. The American liberal intelligentsia interpreted Soviet scientific achievements to mean postwar society had become dangerously anti-intellectual and noncompetitive. McCarthyism's Red-baiting and the country's inattention to serious education as a national priority were hurt-

ing America. Eleanor Roosevelt believed America must get serious about teaching, children, and science to preserve democracy's preeminence.

AUSTIN, TEX., MARCH 3—I wish that the New York Herald Tribune editorial last Friday, entitled "Did Sputnik Wake Us Up?," could be reprinted in every paper in the United States. It called attention to several recent opinion surveys in this country on science, education and history, and commented on the appalling implications of the results obtained. What these surveys reveal is not that we need to copy the Russian system of education and set up more scholarships for scientists, but that we need to change our attitude in this country toward learning and knowledge, its value, and the respect due to those who take the trouble to learn.

This fundamental attitude, for example, is at the bottom of some of the ignorance cited among students of American history in Indiana. You may be shocked to read that, out of 90 university students quizzed on American history, only eight could identify the Bill of Rights! The explanation might be that in the State of Indiana there was for a time, with the help and influence of one of their Senators, so much fear of Communism and so little knowledge about it that few people would have dared to talk of the Bill of Rights for fear of being called Communistic!

That only four students knew what a "right to work" law is does not astonish me so much because the name is a misleading one. These bills have nothing to do with the right to work; they are anti-union bills. They are designed to force concessions upon the unions to a point where they cannot maintain a higher standard of wages for their workers, which is the only way they succeed in obtaining a higher standard for all workers, whether union or nonunion. Also, since the population of the country constantly increases, it might be excusable if there was no great accuracy in remembering the exact estimate. But that no one could name the author of a good history of our country is shocking, for it reveals how little reading our young people now do.

Above everything else, however, the most disturbing revelation is the low opinion people in general have about the teaching profession. There is no question but that in our country we must raise the standards of preparation for teaching, increase the salaries, and recognize teachers in our communities as influential and respected people. Otherwise we will continue to have increasing trouble with juvenile delinquents and uneducated young people. We should remember Thomas Jefferson's admonition that democracy, which we have discovered through the years to be one of the most difficult forms of government, cannot function except with an educated electorate.

The first step is to increase teachers' salaries. The next is to give them better opportunities for education. Finally, every one of us must make it a point, in the locality in which we live, to know the teachers and to give them our support and help. They deserve a place of respect in the community, and they cannot expect to function successfully with their young people unless they are given this recognition.

~

On a fence-mending goodwill tour to South America, Vice President Nixon was the target of insults by anti-American mobs. Angry mobs attacked American libraries in Lebanon. Despite the successful Marshall Plan to rebuild Europe after World War II, the U.S. engendered hostility in certain hot spots, usually in less developed nations where foreign aid was often misused and the military situation was unstable.

Mrs. Roosevelt delineates a foreign policy she believes is better than President Eisenhower's. While it may be inevitable, she argues, for the world's most powerful nation to be resented by poorer countries dependent on the wealthy leader for defense, trade, and humanitarian aid, selling arms never really solves any problems. Eleanor Roosevelt favors a foreign aid policy based on improvement of the quality of life.

EN ROUTE TO LAS VEGAS, MAY 16—We are witnessing these days what it means to be the outstanding power in the non-Communist world. It is our libraries that are burned in Lebanon; it is our Vice President who, on his goodwill tour, is attacked by students and mobs.

The reason is simple. It is not because the attackers dislike Richard M. Nixon personally. Nor is it because the Lebanese have any particular dislike for what our libraries have offered them.

It is because, to them, Mr. Nixon and our libraries stand as a symbol of that which opposes what they have been taught to believe is the great revolutionary movement for the "good" of the peoples of the world.

Our people are justly indignant, and since the kind of power we now possess is rather new to us, we may be inclined to say "Well, they don't want us, so why do we bother to do anything for them or with them?"

This attitude, of course, is a sign that we have gained our power quickly and have not recognized the responsibility that goes with it. If this were to be our official policy, we would do just what the Soviets want and hope for. They would remain as the only ones ready and willing to help the revolutionaries.

I pray that our government, and we ourselves, have grown mature enough to look upon these demonstrations partly as recognition of what our world leadership means and must mean, to regret them but not to let them succeed to the point of forcing us to give the Communist element in the world exactly what it wants.

We believe in freedom and are trying to see that all people obtain freedom. We are not going to look at our interests from the financial viewpoint alone. We are not going to allow our recession to do things abroad that will ruin other economies. We, of course, hold paramount our own interests, but we know that our interests are best served when we consider those of the world as a whole.

No country in our position is loved, but we should make ourselves respected and better understood. Our policy of giving military aid to foreign nations instead of actually raising the living standards in those countries has been a mistake.

This policy may be helpful at home, and it may bring greater financial support from Congress than any other type of foreign aid. For our people do not realize that these shipments of arms are not going to be used against the Communists and will be of no real value, whereas any help we may give in raising, even a little, other people's standards of living will win us friends.

If we now cut down on foreign aid because the Soviets have been successful in stirring up trouble in certain South American countries, in the Near East and in North Africa, we will make a great mistake and lose more friends instead of gaining them.

It may well be that this was not a propitious time for Mr. Nixon to go to certain South American countries. Our State Department should have known that. But we can now be glad that he and his wife have returned safe and sound. These special and spectacular tours had better be given up until we have brought about changes in the feelings of these countries.

I keep repeating that the Moscow challenge is not a military one alone. It is an economic, cultural and spiritual challenge, and sooner or later we will have to face this fact.

∼

By 1958 the postwar baby boom was clogging the nation's schools, which in many communities had not expanded for decades. The issues blocking new school construction were philosophical and political. Heretofore most public education was financed by states and towns. On education bills in Congress, civil rights or segregationist riders were attached, making passage difficult.

Mrs. Roosevelt was once again ahead of her time on the issue of federal aid to education, believing that schools were a far better investment in the

nation's future than new weaponry, or even the space program. Seeing yet
another education bill go down to defeat raised her ire.

HYDE PARK, MAY 24—After a tiring trip in the West, I was happy indeed to
arrive back in my little New York apartment from Bismarck, N.D. I had
planned to write today about the last few days of this trip, but a more important matter has come up that I want to discuss.

This matter is the shelving by the House Education and Labor Committee of the school construction bill that would provide federal money to
help the states improve their school situation by adding more classrooms
before the overcrowding becomes more intolerable than it already is.

How Representative Graham A. Braden of North Carolina, committee
chairman, can permit this is beyond my understanding!

The parents of this country should protest through every organization
at their command, for their children are going to pay the price of schools
so overcrowded that teachers cannot give them adequate attention.

It is a fact that under present conditions the curriculum of the schools
is deteriorating and that children, of necessity, will be less interested in
learning and have less respect for education because the government of
their country does not think it worth paying for.

No democracy can succeed, according to Thomas Jefferson, unless it
has an educated people. And we cannot educate citizens under the conditions that our government is now forcing on the people of the country.

An article in the June *Esquire* magazine tells of some of the things that
happen when people do not consider learning important, and these
things are happening to our young people today.

The author gives an appalling quotation from Dean William C. Warren
of the Columbia School of Law on the shortcomings of college graduates
who are entering law school.

It looks as though it is not until our young people reach graduate school
that they begin to realize that education was not intended to be mere play
but that it is hard work and preparation for life, and that to succeed in the
world of today our children must learn during their educational years to
conquer difficult subjects.

If the federal government does not take its responsibility for helping the
states with their educational problems, or if the states refuse to accept this
aid for fear they will have some type of interference, then we are going to
fall behind.

It is because we are not willing to pay more for our education and to
give it more serious thought that I think we are finding our juvenile delinquency problem constantly becoming more serious.

262 • *My Day*

If we do not pay for children in good schools, then we are going to pay for them in prisons and mental hospitals. There is a distinct tie-up, I think, between the increase of juvenile delinquency and the inadequacy of our public schools.

Of course, this is not the only factor entering into our problem, but it is certainly one of the most important. It seems to me a terrible waste of human material which we are condoning at the present time, but I don't know if it is possible to bring home to our parents how serious this waste really is for our nation.

~

Mrs. Roosevelt's private correspondence in this period confirms she had realized that Adlai Stevenson was not effectively in touch with white or black liberal Americans on domestic issues such as race relations. Admirable as Stevenson was as Democratic intellectual leader, he lacked the political magnetism of a national election winner. Nonetheless, Eleanor Roosevelt still looked to Stevenson for visionary ideas on the global problems of international trade and disarmament.

NEW YORK, JUNE 11—Adlai Stevenson, in urging the free nations to rally to achieve a functioning, expanding free world trading system, has stated what seems perfectly clear to anyone who has studied the situation of the non-Communist nations of the world.

He made this statement in his week-end address at Michigan State University in which he pressed his proposal for a committee of experts comparable to the group that laid the groundwork for the Marshall Plan in 1947.

Mr. Stevenson also pointed out that as Britain and France are laying down the creditor role, the United States must take up this role if economic conditions are to be improved. That is why we should have a committee of experts in this country similar to the Marshall Plan group.

I believe, too, we should go one step further and call together the heads of industries, who will have to implement any plans made by this committee.

If we are to negotiate on a broader scale for better trade in the world, we will have to take a good look at conditions at home. We cannot let people at home suffer because it is necessary to make different arrangements in other parts of the world in an overall scheme for economic well-being on a broad basis.

This means that when certain things become unprofitable to do at home, instead of meeting the problem by putting up a high tariff wall, we will have to meet the challenge by changing our own economy, retraining our people, bringing in new industries. All of this takes real planning.

We have not even taken the trouble to plan economically with our neighbor, Canada. There is one area in which we could begin to make headway at once.

The proposals made by the Canadian Prime Minister, John G. Diefenbaker, for a four-point program deserved careful study because cooperation with Canada, our closest neighbor, should certainly show that we can develop mutually helpful ways of doing things such as dealing with our food surpluses.

To go back to Mr. Stevenson's proposal, he added a suggestion to help bring about a peaceful world which I think has great merit. He wants "an international medical research and health year as another way, similar to the International Geophysical Year, for the world to cooperate for survival instead of destruction."

He goes back to his old proposal of ending the testing of nuclear weapons and of coming to a reasonable agreement with the Soviet Union on matters of inspection against violation.

And, most important of all, he suggests acceptance by the West of the principle of Soviet equality and power so that we could divert our military rivalries into competition in science, education, and economic development.

Mr. Stevenson developed all of his suggestions reasonably and carefully, but the thing that is important is the appointment of committees to begin carrying out these suggestions.

Will the present Administration dare to accept these ideas from a Democratic leader, or will it feel that it must persist in doing nothing?

～

On her visit to the World's Fair in Brussels, Mrs. Roosevelt enjoyed Harry Belafonte's extravagant stage show at the American pavilion. Multilingual, handsome, charming, and black, this entertainer embodied the melting pot culture of the U.S. But the racial discrimination his family faced in New York in their search for housing made Eleanor Roosevelt ashamed. Here she repeats a message stated many times in "My Day." To earn the privilege of criticizing the more conservative South on matters of race, Northerners must first put their own house in moral and legal order.

NEW LONDON, CONN., OCTOBER 20—I am sure that every New Yorker was shocked the other day to read that Harry Belafonte and his charming wife and baby were finding it practically impossible to get an apartment in New York City except in what might be considered segregated areas or in a hotel. I have long been saying that in the North we have only one step to take to meet the Supreme Court order of nonsegregation in schools, and that is nonsegregation in housing. In New York State we have the laws necessary to achieve nonsegregated housing if we saw that they were diligently respected.

There was a time when prohibitions against various racial groups were more prevalent than today. For instance, Jewish groups were much more concentrated in specific areas than they are now; and the same kind of thing was true of the Italians, the Irish or the Germans. Gradually these barriers have broken down, until it now remains for us to see that the barriers against our Puerto Rican and colored population also disappear.

There are beginnings to encourage us. The Committee on Civil Rights in Manhattan, for example, has issued a pamphlet on housing co-ops which may be the answer for a number of people. Some private builders who are planning and constructing co-op apartments are particularly interested in seeing that there is no discrimination in any project where they have invested their money. These cooperatives, of course, vary in price and location; some are in the suburbs, others can be found in the city. Many of them, however, are not in areas conveniently located for individuals of special interests. Therefore it is important that we press for the general freeing from restrictions of all New York City property.

Real estate people often frighten themselves and their clients by saying that property taken over by a Negro family forces the whole area quickly to become a Negro area and that property values go down. This, of course, depends upon the white people in the area. If they move out from places because of prejudice or fear, the character of the neighborhood inevitably will change and the value of the property may decrease. But if they learn to live with their neighbors without discrimination of any kind, they will soon find that their neighborhoods become simply mixed neighborhoods — neither all-white, nor all-Negro, nor all-Jewish, nor all-Italian. We are a mixture of races in New York City, and every neighborhood should in normal course become a mixed neighborhood.

I can think of nothing I would enjoy more than having Mr. and Mrs. Belafonte as my neighbors. I hope they will find a home shortly where they and their enchanting little boy can grow up without feeling the evils of the segregation pattern. Discrimination does something intangible and harmful to the souls of both white and colored people.

~

Eleanor Roosevelt became host of a social issues panel show on NBC-TV, but she was among a tiny minority who, in the early years of television, said

"Stop, let's think this over." She warns her readers about the negative impact of passivity in frequent TV-watching and the positive benefits of a life—like hers—filled with a lively variety of labors and creative pastimes.

NEW YORK, NOVEMBER 5—If the use of leisure time is confined to looking at TV for a few extra hours every day, we will deteriorate as a people.

Actually, preparation for the use of leisure time should begin with our schoolchildren. The appreciation of many things in which we are not proficient ourselves but which we have learned to enjoy is one of the important things to cultivate in modern education. The arts in every field—music, drama, sculpture, painting—we can learn to appreciate and enjoy. We need not be artists, but we should be able to appreciate the work of artists. Crafts of every kind, the value of things made by hand, by skilled people who love to work with wood or clay or stone will develop taste in our people.

These are all things that can give us joy and many of us will find that we are capable of acquiring a certain amount of skill we never dreamed we had, which will give an outlet to a creative urge. But these things must be taught, and in the age now developing about us they are important things. For if man is to be liberated to enjoy more leisure, he must also be prepared to enjoy this leisure fully and creatively.

For people to have more time to read, to take part in their civic obligations, to know more about how their government functions and who their officials are might mean in a democracy a great improvement in the democratic processes. Let's begin, then, to think how we can prepare old and young for these new opportunities. Let's not wait until they come upon us suddenly and we have a crisis that we will be ill prepared to meet.

~

Which was she? The liberal experimentalist, always open to a potentially good new idea, or the habitual traditionalist who liked to do some things the same way, year after year? Mrs. Roosevelt celebrated Christmas with traditionalism, religious and secular. Here, "My Day" describes her best-loved holiday activities.

HYDE PARK, DECEMBER 25—Christmas is here again, and I hope that at this season we will stress the religious side of the celebration. Of foremost importance for the world to remember is that the story of the Christ child is the one that really gives meaning to this day for every Christian everywhere.

I always go to midnight service in our church in Hyde Park because I like to begin the celebration hearing the familiar religious carols and being reminded of the heart of this season, which is "Peace on earth, goodwill to men."

During the day we return, of course, to the enjoyment of all the other traditions which we have absorbed in this country—Santa Claus and his reindeer and the Christmas decorations which every year become more evident in every village and in every city.

I love the Christmas lights and sometime during the Christmas season I always try to drive after dark one night down Park Avenue in New York City where the trees make a long stream of light and many windows are decorated. Then I proceed over to Fifth Avenue and down to Washington Square and up the whole length of Fifth Avenue where so many shops have outstanding decorations.

I love to look at the big tree in Rockefeller Plaza, which is always a joy. This little excursion is one of my annual Christmas pleasures.

1959

$\mathcal{P}$resident Eisenhower's Republican administration was poised to do partisan battle with the 86th Congress, heavily weighted in the opposition party's direction. The Democratic-to-Republican ratios were almost two-to-one in 1959.

The U.S. now recognized Fidel Castro's regime as the legitimate power in Cuba. Eleanor Roosevelt and most Cuba-watchers felt that the dictatorship Castro's forces had overthrown had been the greater of two evils.

The domestic civil rights campaign received a boost in February when public schools in two Virginia towns desegregated without incident—showing that it could be done graciously. That same month brought disaster to St. Louis when one of the worst tornadoes on record struck the city, leaving $12,000,000 worth of damage in its wake.

To surround the Soviet Union with non-Communist Western allies, the United States approved defense agreements with Iran, Pakistan, and Turkey. Eisenhower proudly signed a bill in March admitting Hawaii as the forty-ninth state. The administration lost a key player when Secretary of State John Foster Dulles resigned in April due to ill health and died soon after at the age of seventy-one. Eleanor Roosevelt was not a fan of Dulles's ideas, but she paid him gracious tribute in "My Day" as a loyal public servant.

Canadian neighbors joined in celebration with the United States when the St. Lawrence Seaway opened, creating a usable commercial shipping passage all the way from Duluth to the Atlantic. Some five thousand Japanese nationals who were U.S. citizens prior to World War II but renounced their citizenship during the war had their American status restored, reflecting Japanese and American reconciliation. The new U.S. nuclear-powered submarine to be launched, the *George Washington*, could itself launch a Polaris missile, and this technological step changed the Cold War balance of power.

At Bienhoe, South Vietnam, two American soldiers were killed by Communist guerrillas on July 9. In Laos the political situation destabilized, and by the end of August the State Department began sending significantly increased military aid to that struggling country. Mrs. Roosevelt found herself, like most Americans, divided about the wisdom of these moves. She clearly wanted to thwart the spread of communism but kept searching for ways to do it without tanks and guns.

By summertime the so-called Republican recession was in full swing, with unemployment riding high at 1,400,000 people out of work. A major strike at U.S. Steel had a ripple effect—touching twenty-eight other steel producers and 95 percent of the steel industry. In early October the President invoked the Taft-Hartley Act to break the strike (forcing a resumption of work and arbitration of the dispute). Mrs. Roosevelt opposed the Taft-Hartley legislation for years, but she too believed the current steel strike was unjustifiable. The economic slowdown was substantial enough by fall for the federal government to introduce a food stamp program to help particularly depressed areas.

In the latter part of the year, Nikita Khrushchev, premier of the Soviet Union, visited the United States for six days, including a stop at President Roosevelt's grave at Hyde Park, where Eleanor received him. And Charles Van Doren, an intellectual and professor who impressed the country with his brilliant recall of facts on the TV quiz show *The Sixty-Four-Thousand Dollar Question*, was caught in a conspiracy with the producers. He confessed to having been coached by the network about the questions he would be asked in the "isolation booth" on the show—a disillusioning incident in American popular culture. D. H. Lawrence's famous novel, *Lady Chatterley's Lover,* with erotic scenes too hot for the Post Office to handle, was banned from the mails.

The subject of birth control required a careful dance, even for a liberal like Eleanor Roosevelt. The rapidly expanding world population came up nearly every year in "My Day." Mrs. Roosevelt studied the relationship between population and food supply, concluding that if left unchecked, population growth would run away with itself, creating a tragedy of enormous dimensions, particularly among the poor. Yet she did not advocate family planning as government policy.

NEW YORK, JANUARY 2—There is an organization in Washington, D.C., that will celebrate next month its thirtieth year of work, and yet I think very few people are conscious of the importance of what this particular organization has been doing. It is called the Population Reference Bureau and it publishes the "Population Bulletin," which is used by many newspapers, magazines and colleges as reference material on this all-important question of population.

This organization is trying to tell the public that a crisis really threatens us. It is finally getting recognition and support from some small foundation grants, but it needs much more understanding on the part of the public to really get across to the people the message of the world situation on population today.

The Bureau of the Census recently released population projections that indicate that there could be 100,000,000 more people in this country by 1980. This is approximately half again as many people as there are now in the United States—and this increase would come about in the short period of 22 years.

In 1929, when the Population Reference Bureau was founded, the world population was increasing by about 56,000 each day. By 1945 world population was increasing by about 70,000 each day, and today, every single day, the rate of increase is up to 137,000.

More and more organizations are beginning to see the danger signals. Where is the food coming from? True, we are making new discoveries, and new sources of food will become known in the next few years.

But perhaps the most important thing in the world is a wise and sane approach to the constantly increasing birthrate.

If we read back to the early days of American history, we will be impressed by the fact that out of families that consisted sometimes of 10 to 15 children, only perhaps three or four lived to old age and many more never lived beyond their early twenties. Many women died in childbirth. You can find in many New England cemeteries the names of three wives, each of whom bore their husbands a certain number of children. And frequently the death of the mother and the baby was recorded together on the tombstone.

Science has helped us wipe out these tragedies, but we are still expected to meet the problem that our greater knowledge has created. Fewer people die in other parts of the world through famine and epidemics. And if we are fortunate enough to wipe out war and even eventually to teach people to drive their automobiles more safely, we will gradually eliminate two major causes of death.

It is a challenge to our intelligence to meet this situation on a worldwide basis and find a sane method which will not outrage the religious or physical needs of human beings.

~

She was accustomed to being the one who gave to other people, but Eleanor Roosevelt had a great capacity for enjoying favors done for her. Here we get a journalist's equivalent of a Norman Rockwell painting about the American melting pot and the tradition of kindness among strangers—in one of the toughest cities of them all, New York.

NEW YORK, JANUARY 26—A few days ago I was scheduled to leave New York by plane at nine o'clock in the morning. The weather was bad, however, and when the time came for me to leave the Park Sheraton Hotel, where I live, the rain was coming down in sheets. No taxis were available at either entrance of the hotel, and after ten minutes of waiting I began to grow worried, for I had to reach Idlewild and I was afraid I would miss my plane.

Suddenly a man came up beside me and in a gentle voice said:

"Mrs. Roosevelt, my wife and I live in Woodmere and my car is in the parking lot. We would be very happy to drive you to Idlewild if you would allow us."

I looked at him in great surprise, for we had never met before. I hesitated to put him to so much trouble; but my situation was growing desperate, and so I gratefully said: "If I don't get a taxi before you get your car, I would be most happy to go with you."

He arrived with his car a few minutes later. His wife got in with her bags and I got in with mine, and we started off.

After a few minutes, my host turned toward me. "Don't worry about my driving," he said. "I am an old truck driver."

I smiled, because I was not in the least worried about his driving. I was just wondering if I would make the plane on time.

Then, as we waded through traffic, he said: "Where could it happen but in America? Here am I, an ex-truck driver. I have a nice home now, and a nice wife." He glanced at her. "You can see she is very nice."

I agreed as I looked at the pretty little woman sitting behind us.

"I have two nice children—one in Boston University and one in high school, and both doing well," he continued. "Last night we went to see 'Sunrise at Campobello,' we stayed in the same hotel you live in, Mrs. Roosevelt, and now I am driving you to the airport and talking to you. Where else could it happen but in America?"

I surmise it could happen in some other places in the world. But as I think over the difficulties of getting in touch with government officials, or even with retired individuals like myself, I realize that perhaps this is a country in which contacts are easier. It is good to feel that they are—and to know that, in a way, we still have the feeling which must have existed in the early pioneer days of being a part of a big family. There are many variations, of course, but still the people of the United States are a big family.

This little incident, and the kindness which prompted the offer to take me to the plane, gave me a feeling of warmth and pleasure which I can hardly describe; but many other people must experience the same kind of willingness to help in an emergency. The fact that we had not been previously acquainted was no insuperable barrier because we were part of the American family.

~

Eleanor Roosevelt was no fan of the American Medical Association. She was convinced that psychiatry had little to offer over the clear-cut advantages of having had parents who knew how to balance love with discipline. There were several points in Mrs. Roosevelt's life when psychotherapy might have been helpful (the loss of an infant child, the struggle for family control with her mother-in-law, the discovery of FDR's extramarital affairs). But she saw them all through, with religious faith, love of family and friends, and iron will.

Dr. Karl Menninger co-founded Menninger Clinic in Kansas, where various techniques for treating mental illness were developed.

NEW YORK, FEBRUARY 16—Instead of asking me for a speech, Dr. Menninger said the plan was that he and I would exchange points of view on a variety of subjects. He and his colleagues were the scientists—and they are presented with the problem that exists, namely, mental illness from babyhood through to old age; and they were trying to find the answers and the best answers to every problem put before them. As we talked, I realized that I was of course interested in this problem of treatment, but that fundamentally I was more interested in the problem of prevention. Why was it we had to have mental illness? If we could discover it in children and learned the proper treatment, why couldn't we also study the reasons which brought it about and try to prevent the causes?

I had to confess that at first I had been impatient with the ease with which many people turned to psychiatry to solve personal problems which I felt were problems that self-discipline required one to settle for oneself. But I had come to realize that psychiatry could be of infinite help to people. It could bring about better results and perhaps prevent long struggles which an individual otherwise might have to go through in order to gain self-mastery without any understanding help. But I still believed that it was important for the individual to struggle for himself and to feel the sense of achievement in his own self-reliance and self-control. If this is not one of the results of psychiatric treatment, I am always nervous about the final outcome.

~

Mrs. Roosevelt had seen the face of poverty and hunger many times. She had also crisscrossed the breadbasket heartland of America, witnessing the growth of the country's vast agricultural business and its food surpluses. She studied data about world hunger and population explosion—in her job at the UN and, later, as a concerned citizen. When Eleanor Roosevelt wrote about famine relief, she knew what she was saying.

In 1959 the issue is: Why can't the United States help its neighbor, Haiti? Political factors aside, for Mrs. Roosevelt the issue is hungry people in one country and overfed people, overstuffed grain elevators, in another. She introduces the idea of using food as an international loan. And she praises a man who became one of her favorite Senators because of his humanitarianism, Hubert Humphrey.

FLINT, MICH., MAY 5—It seems to me that we have been left in ignorance of the situation in Haiti which, because of our past history of concern about that land, should be of concern to every one of us.

In the Congressional Record there is a speech by Senator Hubert Humphrey of Minnesota in which he brings out the fact that because of a long drought there has been famine in Haiti which affects 45,000 men, women and children. This condition has existed for over a year and even if the rains were to come now the people would have no seed left with which to plant crops, and no animals left to sell in order to get money to buy seeds. Both a French priest and a Baptist minister report starvation conditions among the people and pitiable conditions among the children.

In his speech Senator Humphrey pointed out the curious fact that we, who are so near to Haiti, not only are slow to act when we hear of such a situation in which our surplus food could be used, but there is no machinery set up by which we can do this. At the same time he points to the fact that in the District of Columbia there are 7,000 children in the grade schools who have an inadequate diet and there is no school lunch program.

The President was upheld the other day by the Senate in his veto of a rural electrification bill and he repeatedly upholds his Secretary of Agriculture, who has allowed a condition to arise where we have no plan either for helping hungry children at home or for helping people who have starved for over a year in a neighboring island. All of this when we ourselves have more food unused than we know what to do with. This looks as though Democrats as well as Republicans must accept responsibility for this deplorable situation.

There was a time when our citizens believed that a good harvest was the gift of God. We needed it and we were thankful for it. Otherwise, we would have no Thanksgiving Day. I think with a little serious planning we could help people all around the world to improve their own food supplies and to profit by our ability to grow food and our luck in having good harvests.

Then we could really thank God again for His rain and His sunshine. We could really be confident again of the value of our land and we would have earned the gratitude of the people in Haiti.

True, we probably recognize in Washington that the government of Haiti under a past President, Col. Paul E. Magloire, got itself into a very bad economic situation by the now-familiar method of having a dictator who exploited the people and made a fortune for himself and ruined the economy of his country. But the people who starve have no realization that this is probably one of the reasons why their government today is unable to help them. They are conscious of only one thing—that they need food and it isn't there.

We could make food part of a loan to help the present government to rehabilitate its economic situation, but I think we have a right to ask for some type of supervision of the economic use of whatever loan we make.

The pattern of dictatorship repeats itself too often and even if they now have a government that has every intention of helping the people and honestly administering the government departments, still they may need some expert financial advice. This could be given on a technical-assistance basis through the United Nations if not through us, but we must not let people so near to us continue to starve.

～

One of the most prominent black families in the world became the object of a racial insult that made Mrs. Roosevelt ashamed of her own country. Dr. Ralph Bunche was the first black division head in the Department of State; he entered the UN in 1946 (the same time as Mrs. Roosevelt) as a director of the Trusteeship Division; and he was awarded the Nobel Prize for Peace in 1950 for his work as principal secretary of the UN Palestine Commission. But his prominence was neither here nor there to Mrs. Roosevelt; the issue was fairness.

HYDE PARK, JULY 13—I don't know how other people feel about the story last week on the refusal of a swank tennis club in Forest Hills, L.I. [Long Island], to permit Dr. Ralph Bunche's son—who has been taking tennis lessons at the club from the pro—to become a member and play there. I can only say I felt mortified that in the North we still have a club, the West Side Tennis Club, which is not ashamed to say that it bars Jews and Negroes from membership.

The members of this club may think themselves better than people of other races, and they may think that in their club and in their homes they can be justified today in refusing admittance to people on a basis of race, color or religion. But I would like to point out to them that bombs do not discriminate in this manner. When these people have helped the rest of us to lose the uncommitted areas of the world where two-thirds of the world's population exist, which are largely of non-Aryan race and of many religions and many colors, then perhaps they will realize what they have done to give us a Communist world—if not to destroy our civilization completely.

I hope that no colored champion and no Jewish champion will play tennis at this club again.

Of course, this kind of discrimination will not hurt the Bunches. They have too many open doors to feel a slight of this kind. But how can we in the North ask of the South the sacrifices that we are now asking if we countenance this kind of snobbish discrimination?

If you can't play tennis with Negroes, how come you are willing to let them be drafted into your army and die for you? I am ashamed for my white people. I am one of them, and their stupidity and cruelty make me cringe.

~

A month before turning seventy-five, Eleanor Roosevelt has the energy and enthusiasm to make professional appearances in two New England cities, driving on two-lane highways between them (no interstate superhighways existed), in the middle of summer without air conditioning—all in the space of eight hours. Her motivation was just as it had been at the UN: to promote international dialogue and to let foreign visitors know America did not want war.

Mrs. Roosevelt's secretary, Maureen Corr, accompanied her. Henry Kissinger would later become President Nixon's secretary of state.

KITTERY, ME., AUGUST 6—On Tuesday Miss Corr and I left Hyde Park at nine o'clock in the morning and drove up to New Haven, Conn., where a summer seminar for foreign students at Yale is in progress. After spending an hour with them, we drove on to Cambridge, Mass., where at 4:30 Mr. Henry Kissinger introduced me to the Harvard summer seminar for foreign students.

It was a long day but one that I enjoyed very much, as I am deeply interested in these students who come to our country to take back to their countries a better knowledge of us and our way of life.

～

Mrs. Roosevelt had great faith in the UN to handle even a political dilemma as old and thorny as the Chinese-Tibetan standoff. Ethnically and religiously distinct from the Chinese, Tibetans had known some degree of Chinese control ever since the eighteenth century and a long period of Mongol control before that. In 1911 Tibet reasserted its independence, maintained until 1950, when the Chinese again invaded. Earlier in 1959 an anti-Chinese uprising was crushed, and in its aftermath the Dalai Lama, Tibetan Buddhism's spiritual leader, fled the country.

Mrs. Roosevelt wrote on behalf of the Dalai Lama because she recognized him as a man of peace and because the Tibetan cause was another facet of the West's struggle against communism.

NEW YORK, OCTOBER 16—I was visited on Tuesday afternoon by one of the Dalai Lama's brothers. He and a second brother have come to the United States to speak before the United Nations on the situation that faces Tibet.

I asked him whether it was true that the people in that mountainous country had been kept at a very low standard of living and that, therefore, the Communist Chinese, who emulate the Soviet Communists, felt justified in moving in to establish what they felt were reforms. He told me that the Dalai Lama had already planned to move on four different fronts to bring some changes into the old agricultural system of the country and to improve the standard of living for the people. And he added that these changes had been opposed by the Communists in the country and that an increasing number of Chinese Communist troops had come in until the people who loved the Dalai Lama had felt that he was in danger personally.

One of the most serious results, of course, of forcing the Dalai Lama to leave Tibet is the fact that a very large number of his people left with him, and they are all now in India. This has added a new problem to the refugee situation. India is finding it extremely difficult to provide the proper kind of food for these thousands of people who must be fed and housed.

I am glad that the situation is being brought before the United Nations and I hope that the nations of the world will give help to these refugees and bring the weight of world opinion to bear on the entire situation. Only thus can peace come to Tibet and the traditional ruler returned in peace and be allowed to try to work out the problems of modernization and contact with the outer world, which now becomes necessary in spite of the remoteness of the people in that country.

It points up to us that there is no area of the world that is remote any more and that all of us are going to feel whatever happens, no matter how far away it is.

~

Senator John Kennedy of Massachusetts had not yet won over Eleanor Roosevelt to his camp. She recognized his growing influence and aspirations, but among the emerging Democratic presidential candidates, Kennedy received less attention from Eleanor than anyone. Nonetheless, she recognized that the senator could handle even the toughest personal and political questions with aplomb. Mrs. Roosevelt's warming to Kennedy was slow, but it had begun.

New York, December 1—The American Roman Catholic bishops made a statement on birth control a short time ago which seems to me the only possible position they could take. I cannot quite understand why the newspapers are making so much of it, and bedeviling Senator John F. Kennedy for a statement.

This is a religious question and has always been understood. In reply to a question on the birth-control issue and its relation to foreign aid, Senator Kennedy gave a wise answer, I think.

It would be unwise for any national administration to grant aid to another nation for this particular purpose. If the other nation finds it essential to its well-being to undertake birth control, that is its own concern, as Senator Kennedy has said. If any organization or individuals in any country feel it is important to help a second country keep down the birth rate, that is the decision of that organization and of those individuals.

The government of a country which has as many people, for instance, as we in the United States have of varying religions and beliefs, should not, as a government, take official action in a subject which enters into the religious and domestic affairs of another nation. It will offend some of its own citizens and it might easily offend some section of the people in the other nation.

No government, however, should have the right to prevent individual citizens or organizations from giving help if they were asked to do so by the government or individuals or organizations of another nation. This practically is the stand which Senator Kennedy stated, and I think it was a sensible and correct stand for him to take, as it would be for any other candidate of whatever religion.

1960

o no one's surprise but to many Democrats' delight, 1960 began with an announcement by Senator John F. Kennedy that he would indeed run for President. Kennedy entered a crowded field of would-be candidates, and he began his formal quest for the White House without Eleanor Roosevelt's endorsement. By summer's end she was in his camp. Mrs. Roosevelt used many of her "My Day" columns in 1960 to comment on social changes she saw coming.

In his January 1960 State of the Union address President Eisenhower reported a $200,000,000 budget surplus and forecast record-breaking prosperity. Vice President Richard Nixon tossed his hat into the ring as a presidential candidate and rode the Republican wave of success almost to victory in November. Eisenhower's trip to Japan in January after the two countries signed a mutual defense treaty, reversing their deadly adversarial relationship in World War II, was canceled when anti-American sentiment ran too high in Tokyo.

In early February, four black people in Greensboro, North Carolina, staged a "sit-in" at a whites-only lunch counter, the first of many such confrontations. As nonviolent civil disobedience, this was an approach Mrs. Roosevelt could support. The Senate ratified the Twenty-third Amendment to the Constitution, banning poll taxes in federal elections. Such taxes excluded poor people from the ranks of registered voters, especially in the South.

In the primary election campaigns, JFK's religion emerged as an issue. A Roman Catholic, his critics claimed, would be a pawn of the Vatican. The Senator replied, "I don't think my religion is anyone's business," but the issue dogged him throughout the campaign. Eleanor Roosevelt saw the religion issue as bogus but also dangerous. She feared for the country should a qualified candidate be defeated because of religious prejudice.

Embarrassments in 1960 for the United States weakened the country's position in world affairs. In May a U–2 spy plane was shot down over Soviet territory, and Eisenhower admitted that the U. S. had flown reconnaissance missions over the USSR for years. At a major-power summit conference in Paris in mid-May, Khrushchev demanded an apology from the U.S. but did not get what he wanted. The Russians promptly withdrew from the meeting. In late June a ten-nation disarmament conference also disbanded after failing to reach any agreements. Fidel Castro, the Cuban revolutionary leader, now President of the Republic, proved increasingly cantankerous. Eisenhower struck back by cutting Cuban sugar imports by 95 percent, a move that may have hurt Cuba but displeased American housewives. These Republican foreign policy setbacks strengthened the Democrats' chances of recapturing the White House.

The national conventions in July nominated Kennedy and Lyndon Johnson (Senator from Texas since 1948) for the Democrats; Nixon and Henry Cabot Lodge, Jr. (former Senator from Massachusetts, defeated by Kennedy in 1952; representative to the UN, 1953–1960) for the Republicans. Television played a bigger-than-ever role in this campaign, introducing the live presidential debate. Although political commentators gave different scores to Kennedy and Nixon concerning their answers to debate questions, almost everyone agreed that Nixon suffered from the stiff image he projected under glaring lights. Kennedy inspired more confidence with his greater finesse.

When the election finally came, Mrs. Roosevelt, a true Democrat, was glad to see another liberal headed for the White House. Selections President-elect Kennedy announced for cabinet and other posts won her approval as well, with the possible exception of Robert Kennedy, the new President's younger brother, as attorney general (Mrs. Roosevelt disliked the apparent nepotism). The year ended on a rising tide of fresh energy in Washington and throughout the land.

On the issue of radioactive waste disposal, Eleanor Roosevelt was one of the earliest lay writers to sound an alarm. She had no easy solutions to offer but recognized a need for public involvement in decisionmaking about how to cope with this worrisome new dilemma.

NEW YORK, FEBRUARY 4—Now I must report on something that has just been brought to my attention. My correspondent writes:

"At least three bills are now before the House of Representatives which would take control of atomic waste sea dumping from the hands of the AEC [Atomic

Energy Commission] and place it where we believe it rightly belongs—in the hands of the United States Public Health Service."

These bills are HR 8187, 8423, and 7014.

My correspondent is temporary chairman of the Lower Cape Committee on Radioactive Waste Disposal, and he lives in Wellfleet , Mass. He says there are several other citizen groups in the East that are urging active Congressional intervention in the problem of radioactive waste disposal in our coastal waters. These other groups have been active in New Jersey, North Carolina, Texas, Connecticut, Florida, and elsewhere.

The dump site off the tip of Cape Cod, which is my correspondent's concern, is barely 12 miles off the Boston shore and in the heart of the Atlantic sea lanes leading into Boston harbor. According to the newspaper story sent to me, there are included among the dumped radioactive material isotopes yielded by the development of the first atomic bomb—the bomb that exploded over Hiroshima.

Hauled out to sea in a metal drum, they were dropped over the side of a vessel in 250 feet of water in 1946. And, until a few months ago, over a period of nearly 12 years, ships returned to the dumping site regularly with more waste cargoes, whose potential hazard can only be guessed at.

It is now discovered that in 1954 the National Committee on Radiation Protection specifically recommended that radioactive waste disposal be carried out in depths of at least 1,000 fathoms, or 6,000 feet. The Lower Cape Committee says:

"If atomic dumping with its grave implications to life and human well-being can be initiated and carried out without the knowledge and consent of citizens of areas which can receive contamination, we believe this is a matter for the U.S. courts."

This situation is one, I think, that very few of the people of the United States have been conscious of, and it is time that we got a little more information.

~

At the end of a long discussion in her "My Day" column of whether capital punishment is a valid way to achieve justice or to deter future crimes (she consistently argued "no" on both points), Eleanor Roosevelt's fearlessness about whether crime and criminals might ever touch her life emerges. Having lived in the public spotlight for decades, she was well aware that a disturbed or angry person could try to harm her husband or her. Attacks on President Truman and on members of Congress in the 1940s and 1950s by disgruntled Puerto Rican nationalists had not frightened her. Not even direct threats to her own life seemed to give her pause.

SARASOTA, FLA., MARCH 14—Our knowledge of human beings is limited. We cannot know all about any other human being. For the protection of society, if a human being seems dangerous we have a right to limit his contacts and thus protect others from the danger. But I doubt if we have a right to take away a gift which we alone cannot give. For that reason I believe the movement against capital punishment is growing stronger in our country. It is a good thing to have people think about the problem at this time. I hope many people will give it serious reflection and come to the conclusion that I have—that human beings have no right to take each other's lives.

On Friday morning my secretary, Miss Corr, and I left New York by air and had a fairly good trip to Tampa, though we ran into a tropical storm just before landing which made us almost an hour late. Trouble with the plane's flaps twice forced us to return to Tampa after taking off, and I finally decided to drive to Sarasota because I was to speak there in the evening and it was getting late. It took so long to arrange for a car that I did not reach the Sarasota airport until 6:30 p.m. A few brave souls who had waited for our arrival escorted me immediately to the dinner where I was to speak, while Miss Corr took our belongings and went to my uncle Mr. David Cray's home.

While we were at the dinner a telephone threat was received against me and one of the gentlemen present. Apparently the sheriffs of two counties were alerted, but we proceeded calmly with dinner and I was unaware of any of the excitement until the morning paper brought me the news. I can't say that such things disturb me much, but I am sorry that my uncle, who lives here and loves Sarasota and the South, has to be dragged in on any kind of disagreeable performance.

~

The debate about South African apartheid, thirty years before it came to a head, was bound to interest Eleanor Roosevelt. Repressive measures were taken against South African blacks as their few remaining civil rights were stripped away and their influential political party, the African National Congress, was eventually banned, with Nelson Mandela, its leader, imprisoned. Mrs. Roosevelt saw a direct link to the civil rights struggle in the United States. Here she recommends actions citizens can take to keep the heat on Southern segregationists.

HYDE PARK, MARCH 26—We have all been very much upset by the situation in South Africa. But equally upsetting has been the news from Alabama, where nine college students were expelled from school for their sit-down strike. A visitor came to tell me that when a sympathy strike was attempted on behalf of these students, the police set up gun posts around the college campus, tapped the telephone lines to the church where meetings were being held, and altogether created an atmosphere so much like South Africa that it is not comfortable for an American citizen to think about.

Fortunately, students in colleges in the North have realized that the students in the South will need help, so within hours $1,000 was expedited from campuses in the North to the beleaguered students in Alabama. I think we should organize to support these students in any way it is possible to do so.

As I have said before, I do not think boycotting lunch counters that are segregated in the North has much value except in letting off our own steam. But I do think that refusing to buy South African goods—such as lobster tails, diamonds, caracul coats, etc., none of which we buy every day—and at the same time refusing to buy anything at all from chain stores that have segregation of any kind in our South will have a very salutary effect.

It is curious that the United States and South Africa have much the same problem. However, the degree, thank heavens, is different. But we must move forward here at home or we cannot protest with sincerity what goes on abroad.

~

When Eleanor Roosevelt saw man's inhumanity to man being passed off as a rational, civilized, and necessary form of behavior, she spoke out to condemn it. Here the issue is chemical and germ warfare. Mrs. Roosevelt's own memories of the horrors of World War I, to which she often returned in her writing, likely inform her thinking.

NEW YORK, APRIL 5—I was very much surprised the other day to be sent a clipping from a March 25 newspaper saying that "the Army asked Congress today to approve an increase in its budget next year for stepped-up development work on the chemical and biological weapons of war."

In World War II it was my understanding that by mutual consent germ warfare was ruled out, but now we see by this clipping that Major General Robert J. Wood, deputy chief of the Army's research and development program, says that the Army feels it necessary to develop germ and gas warfare systems "which can complement the nuclear deterrent."

This seems to me unthinkable. We are becoming less and less civilized every day and also totally impractical. Spending large sums of money on a horrible type of warfare when already we have the certainty that bombs will bring complete destruction seems hardly necessary.

Must we create more and more ways of destroying human beings? Is it really necessary to "complement the nuclear deterrent," which can already give us complete annihilation and cannot deter anything?

~

Senators John Kennedy of Massachusetts, Lyndon Johnson of Texas, and Hubert Humphrey of Minnesota had all three been dedicated supporters of civil rights legislation for years. Congress had done precious little to protect civil rights since Reconstruction. Many proposed civil rights bills collapsed because of filibustering, Southern segregationists. When the Senate passed the 1960 civil rights act, affecting voting rights and other issues, Mrs. Roosevelt applauded. Again, she links the U.S. civil rights crusade to South African apartheid.

NEW YORK, APRIL 11—It is a good thing that the Senate has finally passed the civil rights bill after an eight-week fight, with 42 Democrats and 29 Republicans in favor. This is only the second civil rights legislation to pass the Senate since the Reconstruction Era. The first civil rights act of 1957 was also a voting rights measure. Already those who want a really fair bill giving the Negroes their full rights are denouncing this bill, and I am quite sure that it will continue to be denounced. But I hope that it is at least a step in the right direction.

All of us in the Democratic Party, I think, owe Senator Johnson a vote of thanks. He has risked repercussions among his Southern colleagues and among his own constituents. He has made it possible for the Democrats to claim equal, if not more, responsibility for the passage of the bill, which of course should never have had to be passed for the right to vote should be something which every citizen of this country enjoys without any question. Since it was necessary to pass the bill, however, we are fortunate to have had a parliamentary leader with the skill of Senator Johnson.

My one fear is of intimidation, which I feel sure will be tried to prevent Negro citizens in the South from registering and voting. I hope the Attorney General can find ways of protecting the registration and of preventing retaliation when the Negro citizens of the South exercise their constitutional right.

It is notable that the House of Commons in London unanimously approved the resolution deploring South Africa's racial policies and urging the British government to voice a strong feeling of disapproval at the forthcoming Commonwealth conference. It is difficult to imagine the kind of atmosphere that will exist at this conference—with Ghana, India and Great Britain itself, as well as other Commonwealth countries, protesting the policy of one of their members.

Things seem to go from bad to worse in South Africa, and nothing seems to move the people there but fear. When you have to arrest hundreds of Africans and formally ban two African political groups, you are not living in a safe community or one that has reached a point of understanding where reasonable living conditions can be arranged between the races. It is a very sad situation and one where the fundamental rights of human beings are so clearly involved that world public opinion is turning completely against South Africa.

~

Eleanor Roosevelt, along with a handful of congressional activists showing a serious concern for the environment and the global supply of vital natural resources, was among the first to recommend urgent study of the nation's fossil fuel supply.

NEW YORK, AUGUST 1—A correspondent has drawn my attention to the fact that Concurrent Resolution 73, which calls for the creation of a joint committee to study the need for a national fuels policy, is still awaiting action in Congress. According to my correspondent there is no opposition to this resolution by the small oil companies, but the international group of oil companies is fighting it. Why should they object to such a study?

Vice President William R. Connole of the Federal Power Commission made a statement some time ago that stressed the incredible rate at which our "energy" resources are being used up. He said, "All the fossil fuel consumed in the history of the world prior to the year 1900 would last only five years at today's rate of consumption." Surely there can be no question about the necessity of studying our sources of fuels and carefully watching their rate of depletion.

The coal industry in this country has been a sick industry for a long time. In the last year or so, the deplorable conditions of the people in the mining areas of West Virginia have attracted much well-deserved sympathy. The most shocking part of it is, however, that these conditions are far from new. In the depression years of the early '30s the mining industry suffered terribly in West Virginia, Kentucky, Pennsylvania and southern Illinois. People lived in conditions that should not be permitted, under our American standards.

But we have not yet been moved to make a really fundamental study of the difficulties which must be met, and which I think could be met by a national fuels policy. Certainly this August session of Congress should take up Concurrent Resolution 73 and start a study which cannot be ignored and which will be acted upon.

~

Irresistible force meets immovable object: The Kennedy presidential campaign found a pretext for its candidate to appear in Hyde Park on a day when Eleanor Roosevelt would be at Val-Kill. A luncheon was arranged where she and JFK could talk privately. The air had to be cleared between them, and they both recognized their party's need to rally behind its nominee. Kennedy had little to yield to Mrs. Roosevelt on policy, but he was too astute a politician to run without her endorsement.

In "My Day" the grande dame of American politics shared with JFK her sense of how the presidency actually works. There is one President, and yet his decisions must be informed by listening to many who do not think in his same style. Mrs. Roosevelt was still promoting the idea of an administrative role for her own favorite candidate, Adlai Stevenson.

Luncheon over, Mrs. Roosevelt and Kennedy emerged, beaming. An alliance had been forged. JFK is said to have remarked, "I am smitten by this woman; absolutely smitten."

NEW YORK, AUGUST 17—In my conversation with Senator John Kennedy at Hyde Park Sunday, I was anxious, needless to say, to find out if he and Adlai Stevenson had planned to work closely on foreign affairs during the campaign.

I knew there would be no question of Representative Chester Bowles working closely with the Senator, because it was for this purpose that he withdrew as a candidate for re-election to Congress. And I felt sure that it would be easy for Senator Kennedy and Representative Bowles to work together.

Senator Kennedy has a quick mind, but I would say that he might tend to arrive at judgments almost too quickly. Therefore, it seemed important to me that he should have a good relationship during the campaign with Mr. Stevenson, thereby demonstrating that their philosophies are sufficiently similar so that they could work well together in the future, even though Mr. Stevenson has a more judicial and reflective type of mind.

I was pleased to learn that the Senator already had made plans much along these lines. It gave me a feeling of reassurance.

Our Democratic candidate is a likable man with charm, and I think that already, since the convention, the difficulties and responsibilities that the future may hold for him as President have opened up new vistas for him and brought about a greater maturity.

I think Senator Kennedy is anxious to learn. I think he is hospitable to new ideas. He is hard-headed. He calculates the political effect of every move. I left my conversation with him with the feeling that here is a man who wants to leave a record of not only having helped his countrymen, but having helped humanity as a whole.

I had withheld my decision on joining Herbert Lehman as honorary chairman of the Democratic Citizens Committee of New York until I had a chance to see and talk with our Democratic candidate. After Senator Kennedy's visit, I telephoned my acceptance to serve with Mr. Lehman, and I told Senator Kennedy that I would discuss what help in the campaign I could give, for I have come to the conclusion that the people will have in John F. Kennedy, if he is elected, a good President.

As the weeks go by I hope I will have an opportunity to see our candidate more and to know him better, but I have enough confidence in him now to feel that I can work wholeheartedly for his election.

Senator Kennedy was met by a very large crowd Sunday morning when he landed at Dutchess County Airport on his way to Hyde Park. I had sent my car and two friends, Dr. and Mrs. David Gurewitsch, to meet him.

Dr. Gurewitsch got out of the car to go forward and welcome the Senator. Mrs. Gurewitsch stayed in the car and, while waiting there, asked several people in the crowd if they were Democrats or curiosity seekers. To her surprise, she found that most of them professed to be Democrats. Both she and Dr. Gurewitsch reported to me later that the applause upon Senator Kennedy's arrival was astonishing.

~

In 1960, the popularity of "My Day," although not of its author, was waning slightly. Mrs. Roosevelt's publisher, United Feature Syndicate, agreed that "My Day" should run three times per week instead of six. Like it or not, Mrs. Roosevelt was slowing down, if ever so slightly. She had produced six columns per week for twenty-four years. Following Mrs. Roosevelt's European trip that fall (her last long voyage), the new format would be longer pieces, fewer of them. The syndicate dropped the official name "My Day" because the column was no longer daily and much less a diary of Mrs. Roosevelt's activities. But the "My Day" title was so fixed in everyone's mind that it stayed in common use to the end.

In an early column under the new format, Mrs. Roosevelt took up the Nixon-Kennedy campaigns. Some in the Nixon camp believed Kennedy, a Catholic, would call the Pope in Rome before making important decisions. Some people in both parties held ethnic and religious prejudices such that the idea of an Irish Catholic President made them dizzy with

*distaste. The question was: Would America finally elect a Catholic Presi-
dent, breaking the apparently rigid pattern of entrusting the nation's
highest office only to Protestants?*

*The issue had surfaced in 1928 when Governor of New York Alfred E.
Smith, a Catholic, ran for President and lost to Herbert Hoover. There were
other issues, to be sure, but one that cut down Smith's chances of victory was
the question of his trustworthiness, as a Catholic, in international affairs.
Attacks on Smith's character were unscrupulous but effective. The Roosevelts thought they were scandalous. Kennedy's candidacy gave the country a chance, Mrs. Roosevelt believed, to break an old and harmful habit.*

*Dr. Norman Vincent Peale, a prominent Protestant clergyman, wrote the
influential, longtime best-selling inspirational book,* The Power of Positive
Thinking.

NEW YORK, SEPTEMBER 21—At the start of our national election campaign it seemed that every newspaper I read complained about the dull-
ness of the campaigning, that neither candidate seemed to be able to lift
it out of the doldrums. The people were not being reached, they said, with
anything that really mattered to them.

Since the religious issue was injected, however, by a few clergymen—
some of whom probably thought they were helping the Republicans—
more interest seems to have been aroused. And I was interested to read
that Dr. Norman Vincent Peale some days ago disassociated himself from
the National Conference of Citizens for Religious Freedom, a group that
charged a Roman Catholic President would be under "extreme pressure
from the hierarchy of his church" to align the foreign policy of the United
States with that of the Vatican.

Religious freedom cannot just be Protestant freedom. It must be freedom for all religions. It is a long time since I sat in my office and read the
scurrilous literature that came into the Democratic headquarters in Alfred
E. Smith's campaign. Nothing quite so bad is reaching me now. But some
of the letters sound hysterical and purely emotional.

The question seems to me fairly simple. The Constitution gives us all religious freedom and we are not to be questioned as to our religious beliefs.

Some people maintain that the Catholic Church is not above working to
get certain public privileges for its private institutions. This can be done,
however, only by the passage of certain laws.

To tell a man he cannot run for any office in this country because he belongs to a certain religion or is a member of another race—even though
he is required to fulfill all the obligations of citizenship, including fighting
and dying for his country—is completely illogical and unconstitutional.

I have fought to prevent the Catholic Church from being granted certain school privileges which I think interfere with our accepted beliefs on the separation of church and state, but I will fight equally hard for the right of any American citizen to serve his country in any capacity.

～

On the eve of the election, Mrs. Roosevelt offers observations about the candidates' characters, interpreting the reactions the two men elicit in the crowds who turn out to see them as they crisscross the country, scrambling for votes. Ever more positive in her endorsement of Senator Kennedy, she demonstrates her political flexibility even at seventy-six. Kennedy's character, she thinks, can rouse the nation from an eight-year-long Republican slumber.

ST. LOUIS, NOVEMBER 2—I do not know what will happen on November 8 any more than anybody else knows, but as I go around the country and hear about crowds that have greeted Senator John F. Kennedy and the smaller crowds that have greeted Vice President Richard Nixon, one interesting observation is forcing itself upon me. The crowds that greet Mr. Kennedy want to shake him by the hand, or sometimes they just want to touch him, or sometimes they just want to look at him. This, I think, means a sense of identification between the people and the candidate.

Mr. Nixon has tried to be outgoing and his pretty wife says she loves campaigning because she loves people. But from all that I hear the feeling of the crowd is very different, and I know of only one thing that makes this difference. It is this: When the people finally decide that someone is their man—that he understands them and cares about them—though they may not agree with everything he says or does, they are still close to him and they trust him and they believe in him.

If I am right in this analysis perhaps we are going to have someone who can draw from the people of the United States the greatness that underlies all their everyday concerns. We need it badly at the present time. No one man can meet the problems that are going to face the next President. He must have around him people who are conscious of their greatness, and if we are watching this sense of identification with their candidate and their trust in him we will see a great people rise to the challenge presented in the very difficult days that face us at home and abroad.

This will mean for the United States the greatest opportunity to serve the world that any nation has had and I hope we accept it and rise to the best that is in us as a nation.

1961

wight David Eisenhower did not have an easy time of it during his last month office. He wrestled with cutting off diplomatic relations with Cuba, increasingly restive under Fidel Castro's revolutionary Communist leadership. Eisenhower, in his final State of the Union address, warned that the United States, indeed the Western capitalist world, stood a good chance of being taken over from within by the technocrats who run what he called "the military-industrial complex." He urged that political control over the fate of the nation be revitalized lest big corporations, especially those with vested interests in the arms race, end up dominating the society. Eleanor Roosevelt respected the President's main theme.

Mrs. Roosevelt joined the Congress in granting JFK, the new leader, a honeymoon. He gave the first live televised presidential press conference, and Mrs. Roosevelt recognized that no one who had come along in quite a while in American politics was better equipped to shine in such circumstances.

In March the new President called upon Western Hemisphere nations to join in an Alliance for Progress, a grand economic development program. Kennedy's administration took a stand about the increasing presence of Communist Chinese troops in Laos: The expansion of communism did not fit with the promise Kennedy had made in his inaugural address that the United States would go anywhere and do anything necessary to help preserve freedom. Aiming at the same goal, the President established the Peace Corps. Eleanor Roosevelt was delighted. Late in the year the Agency for International Development was created, another wing of government designed to do what private philanthropy and investment had long done for Third World and other distressed areas. The two new agencies harmonized well with Mrs. Roosevelt's lifelong activities and social values.

Then, in April, one of America's most embarrassing foreign policy disasters hit the headlines. The White House had given its full sanction, through the CIA, for a Cuban invasion intended to oust Castro or at least to make secure the U.S. Naval Base at Guantanamo Bay, Cuba. Most of the participants were Cuban political exiles who wanted to recapture their homeland. The invasion was a military botch within forty-eight hours, and Kennedy absorbed the blame but weathered the storm of criticism with surprising aplomb. Mrs. Roosevelt treated the subject discreetly in her column by emphasizing how well the President had done at cleaning up the public relations mess caused by the failed invasion.

When astronaut Alan Shepard made the first suborbital flight (300 miles up) by an American, the country cheered. The Soviets had sent a man into orbit about a month earlier, to the chagrin of the American space program. Eleanor Roosevelt was not impressed, nor did she applaud Kennedy's bold announcement that the United States would land a man on the moon by the end of the decade. In Mrs. Roosevelt's view there were still far too many unsolved human problems on Earth to justify such huge expenditures as the space program.

Worldwide concern about the potential spread of communism pushed the White House to propose the biggest military budget on record, including a significant buildup of reserve troops. The capitalist-communist standoff solidified when, in August, the Soviets erected the infamous Berlin Wall, shutting off East Berliners from the temptations of so-called decadent life in democratic, capitalist West Berlin. The free world was appalled.

By 1961 Mrs. Roosevelt had begun to slow down somewhat, yet at seventy-seven she could claim proudly to have visited within the year at least thirty cities and towns in the United States and Canada requiring overnight travel from New York. She did take some vacation this year, but the flow of her newspaper columns continued apace.

To Eleanor Roosevelt, bold initiative was synonymous with truly presidential leadership. Her standard, of course, was FDR's administration, especially his first term, when he lifted the country out of economic doldrums with one new program after another. President Kennedy's food stamp program struck her as similarly bold. JFK's key administrator in this area was an unassuming former clergyman from South Dakota: George McGovern. Typical of the young liberal intelligentsia in Washington on Kennedy's team, McGovern combined compassion with political know-how. He served as Senator (1963–1981) and made a famous bid for the presidency as an anti–Vietnam War Democratic candidate in 1972, losing to Nixon.

NEW YORK, FEBRUARY 3—President Kennedy's second press conference was again, I think, a great success. He is being honest in his answers, which is really the one safeguard in a situation where you can be heard by the entire country and where nothing you say will be forgotten.

I am particularly glad, also, to see that a plan for using food stamps in certain areas is going to be worked out and used here at home to bring about a better distribution of our surplus food. Both Agriculture Secretary Orville L. Freeman and Mr. George McGovern, the Administration's director of the food for peace program, must be getting knowledge all the way down the line—from their civil service subordinates who are the ones acquainted with the past and the present most intimately. They no doubt have knowledge that was available in the recent past but which they had not been called on to give.

Food stamps, under the plan now suggested, would be issued through local authorities to needy families who can use them to get designated foods at regular markets, and already the list of foods to be available has been increased. This will be in addition to the expansion of the regular distribution of food to the needy which the President ordered the day after he took office.

All this and much more shows that action is coming in the wake of words and I think the country is beginning to feel the lift of knowing that something is being done to meet our problems. Everything may not work out perfectly, but one does have the feeling that there will be no letup in effort until solutions are found.

~

From Waltham, outside Boston, where Mrs. Roosevelt attended a Brandeis University trustees meeting, she filed a column commending a man destined to become a martyr to one of her own most serious causes, civil rights. The outlines of Dr. Martin Luther King, Jr.'s thinking about race problems in America were already clear, but he was still on the way up to the heights he achieved as an organizer, orator, and preeminent leader in the civil rights movement. Mrs. Roosevelt recognized his talent.

WALTHAM, MASS., FEBRUARY 6—In the past few days I have twice had the opportunity of hearing Dr. Martin Luther King speak—once at the annual Roosevelt dinner of the Americans for Democratic Action, on Thursday night, and again on Friday afternoon in New York at a meeting at Mrs. Dorothy Norman's home.

Dr. King is a very moving speaker. He is simple and direct, and the spiritual quality which has made him the leader of nonviolence in this country touches every speech he makes. He speaks, of course, for that Southern organization which is gradually gaining support all over the United States—the Congress of Racial Equality, known as CORE. Its new national director, James Farmer, impresses me as a very intelligent and capable man.

~

Still sprightly, with a sense of humor, and full of enthusiasm for her favorite political candidates, Mrs. Roosevelt kept on campaigning. She had supported New York Mayor Robert F. Wagner, Jr., since 1954. The mayor's late father was a longtime U.S. senator from New York and an ardent New Deal supporter, particularly on labor legislation. As always she enjoyed the city (here, the Upper East Side) and relished hobnobbing with lively fellow Democrats.

NEW YORK, AUGUST 30—I have been attending meetings this week, some indoors and some on street corners—on behalf of Mayor Robert F. Wagner in his campaign for re-election.

When one is making these short speeches, climbing up a ladder onto a sound truck and trying to speak above other noises of passing traffic, I often wonder how much sense one really makes.

HYDE PARK, SEPTEMBER 1—The other evening in my touring around the city in New York's mayoralty campaign I suddenly found myself a guest with Adlai Stevenson at one stop. This was a rally to raise money for the reform club in the Yorkville section of the city. It happened that Mr. Stevenson, like myself, had a warm interest in young Harry Sedwick, who is running for one of the local district leader offices, and I surmise that our Ambassador to the UN was also brought into this local situation by some younger member of his family!

This happens to us all, but with his usual wit Adlai Stevenson told us how in every political situation he had been admonished not to get into local politics and now his inclination was to rise and say, "Gentlemen, I wish to say a few words to you on disarmament."

However, when it came his turn he explained his particular interest in the young candidate and his genuine interest in good government, and it was as usual a pleasure to listen to him. I think perhaps it gave him an amusing interlude from the more serious business of the special session of the UN.

~

Mrs. Roosevelt always defended the principle of free speech, but it annoyed her greatly when industrial lobbies organized war chests to pay for disin-

*formation campaigns directed at an unsuspecting public. In her opinion
the lobbying effort by the pharmaceutical industry kept consumers believing that only brand-name medicines were effective. The old idea that
generic drugs, priced much lower, might serve just as well found a champion in Congress in Senator Estes Kefauver of Tennessee, Stevenson's 1956
vice presidential running mate.*

NEW YORK, SEPTEMBER 8—Senator Kefauver and Representative
Emanuel Celler of New York have sponsored a drug industry antitrust bill
(S 1552) that will go a very long way toward correcting many of the abuses
and deficiencies of current practice. This bill would have the effect of increasing competition and diminishing the temptation to fix prices. It
would put teeth into the regulation and control of drug manufacture by
the Food and Drug Administration. It would make better known to physi-
cians those drugs which are potentially dangerous and, most important, it
would stimulate prescriptions by generic name through the provision of
long-overdue central control over the naming of drugs.

Prescribing drugs by generic name was first advocated by the Citizens'
Committee for Children of New York in its own intensive study of the impact of modern prescription drugs on the family budget, made some
three years ago prior to the Kefauver investigations.

The director of one large hospital indicated in his testimony before the
committee that prescription by generic name would result in savings annually of tens of millions of dollars and would reduce drug costs in his
own hospital by some 40 percent.

The raising and policing of standards and the encouragement of prescribing by generic name would, in itself, be sufficient reason for enthusiastic support of the Kefauver-Celler bill. But the strong, well-financed
drug industry lobby continues to becloud the issue for the newspaper
reading public.

∼

*A life as rich as Eleanor Roosevelt's could not help but be filled with color-
ful recollections. She had discontinued the summertime family treks to
Campobello Island, New Brunswick, where the Roosevelts spent recupera-
tive time away from the pressures of Albany and Washington. Mrs. Roosevelt never became a sailor, but she admired one salty fellow who had. Her
late husband Franklin had a boat she fondly remembered.*

NEW YORK, NOVEMBER 8—The past few days have been the most beautiful autumn days and I had the good luck to be driving through Connecticut and part of Massachusetts.

I spoke in Mystic, Connecticut, at a meeting sponsored by the Marine Historical Association. The seaport museum there has been considerably developed since I saw it a few years ago and has as many as 4,000 visitors on a summer's day.

Much of the history of the sea and seafaring people in that area of New England can be traced in this museum. And not the least interesting item to me personally is the small sailing boat called the "Vireo," which my husband brought up on the deck of a destroyer to Campobello Island years ago. He had given his own larger schooner to the government during the war, and he wanted a smaller boat in which the children could learn to sail.

Campobello is a good coast on which to learn to be a sailor. The tides are unusually high. They usually run from 20 to 25 feet, and in narrow passageways there may be a succession of small whirlpools. A really knowledgeable navigator, if the winds are out, can often get home by working the eddies along the coast.

This takes long experience but my husband had that, and while he was a careful seaman at times he could be rather adventurous! Seeing the little "Vireo," I am sure, could recall many happy and interesting memories to the boys in our family.

~

The finale to Mrs. Roosevelt's West Coast trip this year was a lecture in Los Angeles, where she encountered picketers and hecklers. But she had seen and heard it all before and was ready to deal with the unruly crowd face-to-face and in print. Over the years she learned that taking rude, ill-informed, or dishonest opponents seriously gave their ideas more credence and attention than deserved. Her preferred tactic was satire and rhetorical dismissal.

She guessed the hecklers were linked to the John Birch Society, an ultra-conservative right-wing group opposed to just about everything Eleanor or Franklin Roosevelt ever stood for. The ACLU (American Civil Liberties Union), an example cited here, was founded in 1920 by social worker–author and Nobel Prize–winning suffragist Lane Addams; by Norman Thomas, the leader of the American Socialist Party; and by Roger Baldwin, who became ACLU's director.

NEW YORK, DECEMBER 15—I was amused to find myself, at a lecture Wednesday night, picketed by a new group—one, I suppose, which is an offshoot of the Birchites.

There were only a few in the group, standing outside and handing out lists of what they said was a part of all the subversive, Communist and Communist-front organizations I have ever belonged to.

Their leaflets were headed by these words:

"Even more than either hell or a woman scorned, there is no fury quite like that of a liberal about whom someone is publishing past performance data."

I can assure the gentleman responsible for the information being handed out, Roger Abel, that I am not in the least annoyed—only vastly amused.

Some of the organizations mentioned I have been connected with for very good reasons at the time. Others I have never even heard of, but that may be because the time is so long past that I have forgotten about them. That they were mentioned on this list as being either Communist, subversive or Communist-front organizations does not make them any one of these things.

I doubt that listing the American Association for the United Nations as subversive makes it so. I think this would be news indeed to a great many on the board of directors. Some of them may even be so excited as to want to take legal action against Mr. Abel, though I hope not, for I feel such accusations are always better met by ridicule and allowing time for the real truth to come out.

I noticed also that this group made the mistake of so many others of listing the American Civil Liberties Union as a Communist-front organization. This long-established and respectable group is repeatedly being confused with the American Civil Liberties Congress, which I believe has been questioned as a possible Communist-front organization.

I am enormously interested in knowing that I have been associated with the National Lawyers Guild. I am not a lawyer, so I wonder just how I served in that organization.

I could pick organization after organization on the list and question the exactness of the information, but the greatest wonder of all is how any group can spare the time or money for such piffling work. What good do they do? This is the question the public sooner or later will decide.

1962

ccomplishments in the civil rights campaign during the last year of Eleanor Roosevelt's life represented the realization of justice after a long period of patient, persistent effort. Rapprochement between the Democratic White House and leadership in the black community accomplished what the Eisenhower administration had not achieved. In January, Roy Wilkins, President of the National Association for the Advancement of Colored People, praised JFK for his active role in civil rights. Kennedy's administration responded with a stepped-up effort.

Speaking in Berlin in February, Robert Kennedy, the new attorney general, denounced the recently erected Berlin Wall as an offense to all freedom-loving peoples. This clear posture won the President's brother some favor in Mrs. Roosevelt's eyes, for she too saw the wall as a symbol of tyranny.

In late March the Supreme Court decided a case called *Baker v. Carr*, empowering federal courts to force reapportionment of seats in state legislatures where patterns of discrimination brought about by gerrymandering had been proved to exist. This gave effective leverage to the federal government to assure more equitable voting for blacks and other minorities previously shut out of the political process. In June, the nation's highest court addressed the religion-in-the-schools issue by ruling that compulsory prayer in the public schools was unconstitutional. Mrs. Roosevelt thought the decision was a good one, but she argued that the history of religion should be taught to students of all ages. When the next school year began, a significant step toward racial integration of higher education was taken when a black student named James Meredith—whom Eleanor Roosevelt admired—was admitted to the University of Mississippi against severe opposition. In November the President issued an executive order that realized a dream long held by the former First Lady. Kennedy directed federal government agencies to eliminate discrimination based on race or religion in federally funded housing.

Mrs. Roosevelt applauded President Kennedy for condemning a steel-industry price hike and forcing a price rollback. As sympathetic as she was to labor, Eleanor Roosevelt could not sanction the inflation in steel prices. She also supported Kennedy in South East Asia. In Laos the threat of a Communist takeover put the containment theory to a test. The U.S. sent naval and ground forces in May to aid anti-Communist Laotians, and Kennedy called it a "diplomatic solution." Neither Mrs. Roosevelt nor many other Americans envisioned the nightmare of an American war over the same issue in Vietnam that was soon to begin.

There were manned space trips in February, May, and October of 1962. Eleanor Roosevelt remained singularly unimpressed; she had simply not developed an interest in seeing the world from on high. Seeing it up close and firsthand in a human way remained Eleanor's priority. In her final year, at seventy-seven, she took numerous trips again across the country for AAUN and other work, and she made one more sweeping visit to England, France, and Israel, each now as familiar to her as home. There were, how-ever, fewer visits to Hyde Park, and finally New York became for her what it had been at the beginning—a magnet, her center of gravity.

By autumn Mrs. Roosevelt's health was deteriorating rapidly. Her last column appeared on September 2. In the November elections the Demo-crats retained their solid control of both houses of Congress; Richard Nixon lost the race for governor in California and another Kennedy joined the exclusive club of senators (Edward Kennedy of Massachu-setts). But the year's major event—the U.S.-Soviet standoff in late Octo-ber over reported missile sites in Cuba, was something Eleanor Roosevelt was too ill to comment upon publicly. Kennedy demanded and won a conciliatory response from Castro and Khrushchev. The world held its breath for a few days as a head-on collision between the two great nu-clear superpowers seemed inevitable, and then shared the world's relief after Kennedy and Khrushchev, for different reasons, decided not to risk war and mutual annihilation.

Mrs. Roosevelt had not known such energy in Washington since the first hundred days of FDR's first term as President: The Kennedy administration had the country hopping with new programs, study groups, and initiatives. Despite lingering testiness between the Roosevelt clan and the administra-tion, Mrs. Roosevelt wanted to be part of the action. JFK clearly wanted her on his team. "My Day" 1962 begins with a typical Eleanor Roosevelt whirl-wind of meetings, social engagements, and travel.

PARIS, FEBRUARY 16—Before coming over here my last two days in the United States were spent largely in Washington, D.C., and I want to tell about them before writing about my current month-long trip.

On last Monday morning in the White House the President opened the first meeting of the Commission on the Status of Women. After very brief preliminaries and upon being introduced by Secretary of Labor Arthur Goldberg, President Kennedy put us all at ease by starting the conference off on a note of levity by remarking that he had appointed the commission in self-defense—self-defense against an able and persistent newspaper-woman, Miss May Craig. No other lady of the press has waged a longer or more persistent battle for the rights of women than has May Craig, and I am sure she is flattered by the President's recognition of her tremendous interest in the field of women's equality.

After the morning session we had lunch in a downstairs restaurant that did not exist in my day there but which must be a tremendous convenience for those working in the White House today. A guide showed us around the White House, telling us about certain things that have been changed under Mrs. Kennedy's direction and which she explained to the American people over two television networks this week.

The basement floor and the first floor for entertaining have certainly been made far more attractive than ever before. Mrs. Kennedy has succeeded in having presented to the White House some really very beautiful pieces of furniture and decorative pictures, which add enormously to the interest of these rooms.

We kept ourselves strictly on schedule all day and opened our afternoon meeting promptly at 2 o'clock at 200 Maryland Avenue, below the Capitol, where the Commission on the Status of Women will have its permanent office.

We soon began to discuss the best way to organize to achieve the maximum of work not only on the six points laid down in the President's directive to the commission but in other situations which will certainly arise. The commission will try to make its influence felt concerning women's problems not only in the federal area but in state and local areas and in industry as well as in women's home responsibilities.

The effort, of course, is to find how we can best use the potentialities of women without impairing their first responsibilities, which are to their homes, their husbands and their children. We need to use in the very best way possible all our available manpower—and that includes womanpower—and this commission, I think, can well point out some of the ways in which this can be accomplished.

I was glad to hear brought up the question of part-time work for women and of better training in certain areas because the possibilities available to women could be more widely publicized and education could be directed to meet and prepare for these new openings.

The Vice President and Mrs. Johnson gave a delightful reception at their home in the late afternoon for the members of the commission.

The meetings continued through Tuesday morning and into early afternoon, and I felt that the discussions had brought us to a point where we could get the staff to continue with the organization and start some of our subcommittees to working very shortly.

I was back at my home in New York City by 5:30 p.m. on Tuesday and a few people came in to say good-bye at 6 o'clock and then I packed and dressed and was ready to leave the house a little after 10 o'clock. My secretary, Miss Maureen Corr, and I left by Air France for Paris at midnight and had a most delightful trip—smooth and comfortable. We are now at the Crillon Hotel, where I always feel at home because of the many months I've stayed here when we used to hold meetings of the General Assembly of the United Nations in Paris.

Henry Morgenthau III met us at Orly Airport and told us of the plans made for doing two educational television programs, and a little later we were joined at the hotel by Professor Alfred Gorsser for discussion of our joint responsibilities on the programs. By this time it was 7:00 p.m. Paris time, though only 1:00 p.m. New York time, and after a delightful dinner we felt well adjusted to the change and feel well prepared for busy days ahead.

~

From her position as the country's most experienced resident of the White House, Eleanor Roosevelt enjoyed commenting upon how First Families present and past fulfilled their public obligations. She gave even-handed sympathy to her fellow First Ladies, Democratic and Republican, knowing how difficult the lob could be. No First Lady drew more enthusiastic applause from Mrs. Roosevelt than Jacqueline Kennedy. As a young mother, serious interior decorator with a respect for history at the White House, and ambassador for the U.S. when traveling abroad, Jackie scored well in every category.

PHILADELPHIA, APRIL 2—I hope that the nation, in welcoming Mrs. Kennedy home, will show her that we are really grateful for her undertaking the strenuous if interesting trip just concluded, because she has certainly enhanced the popularity of America and Americans, and this is not always easy to do.

In London someone asked her if she had really had a chance to sleep enough. With the characteristic resilience of youth, she replied that she had already slept too much! How wonderful it is for us to have a young, intelligent and attractive First Lady with the interest and enthusiasm which she has shown in her trips to India and Pakistan. I am sure the pictures which told of this trip have acquainted many people with these areas and will be valuable in broadening our knowledge of another part of the world.

~

Even at age 78, in the year of her death, Eleanor Roosevelt moved smoothly through several disparate worlds in the course of a single day.

WALTHAM, MASS., APRIL 30—We landed in New York half an hour late. This meant that I had only a short time in which to get tidied up, catch up with what was going on in my own home, and then pick up the Assistant Secretary of Labor, Mrs. Esther Peterson, before going to the courthouse in Foley Square for a hearing that Congressman Zelenko was holding on equal pay for equal work. Mrs. Gladys Tillett, our member on the UN Status of Women Commission, was also present to give her testimony, for this question is one that affects other countries as well as our own. The dignity of women's equality when they meet in government, professional and industrial work is important the world over, not just in the U.S.

I was through by 20 minutes before 11 and on my way to a Brandeis University committee meeting on education, which is always held before the board meeting later in the afternoon. I came home for a hurried lunch and to say goodbye to Mr. Clark Eichelberger, who was leaving for the meeting in Monrovia, Liberia, of the World Federation of UN Associations. Then I returned to the board meeting and some very warm discussions which I thought extremely valuable and interesting.

By 4:40 I was home and quite ready to sleep for an hour and a half before I had the pleasure of having Mrs. Norman bring Mrs. Indira Gandhi to dine here before going to see a play together. What a charming woman Mrs. Gandhi is! Being vitally interested in her country and its policies makes her both knowledgeable and extremely interesting.

I was relieved to find that Tennessee Williams' play, "The Night of the Iguana," beautifully acted as it is, left her—as it did me—a little baffled in trying to figure out what was the message the author meant to give his audience. But at least it left us with much to talk about.

~

Eleanor Roosevelt's reportorial style was heavy on facts and figures. Usually the most literary thing she could manage was a well-told anecdote or scathing one-liner to criticize the ideas or behavior of someone she found harmful to society. Here is a rare instance of Mrs. Roosevelt's use of an extended metaphor that applies, no doubt unintentionally, to her own life.

ATLANTA, JUNE 4—A human life is like a candle. It is lit when a baby is born. It reaches out perhaps at first only in the effect even a very tiny life can have on the immediate family. But with every year of growth the light grows stronger and spreads farther. Sometimes it has to struggle for brightness, but sometimes the inner light is strong and bright from the very beginning and grows with the years.

None of us knows how far it reaches but I am quite sure that even a young life that is not allowed to grow to maturity has left behind it influences for good which will grow and broaden as those who touched this life grow themselves.

The great people of the world spread the major light. They leave behind them accomplishments which touch the lives of thousands, perhaps even millions, of people. But they are strengthened by all the little lights and perhaps could never have accomplished their great ends without the little lights which reached out and inspired them in their own particular circle.

～

Freedom of choice and full tolerance for differences were to Eleanor Roosevelt the sine qua non of a healthy attitude about religion. Thus the furor over the Supreme Court's ruling as unconstitutional a New York State Board of Regents prayer meant for use in public schools seemed to Eleanor Roosevelt unwarranted. She believed in prayer as part of child rearing but rejected imposing prayer on anyone. The conservative zealotry of McCarthyism lurks in the background of Mrs. Roosevelt's concerns here.

HYDE PARK, JULY 5—The nation's governors, in their annual meeting in Hershey, Pa., had a wordy wrangle regarding a resolution to be submitted to Congress for an amendment to the First Article of the Constitution, which of course deals with freedom of religion and the separation of church and state.

All this, it seems to me, stems from a misunderstanding of what the Supreme Court ruled regarding the New York State Board of Regents written prayer and the saying of it in the schools of the state under state direction.

The fact is that this is a prayer written and backed by the government of the state and directed to be used in the schools, and which the Supreme Court has declared unconstitutional. The prayer is innocuous, but this procedure would be an injection of state interference in religious education and religious practice.

Under our Constitution no individual can be forced by government to belong to a special religion or to conform to a special religious procedure. But any school, or any group of people, or any individual may say a prayer if he or they so wish if it is not under the order of the government or con-nected with government direction in any way. This seems to me very clear in the Supreme Court decision and conforms exactly, I think, with the Constitution.

It is my feeling that many of our newspapers put sensational headlines on stories pertaining to this decision, and people have suddenly—without really reading the court ruling themselves—reacted emotionally.

Someone reported to me that he had heard a man on the radio in tears saying that he never thought he would live to see the day when God would be outlawed from our schools. Another told me that a Southern woman wrote to her daughter in New England, saying that she was horrified to find that the Supreme Court was controlled by the Communists and, of course, the Communists were controlled by the Eastern European Jews. Such nonsense, such ignorance is really vicious.

One hears it said, of course, that at present in the South the accusation of communism is rather loosely bandied about and covers whatever you happen not to like. Not to know, however, that the Jewish communities of Eastern Europe are constantly trying to get away from those Soviet-controlled countries because they do not have security or equality of op-portunity makes the accusation of their influence in communism and ad-herence to it a show of complete ignorance of the situation as it really exists. If any people have a reason for disliking communism, it is the Jews.

When unthinking emotions are aroused we usually find that whatever prejudices are held are channeled by the emotions into expressions that have nothing to do with reality but simply are an outlet for the prejudices.

Years ago, in the South, I can remember my husband telling me when he took to Warm Springs the first nurse who had been trained in physio-therapy and had worked for the State of New York that he hardly dared mention the fact that she happened to be a Roman Catholic. He hoped—before anyone discovered this fact—that her kindliness of spirit, her skill and her helpfulness would have won a place among the neighbors where she was going to work.

He was right, but he could not help being amused when an old man came to see him and said: "Miss ——— is such a good woman. But I thought when I heard she was a Roman Catholic she ought to have horns and a tail!"

This attitude has worn off somewhat, but in certain areas, such as where the author of the letter I have mentioned comes from, one can still find astounding beliefs about the Roman Catholics and the Jews.

There is a general lack of knowledge, too, about what communism is and how much influence it may have in our country. And the emotional reaction to a Supreme Court decision, such as we are witnessing, seems to me to be the product of an unwillingness to read with care what is actually said and an unwillingness to look at the Constitution and reread the First Amendment.

I thought the President's comment was one of the very best. The Constitution does not specify that we are not to be a religious people; it gives us the right to be religious in our own way, and it places upon us the responsibility for the observance of our religion. When the President said that he hoped this decision would make us think more of religion and our observance individually and at home, he emphasized a fact which I think it would be well for all of us to think about.

Real religion is displayed in the way we live in our day-by-day activities at home, in our own communities, and with our own families and neighbors. The Supreme Court emphasized that we must not curtail our freedom as safeguarded under the First Article of the Constitution.

～

The seemingly endless flow of "My Day" was interrupted in August for the Campobello vacation and in September, when Mrs. Roosevelt was not feeling well. Then it started once more. None of her final columns address the idea that she was soon to retire and soon, possibly, to die. In her final days and weeks, the same combative moral concern for justice in the world held her attention as it had for decades. A consistent thesis reappears: We cannot make peace by selling instruments of war. Although she slips back into the old-fashioned notion of seeing the U.S. as "a Christian nation," an idea her own ecumenism belies, Eleanor Roosevelt goes out with a bang, urging her countrymen onward in the quest for imaginative new ideas.

NEW YORK, SEPTEMBER 14—I often wonder, as I note how nervous we seem to be about Communist build-up in our world, why our country does not use new initiative to think out fresh approaches to the uncommitted people all over the world.

It has always seemed to me that we never present our case to the smaller nations in either a persuasive or interesting way. I think most people will acknowledge, for instance, that we have given far more military aid to these nations than economic aid. It is not very pleasant to palm off this military equipment on people who really are not looking for it. The fiction is that they are being given military aid so that they will be better able to cope with any Communist attack. But all the nations where we do this know quite well that it is pure fiction and nothing else. Practically none of them could withstand a really determined Soviet attack.

In view of this, why don't we offer them something they really want? For one thing, most of them would like food. Many of them, as they watch the development of the bigger nations, want to establish the beginnings of industry. But they know that wider training of their people is essential before they can make industrial advances, and hence a primary need is aid to their educational system.

Frequently I hear people argue in reply: "Well, look what has happened in Ghana. They are completely under Communist influence." Yet I wonder if this is quite true. Some Communist influence has doubtless proved effective. But we must realize how much more Russia has done in other areas of the world to persuade the young of the efficacy of their system. Unlike the Soviets, we have not established a college for these young foreigners. We have not brought them here at our expense and supported them during their years of study, nor have we indoctrinated them at every turn.

We have allowed them to come to this country on the exchange program arranged by our two governments. But I can't say that we take a great deal of trouble about them once they are here. These students, no matter what their official subjects may be, quite naturally want to study our country as a whole, and they want to find out what may be wrong with our way of life, our government and our people in general. It is important that we prevent them from being disillusioned about us.

It might be profitable to us if we would study what is really good in Soviet education and in their way of life. We can't have a premium on all the good things. We know that there are fundamental differences. We are a Christian nation; they do not believe in God. We are anxious that people should learn to think for themselves and not simply accept what somebody else has told them. But there are good things in the Soviet world and we should give them credit for these. Then, on our own initiative, we should develop a program that we believe will be of greater advantage to the newly developing nations of the world.

Similarly, we might profit by the study of other cultures of the world. The nations of Asia have some of the most ancient civilizations and philosophies, yet rarely does it occur to us that we might learn from them—or that they might offer to the newly developed nations ways of thought that would be far superior to anything we could suggest. In the same way, we might learn from the West African tribes described in Allard K. Lowenstein's "Brutal Mandate." These people are Christians and they have said over and over again that they have no use for communism. But we still persist in thinking of them as bush savages who have nothing to contribute to the rest of the developed world.

I have an idea they have a great deal to contribute. I was struck by the fact that some of the young Harvard graduates working in Tanganyika with the bush people came to have great respect for their ceremonies. For instance, before you could ask them to do any work, they had to welcome you with traditional ceremonies; and they had to ask you about all of your family and you had to reciprocate. This is indeed a gracious custom, and I can see why our young graduates came to respect these people and their customs and to hope that we would not wipe them out.

I would like to see more of such new approaches to people all over the world. If we use new initiative, forget about Russia as a rival, and think about what we can offer as a nation, I am sure we would benefit greatly.

~

Mrs. Roosevelt's health deteriorated rapidly in the fall of 1962. She suffered from tuberculosis. In October the familiar voice that had sustained "My Day" for so many years turned silent. On November 7, resting at her New York City apartment, Eleanor Roosevelt passed away. She was seventy-eight.

Epilogue

In a contest to determine who among all of Eleanor Roosevelt's colleagues and friends admired her most, probably Adlai Stevenson would have won. Adlai and Eleanor shared certain habits of mind and character. Both were passionately rational; both were doggedly loyal to each other and to the liberal cause; both had a certain distaste for the hurly-burly of backroom politics, yet both had what so many politicians lack completely: vision. Stevenson and Roosevelt shared a sense that the world community in their time had sunk lower in terms of moral turpitude and had risen higher in terms of aspirations to achieve peace and fairness than ever before. Each struggled to reconcile the extremes of the century they called their own (the Holocaust, for example, on the one hand, the progress with civil rights, on the other). Eleanor Roosevelt and Governor Stevenson vibrated to the same string. In his capacity as UN ambassador, and as her friend, Adlai delivered the eulogy for her in the UN General Assembly. Paraphrasing a Chinese proverb Eleanor herself loved to quote, he said of her: "She would rather light a candle than curse the darkness. Her light has brought warmth to all the world."

"My Day" was but one of Eleanor Roosevelt's many achievements. A truly full portrait of Mrs. Roosevelt shows her not only as writer but also as mother, presidential adviser, social reformer, diplomat, world traveler, political activist, philanthropist, philosopher, gardener-knitter-homemaker, and lifelong student. As with all great heroes, the story of her life enlarges the scope of our own.

Her biographer and friend Joseph Lash perhaps summarized best why Mrs. Roosevelt was so singularly impressive. Reviewing her years of devoted, indefatigable work for so many good causes and on behalf of so many individuals, Lash remarked that "many of her fellow workers of those days have yielded to age, disillusionment, conformity and comfort." Not so with Mrs. Roosevelt, said Lash, for even in her last busy days Eleanor remained as much as ever "the tribune of the dispossessed and the keeper of the country's conscience."

Eleanor Roosevelt: A Brief Biography 1884–1962

nna Eleanor Roosevelt was born in New York City on October 11, 1884. Her father was Elliott Roosevelt, President Theodore Roosevelt's younger brother, and her mother was Anna Hall, a descendent of the Livingstons, a distinguished New York family. Both of Eleanor's parents died when she was a child, her mother in 1892, and her father in 1894. After her mother's death, Eleanor lived with her grandmother, Mrs. Valentine Hall, in Tivoli, New York. She was educated by private tutors until age fifteen, when she was sent to Allenswood, a school for girls in England, whose headmistress, Mademoiselle Marie Souvestre, had a great influence on her intellectual and social development. At age eighteen, Eleanor Roosevelt returned to New York where she resided with cousins. During that time she became involved in social service work, joined the Junior League, and taught at the Rivington Street Settlement House.

On March 17, 1905, Eleanor married her fifth cousin, Franklin Delano Roosevelt, and between 1906 and 1916, they became the parents of six children, all of whom are deceased—the first Franklin Delano, Jr. (1909), Anna Eleanor (1975), John (1981), the second Franklin Delano, Jr. (1988), Elliott (1990), and James (1991). During this period Eleanor's public activities gave way to family concerns and her husband's political career. However, with the United States' entry into World War I, Mrs. Roosevelt helped the American Red Cross and volunteered in Navy hospitals. After Franklin

Roosevelt was stricken with polio in 1921, Mrs. Roosevelt took an increasingly active role in politics both to help him maintain his interests and to assert her own personality and goals. She participated in the League of Women Voters, joined the Women's Trade Union League, and worked for the Women's Division of the New York State Democratic Committee. Eleanor helped to found Val-Kill Industries, a nonprofit furniture factory in Hyde Park, New York, and taught history at the Todhunter School, a private girls' school in New York City.

During Franklin D. Roosevelt's presidency, Eleanor Roosevelt was a dynamic First Lady, traveling extensively around the nation, visiting relief projects, surveying working and living conditions, and then reporting her observations to the President. She also exercised her own political and social influence, becoming a staunch advocate of the rights and needs of the poor, of minorities, and of the disadvantaged. In World War II, the First Lady visited England and the South Pacific to foster goodwill among the Allies and boost the morale of U.S. servicemen overseas.

After President Roosevelt's death on April 12, 1945, Mrs. Roosevelt continued public life. Appointed by President Truman to the United States Delegation to the United Nations General Assembly, a position she held until 1953, she served as chairman of the Human Rights Commission during the drafting of the Universal Declaration of Human Rights, adopted by the General Assembly on December 10, 1948.

In 1953, following Dwight Eisenhower's election as President, Mrs. Roosevelt resigned from the United States Delegation to the United Nations and volunteered her services to the American Association for the United Nations. She was a U.S. representative to the World Federation of the United Nations Associations, and later became the chairperson of the Associations' Board of Directors. President Kennedy reappointed Eleanor Roosevelt to the United States Delegation to the United Nations in 1961. Kennedy also appointed her as a member of the National Advisory Committee of the Peace Corps and made her chairperson of the President's Commission on the Status of Women. During her many years of public service, Mrs. Roosevelt received numerous awards for her humanitarian efforts.

Eleanor Roosevelt was in great demand as a speaker and lecturer, both in person and through the media of radio and television. She was a prolific writer with many articles and books to her credit including a multivolume autobiography. In late 1935, she began writing "My Day," a newspaper column for United Features Syndicate, which she continued six days a week almost without interruption for twenty-six years until shortly before her death. Eleanor also wrote monthly question-and-answer columns for the magazines *Ladies Home Journal* (1941–1949) and *McCalls* (1949–1962).

In her later years, Mrs. Roosevelt lived at Val-Kill in Hyde Park, Dutchess County, New York. She also maintained an apartment in New York City, where she died on November 7, 1962. She is buried alongside her husband in the rose garden of their Hudson Valley estate at Hyde Park, New York, now a National Historic Site.

Based on materials provided by the Franklin D. Roosevelt Library, Hyde Park, New York.

Eleanor Roosevelt: Time Line

1884	Born in New York City, October 11.
1899–1902	ER attends Allenswood School. Headmistress Madame Souvestre says that Eleanor has a superior intellect and is a born leader.
1901–1909	ER's uncle, Theodore Roosevelt, is President of the United States.
1902	ER makes her debut into New York society.
1903–1904	ER teaches calisthenics and dancing to immigrants in slum areas; joins the Consumers' League and investigates working conditions in garment factories and department stores.
1905	ER marries Franklin Delano Roosevelt (FDR), her fifth cousin.
1912	ER attends her first Democratic Party convention.
1918	ER works with the Red Cross and the Navy Department to help American servicemen in World War I.
1918	ER learns of FDR's affair with her social secretary, Lucy Mercer.
1920	ER joins League of Women Voters and works for women's political gains following the successful suffrage movement. ER delivers first public speeches for the League.
1921	ER nurses FDR after he is stricken with polio and encourages his ambition to return to public life.
1922	ER joins the Women's Trade Union League and the Women's Division of the Democratic State Committee.

1925	ER and friends Marion Dickerman and Nancy Cook co-found the Val-Kill furniture factory at the site of ER's Val-Kill cottage in Hyde Park, New York.
1927	ER befriends Mary McLeod Bethune, black President of Bethune-Cookman College, who helps to develop ER's understanding of black issues and conditions.
1928	ER is named the director of Bureau of Women's Activities of the Democratic National Committee.
1933–1945	FDR is President of the United States.
1933	ER becomes the first First Lady to hold press conferences; only female reporters are admitted. ER helps to establish Arthursdale, an experimental homestead project for West Virginia coal miners.
1934	ER helps to initiate the National Youth Administration, which employs young Americans; arranges a meeting between NAACP leader Walter White and FDR, to discuss anti-lynching legislation.
1935	ER starts publishing her syndicated column "My Day," which she continues until her death.
1939	ER defies state segregation laws by sitting with Mary McLeod Bethune at Southern Conference for Human Welfare meeting in Birmingham, Alabama.
1939	ER helps to arrange a concert by Marian Anderson, a black singer who was banned from Constitution Hall by the Daughters of the American Revolution; 75,000 people attend the concert at the Lincoln Memorial.
1939–1945	World War II.
1939–1940	ER uses her influence to help Karl Frank, who had been active in the German underground movement against Hitler. ER helps relocate to America a number of labor and socialist deputies (and/or their families) stranded in Europe
1941–1944	ER serves as Assistant Director of Civilian Defense with New York City Mayor Fiorello LaGuardia.
1943	ER travels to South Pacific to boost troop morale.
1945	With ER's intervention and pressure from civil rights groups, the Army Nurse Corps opens its ranks to black women.
1945	After FDR's death (April), ER returns to private life at Val-Kill cottage; ER joins NAACP board of directors; President Harry Truman asks ER to serve as a U.S. delegate to the United Nations.

1947	Elected chairperson of the UN Human Rights Commission, ER begins work on drafting the Declaration of Human Rights; spearheads a drive by liberals to create Americans for Democratic Action, which espouses domestic social reform.
1948	ER helps to secure passage of the Universal Declaration of Human Rights by the UN General Assembly.
1952	ER supports Adlai Stevenson in his presidential bid against General Eisenhower; resigns from the United Nations delegation after the election of Eisenhower.
1953	The Women's Division of the Democratic National Committee, which ER served on for thirty-one years, is abolished and the staff is integrated into existing party structure, symbolizing party equality for women.
1956	ER takes a more active and central role in Adlai Stevenson's second unsuccessful bid for the presidency—raises funds, unifies factions, and delivers speeches during the campaign.
1957	ER travels to the Soviet Union for the *New York Post*, interviews Nikita Khrushchev.
1959	Soviet leader Khrushchev visits ER at Hyde Park.
1960	ER meets with Senator John F. Kennedy at Val-Kill, and begins to take an active role in the Kennedy presidential campaign.
1961	President Kennedy reappoints ER to the UN and names her first chairperson of the President's Commission on the Status of Women.
1962	ER chairs an ad hoc Commission of Inquiry into the Administration of Justice in the Freedom Struggle (civil rights). On November 7, ER dies in New York City of complications stemming from tuberculosis and is buried next to FDR at Hyde Park on November 10.

Based on materials provided by the Franklin D. Roosevelt Library, Hyde Park, New York.

About the Editor

avid Emblidge has a Ph.D. in American Studies from the University of Minnesota. He has been a college teacher, editor, publisher, and book packager, and is currently Editor-in-Chief at The Mountaineers Books in Seattle.

Blanche Wiesen Cook is Distinguished Professor of History at John Jay College and the Graduate Center, City University of New York. She is the author of an acclaimed multi-volume biography, *Eleanor Roosevelt*.

Index

Pakistan, aid for, 208
Parks, Rosa, 234
Parochial schools, funding issue and, 148
Pastimes, creative, 265
Peace, xiii, 57, 93, 120, 251
 Ford on, 209
 religious groups and, 104
 return of, 104–5, 111, 248
 women and, 211
Peale, Norman Vincent, 288
Pearl Harbor, viii, 111, 226
 bombing of, 52, 56, 59, 65
Peekskill, riots in, 149
Pennsylvania Station, 233
Pensions, 257
Peterson, Esther, 303
Pharmaceutical industry, lobbying by, 295
Philip, Prince: respect for, 246
Philippines, 60, 111
Photographers, 15, 49
Picketing, 149, 296
Pike, James A.: Declaration of Conscience and, 253
Pillsbury, Mr. and Mrs. Philip W.: baking contest and, 151
Pilot, The: article from, 235
Plog, William: funeral for, 183–84
"Poems of Childhood" (Stevenson), 139
Polish women, 69, 70, 73, 74
Political interest groups, competition of, 148
Political issues, xiii, 199, 236, 251–52
Poll taxes, 232
Poor Richard Club Medal, Ford and, 209
Population, questions on, 269
"Population Bulletin," 269
Population Reference Bureau, 269
Portrait, sitting for, 152–53
Poverty, 272
 crime and, 145
Power of Positive Thinking, The (Peale), 288
Prejudice, 114, 137
 education funding and, 148
 See also Discrimination
Press conferences, 129, 293
Private life, maintaining, 6
"Progressive Education" (CCC), 5
Prohibition, 40

Propaganda, 113
Psychiatry, 271–72
Psychological warfare, 113
Public affairs, 31
Public buildings, 10
Public life, xv, 6, 97, 148, 251–52
 rigors of, 28, 86, 99
Public opinion, 131, 211
Pulitzer Prize, 146

Quakers, 173
Quezon, President, 69

Racial equality, 140, 162
Racial issues, xiii, 80, 114, 262, 293
Racism, exposing, 189, 252–53, 273–74
Radioactive waste, disposing of, 280–81
Ragnhilds, Princess, 202
Ravensbruck Detention Camp, 74
 described, 70
 Polish women in, 69
Reading, lack of, 258
Receptions, 15
Reconstruction, European, 103
Red baiting, viii, 257
Red Cross, 70
 blood labeling and, 162
Red scare, 135, 137, 209
Refugee Relief Act (1953), 224
Refugees, 183, 224–25
 See also Displaced persons
Relationships, 31
Religious affairs, 276, 288
Re-orientation/re-education programs, 113
Republican Party, 131, 175, 232
 Lewis and, 122
 liberals and, 128
Responsibility, 47, 54, 74, 94, 107, 137, 168, 200, 252, 286
 accepting, 273
 civic, 182
 German, 124
 at home, 130
 leadership and, 259, 260
 women's, 301
Retirees' benefits, 257
Revolution, 175, 221
 Western occupation during, 249